NATURAL DISASTERS: FLOODS

A Reference Handbook

Other Titles in ABC-CLIO's

CONTEMPORARY WORLD ISSUES

Series

Agricultural Crisis in America, Dana L. Hoag
Biodiversity, Anne Becher
Endangered Species, Clifford J. Sherry
Environmental Justice, David E. Newton
Genetic Engineering, Harry LeVine III
Indoor Pollution, E. Willard Miller and Ruby M. Miller
Natural Disasters: Hurricanes, Patrick J. Fitzpatrick
The Ozone Dilemma, David E. Newton
Recycling in America, Second Edition, Debra L. Strong

Books in the Contemporary World Issues series address vital issues in today's society such as terrorism, sexual harassment, homelessness, AIDS, gambling, animal rights, and air pollution. Written by professional writers, scholars, and nonacademic experts, these books are authoritative, clearly written, up-to-date, and objective. They provide a good starting point for research by high school and college students, scholars, and general readers, as well as by legislators, businesspeople, activists, and others.

Each book, carefully organized and easy to use, contains an overview of the subject; a detailed chronology; biographical sketches; facts and data and/or documents and other primary-source material; a directory of organizations and agencies; annotated lists of print and nonprint resources; a glossary; and an index.

Readers of books in the Contemporary World Issues series will find the information they need in order to better understand the social, political, environmental, and economic issues facing the world today.

NATURAL DISASTERS: FLOODS

A Reference Handbook

E. Willard Miller
Department of Geography

Ruby M. Miller
Pattee Paterno Library

The Pennsylvania State University

CONTEMPORARY WORLD ISSUES

ABC-CLIO

Santa Barbara, California
Denver, Colorado
Oxford, England

Library of Congress Cataloging-in-Publication Data

Miller, E. Willard (Eugene Willard), 1915–
Natural disasters : floods : a reference handbook / E. Willard Miller, Ruby M. Miller.
p. cm. — (Contemporary world issues series)
Includes bibliographical references (p.).
ISBN 1-57607-058-1 (alk. paper)
1. Floods—United States. 2. Flood damage prevention—United States. 3. Flood control—United States. I. Miller, Ruby M. II. Title. III. Contemporary world issues.
GB1399.3.M56 2000
363.34'93'0973—dc21 00-021512

05 04 03 02 01 00 10 9 8 7 6 5 4 3 2 1

ABC-CLIO, Inc.
130 Cremona Drive, P.O. Box 1911
Santa Barbara, California 93116-1911

This book is printed on acid-free paper ♾.
Manufactured in the United States of America

Contents

Preface, xi

1 Floods: A Perspective, 1
Origin of a Flood, 2
Flood Prediction, 2
Flood Warning Systems, 3
Basic Systems, 3
Flash Flood Forecasting Techniques, 4
Flood Control, 5
Evolution of Flood Control Projects, 5
Types of Flood Control, 7
Floodplain Management, 14
National Program, 15
National Assessment—Unified National Program for Floodplain Management, 15
Interagency Floodplain Management Report, 18
1993 Midwest Flood Evaluation, 19
Flood Insurance, 20
National Flood Insurance, 20
Implementation of a National Flood Insurance Program, 21
Community Responsibilities, 22

Types of Floods, 23
Cyclonic Storms—Midwest Flood of 1993, 23
Dam Breakage—Johnstown Flood of 1889, 36
Thunderstorm Flash Floods—Big Thompson Canyon Flash Flood of 1976, 38
Hurricane Floods—Susquehanna River Flood of 1972, 41
Tsunami Floods—Papua New Guinea Tsunami, 45
Wind and Tidal Floods—Eastern Coast of England, 46
References, 47

2 Chronology, 51

3 Directory of Organizations, 63
Federal Agencies, 63
Private Associations, 68
State Agencies, 74
References, 75

4 Laws and Regulations, 77
Flood Control Acts, 77
Flood Control Act of 1917 (Levee Act), 77
Flood Control Act of 1928, 78
Flood Control Act of 1936, 79
Flood Control Act of 1937, 80
Flood Control Act of 1938, 81
Flood Control Act of 1941, 82
Flood Control Act of 1944, 82
Flood Control Act of 1946, 83
Flood Control Act of 1948, 83
Flood Control Act of 1950, 84
Flood Control Act of 1954, 84
Flood Control Act of 1958, 84
Flood Control Act of 1960, 84
Flood Control Act of 1962, 84
Flood Control Act of 1965, 85
Flood Control Act of 1966, 85
Flood Control Act of 1968, 86
Flood Control Act of 1970, 86

Flood Prevention, 86
Watershed Protection and Flood Prevention Act of 1954, 86
Flood Insurance, 88
Federal Flood Insurance Act of 1956, 88
National Flood Insurance Act of 1968, 89
National Flood Insurance Program Act of 1989, 95
National Flood Insurance Reform Act of 1994, 96
Disaster Relief, 96
Flood Disaster Protection Act of 1973, 96
Robert T. Stafford Disaster Relief and Emergency Assistance Act of 1974, 98
Other Disaster Relief Acts, 103
Proclamation: Contribution to American Red Cross for Flood Relief by the President of the United States of America, 104
Dam Acts, 104
National Dam Inspection Program Act of 1972, 104
Dam Safety Act of 1986, 105
Dam Act of 1906, 106
Specific River Acts, 106
Mississippi River Flood Control Act of 1928, 106
Development of the Coosa River, Alabama and Georgia Act of 1954, 107
De Luz Reservoir, California Act of 1954, 108
Colorado River Storage Project Act of 1956, 108
Colorado River Flooding Protection Act of 1986, 110
River and Harbor Acts, 112

5 Bibliography, 117
Books, 117
Journal Articles and Government Documents, 136
Selected Journal Titles, 230
U.S.G.S. Professional Papers, 243

6 Audiovisual Aids, 265
General, 265
Flood Forecasting, 266

Flash Flood, 267
Disasters, 268
Dams, 269
Rivers, 270

Glossary, 275

Index, 279

About the Authors, 287

Preface

Floods have been a scourge of humankind from the earliest civilizations. Because the level floodplains provide some of the best agricultural land on Earth as well as easy transportation routes, they have some of the highest population densities in the world. Although floodplains may go for decades without being flooded, they are an integral part of the river system and will undergo flooding sometimes. Nevertheless, because of the great value of floodplain lands, the control of the river during high-water stages is a never-ending struggle so that the floodplains can remain inhabited.

This volume begins with an introductory chapter that discusses the origin of floods, flood prediction, flood control, floodplain management, and flood insurance. Floods are classified as to origin—floods caused by excessive rain over a vast area, floods caused by dam breakage, flash floods caused by thunderstorms, floods caused by excessive rain from hurricanes, tsunami floods caused by undersea earthquakes, and floods caused by wind-driven tidal waves.

The Midwest flood of 1993 is described as an illustration of the type of flood that covers vast areas as a result of excessive rainfall over many weeks. Included in the description are the flood's origin, the basic flood control in place for the Mississippi River system, the economic, environmental, biological, transportation, and cultural effects the flood had on the region, and flood recovery issues. The Johnstown flood of 1889 is the classic illustration of a flood caused by the breakage of a dam. The Big Thompson Canyon flood in Colorado in 1972 is an example of a flash flood caused by excessive rain from a thunderstorm. The Susquehanna River flood of 1972 was caused by Hurricane Agnes, which devastated the eastern coast of the United States. The tsunami floods are caused by massive waves on the floor of the ocean, normally as a result of an earthquake. Finally, flooding of coastal areas is frequently caused by winds that create high tidal waves. The initial chapter is followed by a chronology that lists major floods in the United States and the world and provides data on damages and loss of life.

Chapter 3 presents a directory of the wide range of organizations that consider flood problems. Besides major federal and private organizations, each state has some type of organization devoted to floods. Chapter 4 covers laws and regulations concerning floods. Federal legislation has dealt with four types of flood problems—flood control, flood prevention, flood insurance, and disaster relief. The Flood Control Act of 1917 has been amended many times so that there is a flood control program for all major rivers in the United States. The federal insurance program recognizes that the damage caused by floods can be handled only at the national level.

There is a considerable body of literature on floods, and Chapter 5 provides a general bibliography. Studies have been carried out by both private organizations and governmental agencies, at both the state and federal levels. The literature varies from scientific to socially oriented studies. This bibliography provides a list of annotated books, journal articles, and governmental documents as well as the leading journal sources. The final chapter presents an annotated list of the considerable amount of audiovisual material available on floods. These include films on flood forecasting, flash floods, disasters, dams, and characteristics of rivers. A glossary rounds out the volume.

E. Willard Miller
Ruby M. Miller
Pennsylvania State University

1 Floods: A Perspective

Floods are the greatest single natural catastrophe on the Earth. Because floods have created so much human suffering since the earliest civilizations, no other disastrous event has been so well chronicled. The Old Testament story of Noah, the ark, and the deluge indicates the importance of flooding in human thinking at an early time. The first recorded flood was on the Yellow River in China in 2,297 B.C. Since then there have been thousands of floods in the world and hundreds of thousands of people have perished in floodwaters.

Moving water has a tremendous amount of energy that is capable of causing huge amounts of damage. To illustrate, 1 inch of rainfall, dropping from 1,000 feet and covering 1 square mile, has an energy potential of 60,000 tons of TNT, equivalent to three times the force of the Hiroshima nuclear bomb. Once the running water enters a stream, it becomes a battering ram that can destroy buildings and bridges and carry the debris for miles. The velocity of a river is determined largely by gravity. The greater the volume of water and the steeper the grade, the faster the water's flow and the amount of damage. Although the maximum flow of water is only around 20 miles per hour, the potential for damage is staggering.

Since the earliest civilizations, rivers have been major transportation corridors. Because of the ease with which raw materials and finished products could be distributed along rivers, manufacturing was an early activity in floodplains. In more recent years, other economic activities such as communications, trade, and banking have thrived, increasing urban populations greatly. In the United States some 3,800 towns and cities with populations greater than 2,500 are located on floodplains. Some of the world's largest cities, such as Paris, London, Cairo, and Pittsburgh, are on river routes. In the desert areas of the world, notably in Egypt, the country's economy is directly tied to the economic activities on the rivers' floodplains.

Origin of a Flood

Normally a stream is contained in its natural channel. Under these circumstances, not only does surface water flow into the stream, but also ground water gradually seeps into the stream.

When precipitation begins, part of the water flows into the stream, and part infiltrates the ground until the water level reaches the surface. At this point, virtually all of the water will flow directly into the stream. When the flow into the stream becomes greater than the outflow, the stream tops the banks and water flows onto the floodplain, creating a flood.

The flood stage persists as long as the amount of water entering the stream exceeds its natural channel width. The areas flooded can vary from a few acres to thousands of square miles. The flood's duration depends not only on the amount of water but also on the gradient of the stream. If the topography is relatively flat, the water will drain out of the area slowly, extending the flood's duration. If the stream is in a mountainous area, however, it will have a high gradient, and the flood will normally be of a short duration.

Flood Prediction

Although floods will occur in all streams over time, there are no known methods for predicting how often a flood will occur in a given stream. The world's hydrologic cycle does not yield the same amount of precipitation at a given place in a given year; the amount of precipitation can vary greatly from place to place and from time to time, but sooner or later excess precipitation will occur.

Although floods cannot be predicted for any given year, seasonal variations in precipitation and temperature are important determinants of floods in many areas. Many areas of the world have a rainy season, during which floods are most likely to occur. For example, winter is the rainy season in southern California, and summers are dry. Thus, over 90 percent of the floods in southern California are in the cool season.

In the eastern United States, most floods occur in spring or early summer as warm, moist air from the Gulf of Mexico and the Atlantic Ocean is drawn into the continent. As the moisture-laden air is pushed upward over a cyclonic front, massive amounts of rain can occur, and flooding can occur over a wide area as a result.

In the mountainous areas of the West, snow accumulates over the winter. A spring thaw can melt great quantities of snow quickly, causing flash floods in the mountain valleys. Due to changes in altitude from 7,000 to 13,000 feet and latitude extending as much as 1,000 miles north and south, the floods may occur over an extended period. In Arizona and New Mexico floods from melting snows occur as early as March, but in the northern Rocky Mountains they may not occur until July.

In general, there are fewer floods in late summer and early autumn. Floods in these months are mainly associated with intense thunderstorms. Typically they are flash floods, usually covering relatively small areas. In contrast to the flooding of small areas by thunderstorms, hurricanes coming up the Atlantic coast from Florida to Maine can cause massive floods in summer and early autumn. These storms can bring 10 inches or more of water to an area within a 24-hour period.

Flood Warning Systems

Basic Systems

The flood warning systems vary greatly from manually operated to state-of-the-art automated systems. Initially, the local systems, measuring amount of precipitation in a given period, consisted of rain and river stage gauges. Although these systems were simple and very low cost, they were effective in providing many flash flood warnings to areas.

In the 1970s, the Automatic Local Evaluation in Real-Time (ALERT) System and the Integrated Floods Observing and Warning System (IFLOWS) were developed. These techniques are based on sensors, or gauges measuring amount of precipitation, placed in strategic potential flood areas. The sensors transmit the data by radio to a computer located at an Emergency Operation Center (EOC) or at the National Weather Service office. The computer evaluates the data using a river forecast model. Forecasts are updated every few minutes. This technique permits emergency management officials to make critical decisions rapidly. These systems are costly to operate, however, and the federal government has not placed them in all potential flood regions.

Flash Flood Forecasting Techniques

The National Weather Service has also improved the techniques of forecasting flash floods. Advances have been made in radar, satellite, local flood warning systems, and forecast techniques.

Radar Systems

The use of radar techniques is at the core of flash flood detection. In 1972 the concept of manually digitizing radar (MDR) data was established. This technique enabled forecasters to detect the persistence of heavy rainfall in a specific area and made it possible to estimate the amount of precipitation at a given place. To improve the system, computers were linked with the radar, providing the means to estimate rainfall amounts. The Digitized Radar Experiment (D/RADEX) converts radar reflectivities to rainfall rates. The average rainfall is then determined over a specified time period. These data can then be transferred quickly to a map.

In the 1990s the Doppler radar techniques were perfected, providing a means of precisely locating areas of heavy rainfall. The Doppler radar techniques provide a valuable tool for mesoscale system analysis. Their implementation has been possible because of the automation of field operations by the National Weather Bureau. These mesoanalysis programs provide such meteorological parameters as moisture stability, wind vectors, temperature ranges, and many more.

Satellite Imagery

Satellite imagery now provides a new technique for flash flood forecasting. By the use of electromagnetic sensors, radiation reflected from the Earth provides an accurate estimate of rainfall amounts in a storm. Digitized enhancement makes it possible to measure temperatures at the cloud tops in order to assess rainfall rates. Also, certain storm characteristics, such as merging atmospheric cells and cloud line mergers, as well as environmental characteristics such as temperature and wind velocity are used to provide rainfall estimates.

In the early 1980s, the Geofield-Oliver technique was adapted to an interactive flash flood analyzer (IFFA). This computer interface permits forecasters in the Synoptic Analysis Branch at the National Meteorological Center to provide real-time, satellite generated rainfall estimates to National Weather Service field offices. Not only are these estimates essential to the flash flood program, but also they have provided hydrological forecast program quantitative rainfall data for areas where none had existed previously.

Flood Control

Evolution of Flood Control Projects

Flood control efforts in the United States were initially centered on the construction of flood protection levees. After the floods of 1849 and 1850, Congress provided funds for the U.S. Army Corps of Engineers to conduct an extensive study of flood control on the Mississippi River. The study, which took more than a decade, recommended the completion of the existing levee system.

Since flooding continued to be a problem on the Mississippi, in 1879 Congress created the Mississippi River Commission to survey the Mississippi River Basin again and to develop new plans for flood control, including improved navigation. After preparing several alternative plans, the commission agreed that the original levee approach was the only feasible flood control plan for the Mississippi River. The U.S. Army Corps of Engineers continued to strengthen the levee system, and in 1927 the Mississippi River Commission reported that the levee system "is now in condition to prevent the disastrous effects of floods" (Clark 1982).

The great flood of 1927, however, proved that the levee system was imperfect in controlling floods. In that flood most of the levee system failed, and torrents of water flooded the floodplains. At the height of the flood, the river exceeded 100 miles in width from Cairo, Illinois, at its confluence with the Ohio River, to the Gulf of Mexico. The death toll was set at 246, but as many as 500 people may have died. More than 200,000 people were made homeless. Insurance records show that over 139,000 homes and buildings were damaged or destroyed, at a cost of $326 million. For months after the flood, about 325,000 refugees were cared for by the American Red Cross. Nearly 13 million acres of farmland were flooded (Moore and Moore 1989).

In response to the disastrous 1927 flood, Congress provided funds for increased federal assumption of flood control programs. With the Flood Control Act of 1936, Congress recognized that since a flood disaster affects the entire nation, flood control is a federal responsibility requiring a national policy to control floods. In 1938 the Flood Control Act provided that the entire cost of reservoir and channel modification processes be assumed by the federal government. Between 1936 and 1952, the federal government spent more than $11 billion for flood control projects, primarily to create dams to store excess water during periods of high precipitation. This program has substantially reduced flood damages.

The federal plan for flood protection began with the passage of the 1944 Flood Prevention Act (PL 78-354), which authorized installation of upland treatment and flood damage reduction works in selected watersheds. By 1954 the program was expanded to the entire nation. In addition, this act authorized the Soil Conservation Service to participate in comprehensive watershed management projects with cooperation from state and local governments.

Even as the flood programs of the federal government were advancing, many conservationists began to question the widespread wisdom of overreliance on structured measures to control floodwaters. Gilbert White was an early proponent of a new view, which held that flood policy thus far was "essentially one of protecting the occupants of flood plains against floods, of aiding them when they suffered flood losses, and of encouraging more intensive use of flood plains." Instead, he proposed "adjusting human occupancy to the flood plain environment so as to utilize most effectively the natural resources of the flood plain, and simultaneously applying practicable measures to minimize the detrimental impacts of floods" (White 1942, 1958).

In the 1950s, as flooding continued, there was a significant rise in the cost of providing damage protection. At the same time, as the economy developed, the floodplains were increasingly utilized. As a result, the national flood damage potential was increasing at a faster rate than it could be controlled by existing flood protection construction programs. It came to be recognized that the land use type of management was not practical.

Alternatives to controlling flood damages through structural measures were first applied by the Tennessee Valley Authority (TVA). Cooperating with state and local planners, TVA water resource engineers in 1953 began a pioneering cooperative program to manage floodplain utilization. After a few years' experience, the TVA was convinced that floodplain management was superior to previous flood control measures and could be applicable nationally. In 1959 the TVA submitted a report to Congress entitled A Program for Reducing the National Flood Damage Potential. In 1960 Congress enacted the Flood Control Act, which authorized the U.S. Corps of Engineers to provide technical services and planning assistance to communities for wise use of their floodplain. To initiate the program, the Corps developed plans for floodplain use built on the concept of the original TVA experience. The Soil Conservation Service and the U.S. Geological Survey also provided studies on managing floodplains.

A major step in the evolution of this early program to control floods was the passage in 1968 of the National Flood Insurance Program (NFIP). The NFIP came in response to mounting flood losses and the escalating costs to the public. The program provided relief from the effects of flood damages, in the form of federally subsidized flood insurance to participating communities, contingent on flood loss reduction measures embodied in local floodplain management regulations.

Types of Flood Control

Flood control efforts include many types of river alterations, including levees, reservoirs, realignments, widening and deepening of river channels, diversion channels, bank protection, flood walls, and culverts. River engineering now requires considerable modification of the stream.

Levees

Levees, sometimes called flood banks, bunds, or stop banks, are built on the banks of rivers to artificially increase the capacity of a stream so that at times of high volume the water does not spill into the adjacent land. They are intended to protect man's use of floodplains from flood damages. Levees have become the essential component in flood control systems around the world.

The initial construction of a levee on a riverbank requires an investigation to obtain data on the bedrock, the soil top, and the erosion potential. Normally this information is derived from samples extracted through boreholes on the bank. Low-strength bedrock and soil limit the height of a levee. Levee stability is also important, so that it is maintained during high rates of water flow. The effects of water supply through the levee are critical, especially if the levee is built of soft material. In order to maintain the levee, it may be necessary to plant a thick grass cover on it.

The levee's height is determined by the potential flood discharge. However, a levee cannot be built too high, because this would increase the danger to the population if the levee were to break during an extreme flood event. If this were to occur, the loss of life and damage from the flood would be drastically increased.

Reservoirs

The main purpose of a flood control dam is to create a reservoir to store some of the water during the flood stage and then to release it gradually, at a safe rate, when the flood recedes. The reservoir may be a single-purpose flood control reservoir or a multipurpose reservoir—one designed for two or more functions, such as irrigation, power generation, or recreation in addition to flood control.

Reservoir capacity varies greatly. In the development of a reservoir system, the initial step is the attempt to determine the amount of precipitation that would cause a stream to flood. Since the amount of water received by a reservoir can come from thousands of square miles, a ground survey of the physical conditions is necessary. For many streams, rainfall runoff records are now available.

The minimum water storage capacity of a reservoir during a flood depends on the height at which the maximum water level is above the minimum water level. The maximum storage capacity of water in a reservoir is determined on the basis of the time it takes to move the water through the reservoir. When the reservoir spillway capacity is small, the storage required for moderating a flood will be large, and vice versa.

In order to control floods on major rivers, a number of reservoirs may be required. One way of determining the number is by the potential damage caused by a recent flood. The cost of providing various amounts of storage capacity can be compared with the average annual flood control benefits to be expected in order to determine cost-benefit ratios. The determination of a reservoir's flood control capacity also can be based on economic probability analysis of damage losses.

Flood Walls

Flood walls are walls erected to protect urban areas from floods. Usually they are made of concrete and built to a height sufficient to provide protection from the highest known flood of the past. Although they have been highly successful in the United States, they sometimes have problems. If the flood does overtop the wall, the water may not drain quickly from the flooded area. A lake is thus created that might exist for several weeks or even months. In addition, the walls essentially bar all direct access from the river. Not only is recreation reduced, but also the wall is usually unattractive. Although these are all negative aspects, most people tolerate flood walls, for they do control floods. After Lewisburg, Pennsylvania, was saved from flooding by a flood wall in 1972, a sign appeared on the wall: "Thank You Wall."

Channel Widening and Deepening

The purpose of widening and deepening a river channel is to move greater volumes of water at a higher rate so that the river does not overflow its banks onto the floodplain. The extent of the widening and/or deepening is determined by the calculated flood discharge. When a river channel is widened and deepened, usually the levees are also regraded and work on other features such as bridges is required.

The goal of widening and deepening a channel is to create a cross-sectional area that provides the maximum efficiency of flow with a minimum of erosion. In practice, however, this does not always occur, because of such factors as bank instability, porosity of the bed, and proximity of structures, such as bridges, that restrict the width or depth to which the channel can be reconstructed.

In the widening and deepening process, dredging is usually required. In the process, the loose material must be removed from the channel by the stream current or picked up by mechanical dredges and discharged into barges to be dumped on shore. The frequency of dredging thereafter varies with the rate of sedimentation.

The annual growth of aquatic plants is one of the greatest problems in the maintenance of channel capacity in many rivers. Prolific growth of vegetation can clog the channel and impede flow. Plants not only slow the flow but also increase the accumulation of sediments. Plant growth can be controlled by a number of methods, including cutting, using herbicides, and grazing by fish, such as carp.

Fallen trees and debris can clog channels. These blockages decrease the capacity of the stream and are frequently a hazard to navigation. As a means of flood control, all such material must be removed from the channel in order to increase the rate of flow.

Channel Stabilization

Channel stabilization is undertaken to protect against stream abrasion and bank slippage, particularly at locations where the undermining of a bank would result in an impediment to flow, resulting in flooding. Groynes, dikes, or spurs are channel structures built transverse to the river flow and extending from the banks into the channel. Their purpose is either to guide or to deflect the axis of flow in order to create a desired channel width, to increase scour, and/or to build up the riverbanks by trapping the sediment load and its deposition.

Groynes may be permeable or impermeable, depending on whether they are intended to trap the bed material or to allow water to pass through the materials, thereby permitting the deposition of suspended material between the groynes. The width, slope, shape, and spacing of groynes and the location of their axes in relation to the current varies with the purpose for which they are built.

Controlling fences, constructed as a line of piles driven parallel to the banks, may be built in order to increase accretion by allowing a river to deposit material behind the fence, thus building up the bank. Permeable groynes are often built of timber or lines of stakes interwoven with willows or other trees. Impermeable groynes are constructed of concrete, earth-fill, boulders, or gabions.

Revetments provide direct protection to the channel by stabilizing the banks and protecting the underlying soil layers against erosion. In the construction of reventments, the irregularities are first removed and banks graded to acceptable slopes so that the structure will not be damaged as a result of excessive erosion. The shear stress and the weight of the revetment must be taken into consideration as well. A general recommendation is that revetments be extended to the bottom of the stream to prevent failure through continuous scouring of the stream bed.

Depending on the construction materials, revetments may be permeable or impermeable. If the ground water table is the same as the water level of the stream, an impermeable revetment built of concrete, stone, or plastic sheet serves best to control the water pressure that develops behind the structure.

Spillways

Spillways are built in storage dams for safe disposal of the excess water flowing into a reservoir after it is filled. Spillways may have simple overflow channels or may control crests with gates. The spillway thus allows controlled release of surplus water in excess of the reservoir capacity. The goal of controlled release of water is to channel the water downstream or into drainage areas in order to protect the foundation of the dam from erosion and scouring. Water cannot be released at flood stage unless the river is capable of handling the additional rapidly flowing water. Many failures of dams have been attributed to inadequate spillway capacity, resulting in overtopping of the dam. In the case of earthen dams, if the water overtops, there is no possibility of preserving the dam from failure. The adequate design of dam spillways is crucial to the satisfactory design of the dam.

There are a number of types of spillways. The overflow type, the most common, is found in masonry dams having sufficient crest length to provide the requisite capacity. Overall, spillways with crest gates will act as orifices. The chute or trough spillway is used to direct water flow over the crest of the dam into a steep-sloped open channel—the chute or trough. The channel is usually cut into a rock abutment and either left unlined or lined with concrete slabs. The rate of flow of the water from the dam is critical to the controlling of floods downstream, and therefore the width of the spillway is determined by the required discharge. When the slope of the chute conforms to the topography, minimum excavation is required. In a shaft spillway, the water drops though a vertical pipe that conveys it down a horizontal shaft or tunnel. In cases where there are limitations on space and where the discharge is not extremely large, the siphon spillway prevails. The siphon spillway consists essentially of a siphon pipe that is kept on the upstream side of contact with the reservoir, with the other end discharging water to the downstream side. The siphon spillway is also satisfactory in providing automatic regulation of water within fairly narrow limits.

Sometimes an emergency spillway is provided against the possibility of a flood that is higher than expected. For this purpose a suitable spillway capacity up to, say, 25 percent of the normal operation is provided. In the event of an extraordinarily large flood, the damage caused by the operation of the emergency spillway may vary from the loss of the control apparatus to the complete washing out of the spillway structure and its foundation.

In essence, the goal of spillway design must be to attempt to provide a safe and adequate spillway structure at the most economical cost without impairing the safety of the dam. Dam failure as a result of an inadequate spillway may result in loss of property and life.

Cutoffs

In alluvial areas with a gentle gradient, streamwide bends may develop. These bends become large loops with a narrow neck, called oxbows. After a limit is reached in the narrowing, a breakthrough occurs, resulting in the formation of a chute channel known as a cutoff.

This process reduces the length of the stream, increasing its gradient. With the increased gradient and increased velocity, flood crests reach downstream more rapidly, because of the shorter distance the water has to travel. For some distance above the cutoff, there is an increase in velocity, resulting in a lowering of flood heights. Thus, the flood danger above a cutoff is diminished because of the increased efficiency of flow of the stream. Below the cutoff, however, the floodplain may be more liable to flooding, for not only is more water passed downstream more quickly than before, but also the storage capacity of the old channel can no longer be used.

An effect of cutoffs that may extend far downstream is that resulting from a change in the direction of the current as it comes out of the cutoff as compared with its direction in its natural condition, when the bulk of the stream flows around a bend. Deflection of currents may give rise to a whole new series of downstream bends initiating new meanders.

When a cutoff occurs, some areas that previously had little erosion may have greater erosion. Any lengthening or shortening that changes the gradient of a stream disturbs the profile of equilibrium. As a result, the stream starts building up (aggrading) or scouring until a new profile of equilibrium is established. A stream is said to be graded, or to reach its profile of equilibrium, when its slope and volume are in equilibrium with the sediment transported.

The U.S. Army Corps of Engineers has completed a series of cutoffs on the Mississippi River from Cairo, Illinois, to its mouth, a distance of nearly 800 miles. In these endeavors, over 300 miles of river channels were shortened by 130 miles. A comparison of the height of the 1929 flood with that of January 1937 indicates that the latter flood was 2 to 12 feet lower. However, because of the difficulty of comparing the two flood levels, it is not possible to state quantitatively how effective the cutoffs have been.

There are practical limits to the effects of cutoffs. They are generally used in conjunction with the control system of the entire river. Any channel improvement may have adverse effects if the downstream channel was not improved to pass the greater flows of water produced by upstream channel improvements. Hence channel improvements should be considered a part of the overall development plan for the entire stream and must be planned and developed such that the benefits at one place are not offset by higher levels of damage elsewhere.

Diversion Channels

A diversion is a flood control measure that opens up a new exit channel that carries excess flow safely around the area that is protected. On occasion, the floodwater of one river has been diverted to another river system. This is an ancient technique. Amenenhot, King of Egypt, is said to have diverted the floodwaters of the Nile into Lake Norris.

The diversion of floodwaters is normally for a limited period. After the flood in the main stream has receded, the water standing in the temporary depression is permitted to flow back to it. The effect of this type of diversion, in which the diverted water returns to the main channel some distance downstream of the protected area, depends on the distance between the point of diversion and the point of return. When this distance is small, the backwater effect may somewhat negate the effect of the diversion. However, if a large backwater effect exists over a relatively small distance, the diversion will be effective in reducing the flood stage. Another consideration is the availability of an adequate gradient for the diversion channel to develop the necessary velocity. If the gradient is low, a dam can be built to raise the water level and create an adequate flow to remove the water.

Bypass Channels

The particular application of bypass channels is in highly developed areas where it is impossible to increase the size of the existing river during the flood stage. For this method to be completely economical, the existing river must carry the maximum volume possible without flooding and the bypass channel must be designed to carry the balance. Theoretically, the river should carry all water up to the point of flooding and then the bypass should carry the excess water. In practice, however, the value of the bypass in controlling flood water is impossible to predict or calculate accurately. Models are now available to determine the amount of floodwater due to the construction of bypass channels.

Floodways

Floodways serve two functions in flood abatement: they provide additional channels for storing a portion of the floodwater, and they open new channels to carry part of the main stream flow. The development of floodways often is limited by the unavailability of low-cost land and sometimes by unfavorable topographic conditions.

Floodways are ordinarily used only when there is a major flood. Nevertheless, for floodways to be effective, periodic floodings are necessary to scour any sedimentary deposits so that the channel does not aggrade. Water is admitted from time to time to remove sediment in one of several ways: a low section of the levee may be opened so that a washout of sediment occurs; a concrete channel may direct a flow of water through the floodway; or the spillway may have gates to control the flow of water. Gates provide greater control of flow but are costly to construct. The cost can usually be justified only when floods are frequent.

Overflow Land

In order to control a flood, water may be diverted onto large flat land areas that are capable of absorbing water at relatively high rates. Overflow areas are also important to reduce the amount of water flowing downstream at a given time. These areas are also important in replenishing underground reservoirs. In dry regions, these floodwaters sometimes are used for irrigation. In coastal areas, the overflow areas are used not only for a water supply but also to suppress salinity intrusion from the ocean.

Floodplain Management

Because floodplains provide relatively flat transportation routes, rich alluvial soils for a productive agriculture, and a level terrain that is easy to build on, they have some of the highest population densities in the world. Although floodplains provide an excellent environment for development, all floodplains are subject to flooding. As the cost in life and property increased, it was recognized long ago that the use of floodplains needs to be managed. In 1937 the journal *Engineering News-Record* raised the question, "Is it sound economics to let such property be damaged year after year, to rescue and take care of its occupants, to spend millions for their local protection, when a slight shift in location would assure safety?" The increasing use of floodplains disregards the basic fact that floodplains are a fundamental part of the river. Despite the repeated flood damages, the physical and economic attractiveness of floodplains during normal river stages has encouraged human occupancy. As a result, there has been unhindered development of the floodplains with the hope that flood control measures will reduce the risks of floods (see Table 1.1).

National Program

In establishing the National Flood Insurance Program in 1968, Congress stated that "the objectives of a flood insurance program should be integrally related to a unified national program for flood plain management" and directed that "the President should transmit to the Congress for its consideration any further proposals necessary for such a unified program." The initial report, issued in 1976, provided a conceptual framework of general and working principles and established "strategic" goals and "tools" to guide local, state, and federal agencies to make decisions in implementing a unified national program for floodplain management. The report was updated in 1979 and again in 1986 by a federal interagency management task force.

The 1986 report established two broad goals for floodplain management: (1) to reduce loss of life and property from flooding, and (2) to reduce losses of natural and beneficial resources from unwise land use. Four primary strategies were outlined to achieve these goals. Under each strategy a set of floodplain management tools was established (see Table 1.2).

National Assessment—Unified National Program for Floodplain Management

A major recommendation of the 1986 report was to "provide an evaluation of floodplain management activities with periodic reporting to the public and to Congress on progress toward

Table 1.1
Natural Resources of Floodplains

Water Resources

Water Quality Maintenance
- Filter nutrients and impurities from runoff
- Process organic waste
- Moderate temperature fluctuation

Groundwater Recharge
- Promote infiltration and aquifer recharge
- Reduce frequency and duration of low surface flows

Natural Flood
- Provide flood storage and conveyance
- Reduce flood peaks
- Reduce sedimentation

Biological Resources

Biological Productivity
- Support high rate of plant growth
- Maintain biodiversity
- Maintain integrity of ecosystem

Fish and Wildlife Habitats
- Provide breeding and feeding grounds
- Create and enhance a waterfowl habitat
- Protect habitats for rare and endangered species

Societal Resources

Harvest of Wild and Cultivated Products
- Enhance agricultural lands
- Provide sites for aquaculture
- Restore and enhance forest lands

Recreational Opportunities
- Provide areas for active and passive uses
- Provide open space
- Provide aesthetic pleasure

Areas for Scientific Study and Outdoor Education
- Contain cultural resources (historic and archaeological items)
- Provide opportunities for environmental and other studies

Source: A Unified National Program for Floodplain Management, Washington, DC: Government Printing Office, 1994.

Table 1.2
Strategies and Tools for Floodplain Management

Strategy: Modify Susceptibility to Flood Damage and Disruption

1. Floodplain regulations
2. Development and redevelopment policies
3. Disaster preparedness
4. Disaster assistance
5. Floodproofing
6. Flood forecasting and warning systems and emergency plans

Table 1.2 *continued*

Strategy: Modify Flooding
1. Dams and reservoirs
2. Dikes, levees, and flood walls
3. Channel alterations
4. High flow diversions
5. Land treatment measures
6. On-site detention measures

Strategy: Modify the Impact of Flooding on Individuals and the Community
1. Information and education
2. Flood insurance
3. Tax adjustments
4. Flood emergency measures
5. Postflood recovery

Strategy: Restore and Preserve the Natural and Cultural Resources of Floodplains
1. Floodplain, wetland, coastal barrier resources regulations
2. Development and redevelopment policies
3. Information and education
4. Tax adjustments

Source: A Unified National Program for Floodplain Management, Washington, DC: Government Printing Office, 1994.

Table 1.3
Floodplain Management, 1992

• *Individual Risk Awareness.* Although substantial progress has been made in increasing institutional awareness of flood risk, individual awareness falls far short of what is needed, resulting in unwise use and development of flood hazard areas.

• *Migration to Water.* People are attracted to riverine and coastal environments but not usually out of economic necessity. In recent decades, the annual growth rates in these areas have greatly exceeded the national rate.

• *Floodplain Losses.* Despite attempts to cope with the problem, the large-scale development and modification of riverine and coastal floodplains have resulted in increasing damages and loss of floodplain resources.

• *Short-term Economic Returns.* In many instances, private interests develop land to maximize economic return without regard to long-term economic and natural resource losses. This increases public expenditures for relief, recovery, and corrective actions.

• *Enhanced Knowledge and Technology.* Institutions and individuals that deal with floodplain problems require a broad range of information, a variety of technologies to deal with emerging problems, and standards to which they can refer for guidance. Research enhances our knowledge about these areas.

• *National Flood Protection Standard.* Protection from the effects of greater, less frequent flooding is still needed in areas where such flooding will cause unacceptable or catastrophic damages.

• *Limited Governmental Capabilities.* Many states and most communities lack the full resources necessary to bring about comprehensive local action to mitigate flood problems without federal support. Local governments invariably misjudge their ability to deal with severe flood events. However, they are necessary partners to any successful solution.

• *Need for Interdisciplinary Approaches.* Plans to solve flood problems must encompass the entire hydrologic unit and be part of a broader water resources management program. Training in a variety of disciplines is required to devise and carry out mitigation strategies.

• *Application of Measures.* Measures implemented locally typically involve only floodplain regulations (to meet the requirements of the NFIP and state programs) and eligibility for individuals to purchase insurance. Communities typically have not implemented other floodplain management measures.

• *Effectiveness of Mitigation Measures.* Structural flood control measures have been effective in reducing economic losses. The application of additional structural measures is limited because of economic and environmental

Table 1.3 *continued*

considerations. Land use regulations required by some federal programs and implemented by state and local governments have reduced the rate of floodplain development. Compliance with regulatory controls is a significant problem. New technologies and techniques associated with risk assessment, forecasting, warning, and construction practices have substantially improved these activities. The potential of the NFIP has not been realized: less than 20 percent of floodplain residents have insurance.

• *Role of Disaster Assistance.* Liberal federal assistance in postflood relief and recovery has reinforced expectations of government aid when flood disasters occur. This view has resulted in limited mitigation planning and actions by communities and individuals.

• *National Goals and Resources.* Despite significant progress, the United States still lacks a unified national program for floodplain management. Ambiguity in national goals has hindered the effective employment of limited financial and human resources.

Source: Federal Interagency Floodplain Management Task Force. Washington, DC: Government Printing Office, 1992.

implementation of a unified national program for floodplain management." Consequently, in 1987 the Federal Interagency Floodplain Management Task Force initiated an assessment of the nation's program for floodplain management. A special National Review Committee, composed of professional planners, provided an evaluation of the effectiveness of floodplain management for the task force. The task force reported a number of important findings in 1992 (see Table 1.3).

Interagency Floodplain Management Report

To implement the report, the Federal Interagency Floodplain Management Task Force developed proposals for a Unified National Program for Floodplain Management in 1993. The report established intermediate and long-term goals that would ultimately result in sound floodplain management. The report is based not only on the task force report but also on national and global perspectives.

Four broad goals are recommended for achieving a unified national program for flood control (see Table 1.4). A target date is given for each goal in order to set an "action agenda" and to make estimates of feasible progress. As the program proceeded, it was recognized that the various objectives would need to be refined. Although the task force submitted the established goals in 1994, there has been little implementation. By 1999 no organization had been established to act on the report's recommendations and those of the previous national assessments. In short, there has been much discussion of floodplain use and management, but no change in their functions has yet occurred.

Table 1.4
Action Agenda for a Unified National Program for Floodplain Management, 1998–2000

Objective	Completion Date
Goal Setting and Monitoring	
1. Devise a mechanism for setting, monitoring, and revising national goals.	1995
2. Hold a national forum on "Floodplain Management for the First Quarter of the 21st Century," to discuss and modify the mechanism as needed.	1996
3. Institutionalize the mechanism through legal, legislative, or administrative measures.	1997
Mitigation of Risk	
1. For all metropolitan floodplains, complete an inventory of	
a. all existing structures.	1996
b. all natural resources.	2000
2. For all nonmetropolitan floodplains,	
a. inventory existing structures.	2000
b. identify areas with high potential for development.	2000
c. inventory all natural resources.	2005
3. Mitigate the risk of flood damage for at least half the nation's highest-risk floodplain structures.	2020
4. Reduce, by at least half, the risk of degradation of the most important natural resources of the nation's floodplains.	2020
Public Awareness	
1. Develop a simple concept and definition of floodplain management to improve public understanding and support.	1996
2. Lay out a leadership strategy to encourage initiative and acceptance of responsibility.	1996
3. Establish new incentives that give credit for integrating different floodplain management programs, strategies, and tools.	1996
4. Devise a national strategy to foster public understanding of the need for mitigating action when floodplain development potentially damages public or private property or natural resources.	1997
Professional Capability	
1. Make available enhanced training, especially with a comprehensive view of floodplain management.	1996
2. Establish in-house, professional floodplain management capability in all states and metropolitan areas.	1998
3. Provide professional floodplain management services to nonmetropolitan areas.	2000
4. Establish professional standards for floodplain management expertise.	2000

Source: A Unified National Program for Floodplain Management, Washington, DC: Government Printing Office, 1994.

1993 Midwest Flood Evaluation

In January 1994 President Clinton assigned to the Federal Interagency Floodplain Management Review Committee the task of evaluating the property damage created by the 1993 Midwest floods and then to evaluate the performance of existing floodplain management and related watershed management programs. The resulting report was based on the committee's research and interactions with local, state, and federal officials, businesses, interest groups, and individuals. It provided a further blueprint for managing the use of floodplains (see Table 1.5).

Table 1.5
Floodplain Management Assessment of 1993 Midwest Floods

- *The goals for floodplain management are clear.* The means to carry out effective floodplain management exist today but need improvement and refocusing. It is time for responsibility and accountability for accomplishing floodplain management to be shared among all levels of government and with citizens of the nation.
- *Full disaster support for those in the floodplain [should be] contingent on their participation and self-help mitigation programs such as flood insurance.* Measures that internalize risks reduce the moral hazard associated with full government support.
- *State and local governments must have a fiscal stake in floodplain management.* Without this stake, few incentives exist for them to be fully involved in floodplain management.
- *People and property remain at risk throughout the nation.* Many of those at risk neither fully understand the nature and the potential consequences of that risk nor share fully in the fiscal implications of bearing that risk.
- *The lessons of the flood of 1993 are clear.* The nation should not carry the burden of massive federal flood disaster relief costs that current policies generate each time a major flood occurs.
- *The dominant federal role in funding flood damage reduction and recovery activities limits the incentive for many state and local governments, businesses, and private citizens to share responsibility for making wise decisions concerning floodplain activity.*
- *Increased state involvement will require greater state technical capabilities in floodplain management.* Few incentives exist for the state to build this expertise.

Source: Federal Interagency Floodplain Management Review Committee, Washington, DC: Government Printing Office, 1994.

Flood Insurance

National Flood Insurance

As early as the 1920s it was recognized that a flood insurance program should be developed for the nation. Although there was a long debate in Congress on the need for a federal program, it was not until after the 1951 and 1955 floods that Congress acted. In 1956 the first federal Flood Insurance Act was passed.

However, largely because of the opposition of the private insurance industry, which felt that federal land insurance was impractical and financially unsound, Congress refused to pass appropriations necessary to implement the act (Mrazik and Kinberg 1991).

However, after major flooding and flood losses in the 1960s resulting in the disbursement of massive amounts of federal relief funds, a 1966 task force for the development of a federal flood control policy recommended the establishment of a federal flood insurance program. The report noted that "a flood insurance program is a tool that should be used expertly or not at all. Correctly applied, it could promote wise use of flood plains. Incorrectly applied, it could exacerbate the whole problem of flood losses" (Task Force on Federal Flood Control Policy 1966, 17). In response, Congress passed the National Flood Insurance Act of 1968, creating the National Flood Insurance Program.

Implementation of a National Flood Insurance Program

The development of flood probability standards and the implementation of the National Federal Insurance Program constituted a major attempt to change the management of floodplain use. In order to secure federal insurance, the local governments that managed floodplain use were required to provide information on the probability of how often the floodplain could be flooded. A fundamental weakness of the law, however, was that no procedure exists that can accurately define the flood potential of a given area.

Nevertheless, quantification of the risk is a fundamental necessity in order to determine the cost of flood insurance as well as to control the use of the floodplain. Although accurate quantification was impossible, Congress stipulated that the NFIP fulfill six primary objectives:

1. To make nationwide flood insurance available to all communities subject to periodic flooding
2. To guide future developments, when practical, away from flood-prone locations
3. To encourage state and local governments to make appropriate land-use adjustments to restrict the development of land that is subject to flood damage
4. To establish a cooperative program involving both the federal government and the private insurance industry
5. To encourage leading institutions, as a matter of national policy, to assist in furthering the objectives of the program
6. To authorize continuing studies of flood hazards

An important provision of the legislation was the identification within five years of all communities prone to flooding, and the establishment of flood-risk zones in those communities within fifteen years. The NFIP adopted the 100-year flood standard. Through this procedure, it was able to secure standardized comparisons of areas of risk between communities. The 100-year flood standard refers to a flood area that has a 1 percent chance of being flooded in any given year. It does not refer to a flood that occurs on average every 100 years. In fact, for a home in a 100-year flood zone, there is a chance in excess of 20 percent that a 100-year flood will occur once every 30 years. The general formula is (1 – P)N(C), where N equals the number of years from now, P is the annual flood probability, and C is the cumulative probability over period N (P is assumed to be constant, and events are independent from year to year). By choosing values for P and C, one can assess the number of years that the cumulative probability (C) covers.

Community Responsibilities

Because the federal insurance program left the management of floodplain use with the local government, eligibility to secure flood insurance depends on adoption of local ordinances consistent with the NFIP criteria.

The NFIP has evolved a set of guidelines for communities:

1. A permit for all flood plan development must be secured.
2. The lowest floor of all residential construction and housing must be elevated to or above the base flood level.
3. Floodproofing of all nonresidential construction must be elevated to the base flood level.
4. Development is prohibited unless planners can demonstrate that there will be no increase in the base flood level.

These standards have been widely accepted as the principal guidelines for flood loss reduction. The requirements for participation in the NFIP included (1) that the NFIP standards be administered at the level of the local government, rather than by the federal government; (2) that the local ordinance adoption be one of the rare examples where local taxes are required for implementation; (3) that the NFIP standards for managing future floodplain development not affect existing developments; and (4) that the NFIP provide a balance between development and flood management interests. In order to develop the program, Community Assistance and Program Evaluations providing on-site review of local floodplain management programs were initiated in 1978. These standards provide the basic guidelines for the issuance for federal insurance.

Although by the middle of 1999 about 20,000 floodplain plans had been approved for federal flood insurance, problems persist. Most important is that the program does not apply to past development of the floodplain. The U.S. Army Corps of Engineers has indicated that the cost of evaluating existing construction above the possible flood level is so costly that it can be done only in areas of frequent flooding.

There have been lesser problems, too, in implementing the insurance program. Because of limited numbers of skilled personnel in local areas to evaluate the floodplain hazard, the NFIP has had to rely on local visits to perform evaluations for issuance of insurance policies. In addition, the national standards may need to be modified to address unique local situations. This has been recognized, and most communities have developed standards for future floodplain use that now exceed the national requirements.

Types of Floods

There are six major types of environmental disasters that cause floods. The largest floods are caused by excessive precipitation over an extended period from cyclonic storms. These floods may cover several hundred thousand square miles and persist for weeks. The damage from these floods can run into billions of dollars and considerable loss of life. The second type of flood occurs when rivers overflow man-made structures such as dams. The third type of flood occurs from the excessive rains from hurricanes. Hurricanes frequently create floods when they bring massive amounts of rain to a land area, such as the eastern coast of the United States or the western coast of Asia. The fourth type of flood develops when excessive rainfall occurs within a short period and is channeled into a narrow valley. This is known as a flash flood. The fifth type, the tsunami flood, results when an earthquake occurs under the ocean, creating waves that cause a flood when they hit a shore. The sixth type of flood occurs when wind creates surface tidal waves that flood adjacent shorelines.

Cyclonic Storms—Midwest Flood of 1993

The Midwest flood of 1993 was possibly the greatest flood suffered by the people of the United States. It caused more than $18 billion of property damage and at least fifty deaths. The 1993 flood lasted longer, covered a larger area, and involved a greater volume of water than any recorded flood. It severely tested the nation's ability to manage national emergencies.

Origin of the Flood

During the summer of 1993, unusual weather patterns existed across the central United States, bringing copious rainfall almost daily to the Midwest. The rainfall of June, July, and August totaled double or even triple the normal amounts. The entire upper Mississippi Basin, an area covering more than 300,000 square miles, received an average of nearly 20 inches of rain from June through August, 2.5 inches more than any previous three-month period dating back to 1895. Within the region, there were seventy-seven large rainfall locations in an area 400 miles wide and 600 miles long. Within this enormous area there were 175 areas of heavy rainfall, each having more than 6 inches of rain in short periods, creating local flash floods.

In addition to the excessive rainfall, a number of other factors increased the flood intensity. From June through August, the interval between the storms varied only from three to seven days, allowing no time for the land to dry out. In addition, the heaviest rain of the summer fell during the twelve-day period from June 29 to July 10, during which time excessive rains fell every day. During the 92-day period from June 1 to August 31, rainfall amounts below 0.05 inches fell on only 17 days, and more than 9.25 inches was recorded across the large area on 36 days, setting new records. In early September, rain abated for a short period. But from late September until November, an additional 3 to 8 inches of rain fell, creating new flooding along the Mississippi and Missouri Rivers and their tributaries.

General Flooded Areas

Flooding occurred in nine states: Illinois, Iowa, Missouri, Kansas, Nebraska, Wisconsin, Minnesota, North Dakota, and South Dakota. The flash floods were most extensive in western Illinois and Iowa. In the Mississippi Basin, 1,800 miles of rivers had record flooding, including 520 miles on the Mississippi, 415 miles on the Missouri, 190 miles on the Des Moines, 185 miles on the Kansas, 165 miles on the Iowa, and shorter portions of eight other Midwestern rivers.

Flood Control

Because of the recognized flood damage in the Mississippi Basin, a system of levees and reservoirs was present to control floods.

Levees

In 1993 there were 1,576 levees on the upper Mississippi River, of which 1,082 were damaged. Only 15 of these had been federally constructed and maintained, of which only 3 were damaged. In addition, 214 were federally constructed but locally maintained;

only 36 of these were damaged. In contrast, 1,347 were constructed by local or state agencies, of which 1,043 (77.4 percent) were damaged.

A number of factors caused the levees to break. Most significant was the extended period of flooding. As the floodwaters rose, so did the saturation level. With saturation, seepage began. As the water continued to rise, sloughing occurred, and this was followed by a breakage of the levee. Once the breakage occurred, the water poured onto the floodplain.

The levee's ability to hold the excess water of a flood depends considerably on the type of material used in its construction. Almost all sand levees suffered some sort of damage, and some were even swept away. Levees constructed of rocks and heavy clays had fewer breaks.

After the initial breakage occurred, the size of the levee channels varied from a few yards to well over a mile wide. The size depended on the height and velocity of the river water. In general, the higher the velocity, the greater the size of the breakage channel.

After the water entered the floodplain, erosion of the surface began. At the break the water reached speeds of 20 to 25 feet per second. The scouring of a floodplain continues until the water surface levels on both sides of the levee become equal and the water becomes calm. At this stage the sediments carried by the water begin to settle, creating the new alluvial surface of the floodplain.

The levee system of the upper Mississippi Basin had a minimal influence in controlling the 1993 flooding of the region. They did, however, hold the excess water long enough for the people of the region to be warned of the flood danger.

Reservoirs

The flood's magnitude was lowered by the control reservoirs in the headwaters of the rivers. The flood and the resulting damage would have been greater had some of the floodwaters not been retained in the reservoirs built by the U.S. Army Corps of Engineers, the Bureau of Reclamation, and the Soil Conservation Bureau. These reservoirs stored large volumes of floodwater, reducing the damage to agricultural lands and urban areas, and possibly also reducing the loss of life.

At some of the reservoirs the spillways were used for the first time to release excessive floodwater. It was estimated that the volume of runoff from the land was equal to about twelve times the capacity of each reservoir. Although the inflow far exceeded the outflow, they did reduce the flood's magnitude. It is estimated that they reduced the peak flow of the Mississippi River at Quincy, Illinois, by 2 feet, and by 1.5 feet at Hannibal, Missouri.

Effects of the Flood

Economic Effects

The 1993 floods had a profound effect not only on the economy but also on many other aspects of life in the Midwest, such as agriculture. Here every aspect was affected, from the initial erosion of the soil to the eventual reduction of crop yields.

The 1993 decline in corn and soybean yields reflects the major effect of flooding on crop yields. The corn yield in Iowa was only 80 percent of the 1988–1992 average yield. In Minnesota corn yields were down nearly 30 percent, in Wisconsin 13 percent, and in Missouri 11 percent. By contrast, in Illinois, where most of the agricultural land was not flooded, the additional rainfall increased the yield (see Table 1.6).

Soybean production reflected the same trends, with output in Iowa down 20 percent, in Minnesota 36 percent, and in Wisconsin 2 percent. However, in Missouri and Illinois, the unflooded areas maintained their production levels of 1988–1992.

These declines in crop production not only lowered the total value of crops but also reduced livestock production because of lack of feed. It was estimated that the total value of agriculture losses was $8.454 billion in 1993 (USDA 1994) (see Table 1.7). In Iowa the ripple effect in the state's total economy was calculated at 2.2 times the loss in agriculture. If this calculation is applied to the other eight states, the total losses reach $18.1 billion.

Because this region contains some of the most productive farmland in America, the recovery of the farm economy began as soon as the flood ended. The flooding created benefits as well as problems. In many areas, new sediment revitalized the agricultural potential of the land. In others, agricultural land was heavily damaged by the deposition of sand or by erosion from the flowing waters. With the use of modern earth-moving equipment, vast amounts of sand were removed from the fields, and in many places new soil was imported. In numerous areas, eroded lands were converted to wetlands. In the process, the ecosystem was altered as a result of the new supply of water. The agricultural recovery from the flood was dramatic, however. In 1994 the Midwest produced the largest corn and soybean crops in the region's history.

Table 1.6
Corn and Soybean Yields

State	1988–1992 Bushels per Planted Acre	1993 Bushels per Planted Acre
Corn		
Illinois	116.0	130.0
Iowa	118.0	80.0
Minnesota	115.0	70.0
Missouri	101.0	90.0
Wisconsin	100.0	92.0
Soybeans		
Illinois	37.1	43.0
Iowa	39.1	30.0
Minnesota	34.5	22.0
Missouri	30.5	33.0
Wisconsin	35.7	35.0

Source: U.S. Department of Agriculture, Washington, DC: Government Printing Office, 1993.

Table 1.7
Agricultural Income Lost 1993

State	Income Loss ($ billion)
Missouri	1.79
Iowa	1.70
Minnesota	1.50
Wisconsin	0.80
South Dakota	0.57
Illinois	0.56
North Dakota	0.50
Kansas	0.44
Nebraska	0.38

Source: U.S. Department of Agriculture, Washington, DC: Government Printing Office, 1993.

Environmental Effects

The excessive rainfall of 1993 increased the rate of soil erosion, resulting in an increase in sediment transport rates and deposition. Most of the erosion was in the form of sheet and rill erosion. Although it is difficult to measure this type of erosion, it is estimated that about 4 million acres of tillable land were severely eroded by the floods. In Iowa alone, 2.4 million acres lost 20 tons or more of topsoil per acre. This rate of loss is approximately four times the soil tolerance of 5 tons per acre per year at which soil is seasonally regenerated.

The effects of the floods on groundwater levels was generally favorable. The floodwaters led to increased infiltration, renewing the groundwater. Large quantities of groundwater are required for domestic, municipal, and industrial development in the Mississippi Basin, and water withdrawal from the permeable sands and gravel frequently exceeds replacement.

Water Quality

The floods increased tremendously the amount of water flowing into the Gulf of Mexico in 1993. The floodwaters carried not only sediments but also vast quantities of chemicals, either as dissolved matter or in suspension. The total amount of herbicides (atrazine, alachlor, and metolachlor), insecticides, and fungicides carried by the Mississippi River increased greatly. For example, the total amount of atrazine delivered to the Gulf of Mexico by the Mississippi River from April to August 1993 was 1,185,800 pounds. This was 85 percent and 235 percent higher than loads delivered during the same period in 1991 and 1992, respectively. About 909,700 tons of nitrate-nitrogen were discharged in the Gulf of Mexico from April to August 1993, which was 3.7 percent and 11 percent higher than the loads in 1991 and 1992, respectively (Goolsby and Battaglin 1993).

Although the physical effects of the 1993 flood on river processes were many and varied—erosion, sedimentation, pollution transport, and so on—there is little evidence that the waters of the rivers or the Gulf of Mexico have been permanently affected. The excessive amounts of fresh water diluted the material carried, and the floodwaters mixed with the waters of the Gulf of Mexico and were soon dissipated.

Impact on Transportation

The 1993 Midwest flood caused more damage to railroads, the river barge industry, and all other forms of surface transportation than any previous disaster in the nation's history. The total loss to all transportation facilities was estimated at $1.9 billion.

The U.S. barge industry hauls 15 percent of all freight shipped in the United States, nearly all of which is on the Mississippi River system. The barge industry transports about 30 percent of the nation's petroleum products, 65 percent of the grain, 25 percent of the coal, and 20 percent of the wood products.

On June 25, 1993, the flooding reached a stage that prompted the U.S. Army Corps of Engineers to stop all barge and pleasure craft operations for a 215-mile stretch from Clarksville, Missouri, just north of St. Louis, north to Rock Island, Illinois, and then on June 28 the river was closed from Rock Island north to Minneapolis. Between July 2 and July 5 the U.S. Army Corps of Engineers closed the Missouri River between St. Louis and Omaha. In early July it was estimated 2,000 barges and 50 towboats were trapped along the flooded rivers. Because of a lack of transportation, losses of revenue rose to $1 million per day.

Initially it was thought the flood would last no longer than several weeks. When it became evident that it would persist much longer, shippers began seeking other types of transportation to move their goods. There was deep concern that several on-river coal-powered plants could not be supplied with fuel. By July 12, 2,900 barges were idled and loss of revenue had risen to $2 million per day.

As the flood persisted, the costs increased. By July 25, a tally showed that 7,000 barges containing cargoes valued at $1.9 billion were stranded on the two rivers, with losses of $3 million to $4 million per day. At St. Louis alone, over 3,000 dock workers were idled. Barge industry leaders announced that "the economic impact on the barge lines is catastrophic." During the flood, shippers who rely on barges turned to the railroads, to truckers, or both, to maintain delivery of goods. Mounting losses to the barge industry led to rate increases as high as 25 percent.

Navigation was not resumed on the Mississippi River until August 22, when 830 miles of limited barge traffic opened. During the following month new courses had to be charted, sand bars removed, and new navigation buoys placed. Congestion on the rivers prevailed for weeks. Total revenue losses in the barge navigation industry were assessed at $600 million (Interagency Floodplain Management Review Committee 1994). This far exceeded the previous record loss to the barge industry of $288 million during the 1988 drought when barges were stranded because of low river levels. It is also estimated that the closed rivers cost the economies of the flooded states $320 million (St. Louis Post Dispatch, August 18, 1993).

Not only did the 1993 flood halt barge traffic, but also, since most railroad routes were on floodplains, it curtailed—and in many areas stopped—rail service. The problem began on June 19 when a portion of the Green Bay and Western line in Wisconsin was washed out. On June 24 the Canadian Pacific removed all its cars from the St. Paul rail yards before the flood submerged them (Pacific Rail News, August 1993). By early July, high waters along the Mississippi River had inundated low-lying rail lines built parallel to the river. Bridge problems slowed or stopped trains at seven major crossings. Continued heavy rain caused washouts, severing several major lines for periods of two weeks or longer. Flooding halted rail traffic from time to time on seven main lines crossing the Midwest.

It is estimated that the damage to the railroads exceeded more than $240 million. This figure included $96 million for repair of tracks (60 miles were washed out, at a replacement cost of $1 million per mile, and 820 miles of tracks were under water, at a repair cost of $100,000 per mile), $15 million for bridge replacement and repair, $14 million for signal repairs, $9 million for repairs for train cars and engines, and $55 million for labor and fuel costs.

The flooding of highways in the Midwest began in late May in southern Minnesota and Wisconsin. Flooding of highways continued in the nine-state flooded zone well into October, with the greatest impact occurring from June through August. The closure of bridges across the Mississippi and Missouri rivers created additional problems. For example, the bridge across the Mississippi at Hannibal was closed July 2, the bridge at Keokuk on July 5, and the bridge at Quincy on July 15, leaving no way to cross the Mississippi along a 250-mile stretch north of St. Louis.

The closure of the bridge at Quincy involved a bizarre and tragic story. On July 15, floodwater overtopped a levee just west of Quincy. The rapidly flowing water swept a barge and its tow into the breach, and these in turn hit the fuel tanks of a filling station, which exploded in a ball of fire. The swirling water quickly covered five miles of U.S. Highway 36, the west approach to Quincy bridge. It spread across 14,000 acres of farmland. The 200 residents of West Quincy were evacuated as the flood destroyed many houses and buildings. A man named James Scott, who claimed to be a firefighter and an eyewitness to the levee break, was interviewed for a local television show. A sheriff recognized Scott as a parolee. After an investigation, it was determined that someone had purposefully removed the plastic topping and sandbags, thus sabotaging the levee and causing the break. Scott, the only one present at the time, was charged with the act of sabotage. After a lengthy trial, he was sentenced to life in prison (*USA Today*, December 6, 1994).

As the floodwaters receded, the damage to roads and highways was found to be much more extensive than had been expected. Illinois authorities calculated that the flood had closed 121 miles of state highway, 870 miles of county roads, and twelve state bridges. Repair costs were placed at $98 million.

Missouri highway officials reported that their damages included 350 miles of inundated state roads and 2,000 miles of flooded rural roads, of which 14 miles of state roads had to be totally rebuilt and 100 miles resurfaced. The repair cost was $110 million ($62 million for federal roads and $48 million for nonfederal). Rural and highway repairs in other states were $122 million in Iowa, $31 million in Minnesota, $22 million in Nebraska, $19 million in Wisconsin, $17 million in Kansas, and $16 million in North and South Dakota. Repair costs for highways and roads in the nine-state area was $434 million.

Federal aid for highway and road repairs from the Federal Emergency Management Agency (FEMA) and the Department of Transportation amounted to $275 million. Losses resulting from lost jobs, costs of altered commuting, delayed shipments, costs of rerouting shipments, and transfer of goods to other means of transportation were estimated at an additional $150 million.

The flood had a minimal impact on airports and air travel. In all, it affected a total of 33 airports, including 16 in Missouri and 12 in Iowa. The impact was small. There was no impact at major airports in urban areas. The total repair cost was $5.4 million. The only sector that had any effect due to flooding was the limited commercial air traffic.

Biological Effects

There were both positive and negative effects on the ecosystem of the flooded region. In general, mobile organisms, such as fish and birds, adapted to the seasonal floods. For example, because the flood endured for an exceptionally long time, extending through the spawning season for virtually all fish species, the fish sought new spawning sites in the flooded area. Given the larger area in which the fish could spawn and a better food supply, the spawning sites were of a higher quality. As a result, a large number of young fish were produced, which in turn provided a large source of food for the area's wading birds.

The flood changed the environment for a number of species. Some mosquitoes that are vectors of human disease thrived in temporary pools, water-filled containers, and tree holes. The population of zebra mussels increased enormously, with densities approaching 100,000 mussels per square yard on the river bottom. The larvae were spread across the flooded floodplains. The zebra mussel crowds out other species and hence is undesirable in large numbers. The cost of killing the excess zebra mussels has been estimated at several hundred thousand dollars.

In contrast, the vegetation, especially trees, underwent severe stress, and many trees died as a result of the exceptionally long period of inundation. A 1994 survey in the St. Louis area showed that the percentage of trees that died within the year varied from 3.7 percent near Bellevue, Iowa, to 37.1 percent near St. Louis, and 32.2 percent at Cape Girardeau. The mortality of saplings was even higher, increasing from 1.8 percent in Minnesota to 80 percent near St. Louis. Saplings are more vulnerable than mature trees, because they are shorter and more of the plant is submerged in floodwaters. However, because the mature trees survived, there is a source of seeds to regenerate the forests. The forest regeneration will actually be speeded in areas where the competing vegetation was eliminated and where nutrient-rich sediments were deposited, and sunlight can reach the forest floor where the canopy trees were killed.

Some of the mature trees were so weakened by the flood that they will die in later years as a result of insect attacks, diseases, and stress. In many instances the trees will leaf out but then die later in the season. For example, in 1994 over 90 percent of the black willows in the St. Louis area died.

The 1993 flood created conditions favorable to the removal of oxygen from the water. Fertilizer that was washed from the flooded agricultural lands carried a great amount of nitrogen, which stimulated plankton blooms on the Mississippi River and on into the Gulf of Mexico. When the blooming algae died and sank, the decaying organic matter consumed the oxygen in the bottom layers of the river waters, thereby lowering oxygen levels to less than 2 parts per million over an area of about 6,000 square miles in the Gulf of Mexico. This in turn affected valuable fisheries. It was estimated that the rivers carried 22,000 tons of nitrates downstream to the Gulf of Mexico daily in 1993, compared to about 4,000 tons per day during typical river flow.

Cultural Effects

There were many Native American archaeological sites in the flooded area. Most of the native settlements were built along water routes, for they provided water, food, and transportation to the tribes. In a survey of sites, it was found that of 28 sites in North Dakota, 10 sites had suffered significant erosion damage from the flood. In Iowa, 23 of 96 sites were damaged, and in Wisconsin, 10 of 82. At seven archaeological sites, sediment deposition and removal of vegetation caused damage. Loss of trees at archaeological sites, and hence loss of riverbank stabilization, has resulted in further erosions.

Recovery Issues

As the floods receded, there was intensive debate on how the region would proceed in its recovery from the flood. Several broad questions figured prominently in the debate: Is there a way to control the flow of water during floods? What is the best way to repair or rebuild the thousands of damaged buildings and homes? What is the role of community planning? With financial assistance, were there alternative mitigation strategies in the typical tear-down or repair-rebuild scenarios? How does risk insurance serve as a mitigation tool?

Federal Governmental Aid

Traditionally the federal government has played a significant role in dealing directly with economic catastrophes. Until 1950 Congress periodically enacted relief bills to aid victims of specific disasters. In legislation enacted in 1950, the president was authorized to define what constituted a major disaster and then to direct federal agencies to provide aid to the victims. This law formally stated that natural disaster relief was a local responsibility, but the severity of some disasters would put relief and rehabilitation efforts beyond the financial capabilities of state and local governments.

The Robert T. Stafford Disaster Relief and Emergency Assistance Amendment of 1988 made important changes to existing disaster relief programs in an attempt to increase postdisaster mitigation measures and to reduce vulnerability to damage from further disasters. Hazard mitigation is emphasized, including funding for acquiring destroyed or damaged properties and for reducing exposure to flood risks in reconstruction.

The large area of the 1993 flood provided the basis for the president to declare a disaster for 532 counties in the nine-state area. This declaration allowed the designated counties to receive federal disaster aid from various federal agencies.

On August 12, 1993, Congress appropriated $1.7 billion for "relief from the major, widespread floods in the Midwest of 1993" (P.L. 103-75). To develop the aid program, the president issued a statement in September that described the federal role in the "cost-share adjustment for Midwest flood recovery." It stated that the unprecedented degree of damage to the Midwest's economy led the president to revise the apportioning of reimbursement of eligible public assistance disaster costs for the Midwestern states affected by the flooding. Whereas the original ratio of federal to nonfederal funds was 75 percent to 25 percent, in this case it would be 90 percent to 10 percent. With the passage of the Hazard Mitigation and Relocation Assistance Act in December of 1993 (P.L. 103-181), there was a significant increase in both cost-sharing and funding for hazard mitigation.

1993 National Flood Insurance Program

The National Flood Insurance Program played a major role in the recovery from the damages of the 1993 flood. Insurance industry payments for damaged property in the region totaled $1.017 billion, and crop insurance payments totaled $1.65 billion. Despite the large losses in such a short period, "there were no reports of insolvencies for companies writing crop insurance as a direct result of the 1993 flood losses (Zaccharias 1996, 176). At the end of the 1993 fiscal year, the Federal Insurance Administration (FIA), which oversees the NFIP, had obligated in excess of $110 million more than it had available (General Accounting Office 1994). Consequently, the FIA had to borrow from the U.S. Treasury to cover the difference.

Of the claims filed after the Midwest flood, 14.9 percent (2,413 of 16,167) of these federal flood insurance claims were for structures located outside the area of the 1 percent annual flood probability (U.S. Army Corps of Engineers 1995). This means that 99 percent of the property in the floodplain area had an annual chance of floods in excess of 1 percent. In addition, another study revealed that half of the mortgaged houses in the flooded areas did not have flood insurance (Bipartisan Task Force on Funding Disaster Relief 1995). Another study found that fewer than 42,000 households of a total of 803,000 in the flood hazard area had purchased insurance at the time of the flood (Kunreuther 1996, 173).

The problems of reclamation and rebuilding were so great that many communities did not know how to cope with the devastation. There was a general consensus, however, that rebuilding in flood-prone areas was not an acceptable procedure.

The NFIP provided the guidelines for reclamation and rebuilding. When NFIP funds were used, the reclamation and rebuilding had to conform to the NFIP standards. The structure had to be damaged beyond 50 percent of its value, and the lowest floor had to be at or above the level of a flood that had a 1 percent chance of occurrence in any given year. These requirements were intended to reduce future exposure to flood risk through elimination of the structure in place or its relocation outside the regulated floodplain.

In addition to NFIP funds, funds were available from about three dozen other federal programs. By October 1994 the federal government had approved projects to purchase as many as 7,500 buildings. It was the first time buyouts had been attempted on such a scale.

Effects on the National Flood Insurance Program

In light of the problems encountered in providing aid to the victims of the 1993 flood, the federal government recognized that there was a need to reevaluate its flood insurance policies. In January 1994 the Executive Office of the President, through the administration's Floodplain Management Task Force, assigned to the Interagency Floodplain Management Review Committee the mission of determining the major causes and consequences of the Midwest flood and then of evaluating the performance of existing floodplain management and related watershed management programs. In response to this investigation Congress enacted the Community Development and Regulatory Improvement Act of 1994 and the National Flood Insurance Reform Act of 1994.

Some of the major changes recommended were:

1. Improve compliance with the mandatory requirements of the program
2. Prohibit federal disaster relief in flood disaster areas to those who fail to obtain and maintain required federal flood insurance
3. Create a supplementary mitigation insurance program to provide expanded coverage for new buildings that were constructed to current building code standards
4. Create mitigation assistance guidance for activities that are technically feasible and cost-beneficial
5. Prohibit the nonwaiver of flood insurance purchase requirements of recipients of federal disaster assistance to repair or rebuild structures damaged by floods
6. Decree that agricultural structures are no longer eligible for federal disaster assistance. However, other acts prohibited such assistance to anyone if the previous recipient let a flood insurance policy lapse
7. Establish civil monetary penalties for insurance lenders who fail to insure borrowers who are required to purchase flood insurance

However, as the recent history suggests, these provisions could easily be waived by future flood response and recovery legislation.

Dam Breakage—Johnstown Flood of 1889

The cataclysmic flood of the Conemaugh River on May 31, 1889, which caused over 2,200 deaths and the destruction of thousands of homes, resulted from the failure of the South Fork Dam, 14 miles upstream from Johnstown, Pennsylvania.

History of the South Fork Dam

The South Fork Dam was built by the state of Pennsylvania. When completed in 1824, it was the largest earthen dam in the world, holding back the largest man-made lake. The crest of the dam stood 100 feet above the old creek bed. It was 272 feet thick at its base, diminishing to 10 feet at the top. From rock wall to rock wall, it stretched 931 feet. Four cast-iron pipes, regulated by valves, discharged excess water from a reservoir 2 miles long, 1 mile wide, and 70 feet deep that contained about 5 billion gallons of water. In addition, a spillway 72 feet wide was cut 9 feet deep into the rock abutting the eastern end of the dam. The dam was part of a system of rivers and canals that extended river navigation from Pittsburgh to Johnstown.

Soon after the dam was completed it was part of an obsolete canal transportation system. The railroad had replaced most of the water links in the system. In 1879 the state of Pennsylvania sold the dam and reservoir to a private investor, who created the South Fork Fishing and Hunting Club and sold $2,000 memberships to such luminaries as Andrew Mellon, Andrew Carnegie, Henry Clay Frick, and Philander C. Knox. Cottages and a clubhouse were built, and makeshift repairs were made on the deteriorating dam. Tree stumps, straw, and hemlock branches were used to fill holes. The discharge pipes were removed, and the crest of the dam was lowered by 20 feet to permit the construction of a road. In 1880 the Cambria Iron Company retained an engineer to inspect the dam. His report indicated that the dam needed extensive repairs, but the owner of the South Fork Fishing and Hunting Club, Benjamin R. Ruff, assured the Johnstown public, "You and your people are in no danger from our enterprise."

Dam Breakage

In May 1889, unusually heavy rainfall occurred in the 12,000-square-mile basin of the Conemaugh River. In addition, warm weather quickly melted a snow cover of 14 inches. Rivers were swollen and the lake above the South Fork dam was filled to capacity. About 75,000 gallons of water per second were flowing into the lake, but the restricted spillway was capable of discharging only about 45,000 gallons per second.

The danger of a dam breakage grew, and on the morning of May 31 a crew of some thirty men attempted to shore up the swollen dam. By 11:00 A.M. it became evident that the dam would break. In response, a lone rider began a solitary ride through the valley to warn residents to evacuate.

Effects of Dam Breakage

At 3:10 P.M. the dam gave way. A wall of water 150 feet high rushed southward through the valley at about 50 miles per hour. In the villages, the water plunged forward, picking up trees, houses, and other flotsam. Not only was there devastating property damage, but also the floodwaters moved in so quickly that people did not have time to flee. In East Conemaugh in the Pennsylvania Railroad yard there were 33 Consolidation model locomotives with a tender, each weighing 170,625 pounds. These, along with 315 freight and 18 passenger cars, were tossed about as though they were toys. One engine was carried nearly a mile and embedded in rock and sand.

After moving through East Conemaugh, the flood careened through the town of Woodvale, where it uprooted 800 buildings, smashing 255 of them to timber, and killing nearly 1,000 people. Hundreds of people saved their lives by hanging onto rooftops.

Moments later the flood roared though the steel mill of the Gautier Wireworks. The plant's boiler burst, sending towering plumes of steam hundreds of feet into the sky.

A little after 4:00 P.M. the enormous wave, carrying an enormous amount of debris, reached Johnstown. It sped through the city in minutes, killing more than 1,000 people. Not only were small houses destroyed but enormous stone buildings collapsed, trapping hundreds who thought they had safe havens. All of the municipal buildings were flattened. The Hulbert House, a large brick hotel, collapsed, drowning all of the sixty guests who were trapped on the third-floor staircase leading to the roof and supposed safety.

Families were separated and whole families died as they were swept from rooftops into the rapid waters. Some were saved as they were transferred from one swirling mass of debris to another; others were drowned along the way.

At the southern edge of Johnstown the floodwaters encountered a stone bridge that was normally 32 feet above the riverbed. Mountains of debris soon clogged the bridge. The rushing mass of debris contained human beings, both alive and dead. Within the debris, burning coal from the factories soon created a burning mass of flames. One woman later reported, "As the fire licked up house after house and pile after pile, I could see men and women kiss each other good-bye and fathers and mothers kiss their children. The flames swallowed them up and the water moved them from my view but I could hear their shrieks as they roasted alive."

The flood was through Johnstown by 6:00 P.M. People were pulled from buildings for days. For weeks, bodies floated downstream, threatening the spread of disease. Against all odds, a live five-month-old baby was found 100 miles downstream in Pittsburgh, floating inside a ravaged house.

The devastation was that much greater because Johnstown was a major iron and steel center where the mills were located on the floodplain surrounded by the closely packed homes of the workers. The rebuilding of Johnstown and the villages progressed rapidly, however, and the iron and steel operations and the coal mines were operating again within a few months. Within a few years, the area was restored and the pace of life was restored to what it had been before the flood.

Thunderstorm Flash Floods—Big Thompson Canyon Flash Flood of 1976

The Big Thompson River rises in the Colorado Rocky Mountains and flows 78 miles downstream to the point where it enters the South Platte River. Under normal conditions, it is a small stream, barely 18 inches deep and several feet wide. Through the first 21 miles of its course it descends over 5,000 feet. At Estes Park it drops into a 25-mile-long gorge known as the Big Thompson Canyon. In this narrow gorge it falls about 2,500 feet. After it leaves the canyon it wanders on the flat Great Plains to its junction with the South Platte.

The Big Thompson Canyon is a sparsely inhabited wilderness area with about 600 ranches. It is also a popular recreational area not far from Denver. On July 31, 1976, a three-day celebration began marking Colorado's centennial. The motels and campgrounds in the canyon were filled to capacity. The population was estimated to be more than 3,500.

Origin of the Flood

Late in the afternoon of the 31st, a line of thunderstorms ran from central Kansas to the Rockies in Colorado. Around noon an intense thunderstorm developed in this area at the foot of the mountain and continued unabated for four and a half hours. In the upper area of the canyon, 12 inches of rain fell, exceeding the normal amount for one year.

By 8:00 P.M. the water was rising so rapidly in the stream that flood conditions were evident. Because heavy thunderstorms occur frequently in the Rockies, many who had been told by police to leave the area did not believe that there was any real danger. By 7:00 P.M. floodwaters were moving so rapidly that police could not spend more time trying to convince people to leave. Shortly after 8:00 P.M. most of Route 43 in the canyon was washed out.

Effects of the Flood

Around 8:30 P.M. the river water raced out of the canyon mouth at a velocity of more than 20 feet per second, or more than 230,000 gallons per second. By this time the water contained dirt, rocks, buildings, cars, and other debris. Route 43 was being ripped apart, sending 10- to 12-foot chunks of asphalt high into the air. Dorothy Venrick, an observer who lived 250 feet from the river, later related, "You could hear people inside cars screaming for help. Above the roar of the river and the sound of homes smashing into each other, you could hear (them). . . . It made your heart sick to stand there and know that there was nothing you could do." An ambulance crew had entered the canyon to aid people. As they were trying to turn the ambulance around, the driver later reported, "There was a huge, choking dust cloud ahead of the water. Then the water hit us like a big freight train. It picked up the ambulance about fifteen feet into the air and slammed it into a V-shaped wedge on one of the canyon walls." The men left the ambulance and climbed the canyon walls to a perch 50 feet above the highway. The water rose to their level, but they clung to the hill until morning, when a helicopter rescued them. Hundreds were rescued from the canyon walls by helicopters.

The toll in death and property destruction was enormous. Officially, there were 139 deaths by drowning, but over 600 people were never accounted for. For example, a motel registration log was found with 28 registered guests. The motel had been completely washed away and many of the guests were never found.

Governmental Response

The governor of Colorado responded to the flood immediately, that night, to provide aid to victims. In 1973 the Colorado legislature had given extraordinary power to the governor to "meet the disasters of the state." Under the Colorado Emergency Act, the governor immediately appointed an advisory committee to develop a complete disaster recovery program for victims of the Big Thompson Canyon flood. At the same time, the Colorado Water Conservation Board made an aerial survey of the flood to determine any water problems.

After a year's study, a final report was prepared. In order to implement the comprehensive plan, a set of goals and objectives was established. The goals for the Big Thompson Advisory Committee, adopted on August 23, 1976, were precise:

1. Economic and social: to assist survivors, property owners, and communities in readjusting
2. Physical and public works projects: to support the recovery and rehabilitation of the canyon in a safe and orderly manner
3. Planning: to achieve positive results and avoid duplication of past mistakes
4. Financial: to assume maximization of planning and public works financial assistance

Several years after the recovery plan was initiated, a survey revealed some strengths and a few weaknesses in it. At the state level, the recovery was placed in the hands of department heads. By this procedure, the state government developed a uniform approach. This provided a logical resolution of many disaster problems. In contrast, there was sometimes a leadership vacuum at the local governmental level. The *Estes Park Trail Gazette* wrote, "The Governor really tried to let the county run the program, but they were not ready for the disaster and they came off like they were campaigning rather than trying to solve the problems." Part of the problem was that the local leaders, who had been in office for years, thought they knew what was best for the people. However, they were unaccustomed to dealing with disasters. In spite of some problems, the state and local governments did make progress in the area's economic recovery. By 1979 over $57 million had been spent on the recovery of the canyon economy.

At the time of the flood, only one federal flood insurance policy was in effect in the Big Thompson Canyon, and only twenty-three policies had been issued in Larimer County. The importance of flood insurance became evident with this flood, and in 1974 Larimer County joined the National Flood Insurance Program.

Hurricane Floods—Susquehanna River Flood of 1972

As Atlantic hurricanes move northward along the Atlantic coast from Florida to Canada, flooding is a common phenomenon. Some recent hurricanes are listed in Tables 2.4 and 2.5 (see pp. 59–60). One of the most devastating such floods occurred in 1972 in the Susquehanna River Basin and adjacent areas. The crest stages of the Susquehanna River exceeded the previous record by several feet. Most levees built to contain the highest floods overtopped.

Origin of the Flood

The Susquehanna River flood of 1972 was caused by an Atlantic coastal hurricane. On June 16 Hurricane Agnes was spawned on the eastern coast of the Yucatan Peninsula in the Gulf of Mexico. As the storm moved westward, it gained strength. Moving through the west end of Cuba and the panhandle of Florida, it killed dozens of people and caused considerable property damage.

From there the storm moved inland over Georgia and the Carolinas, where it did little damage. It then moved outward over the Atlantic Ocean, once again gaining moisture and energy. But as it moved northward it veered inland over the Middle Atlantic states, where it stalled over Pennsylvania from June 20 to June 25. During this period, rainfall recorded in Pennsylvania ranged from 4 inches to more than 19 inches. The greatest amount fell in the Susquehanna Basin from Maryland to Wilkes-Barre, Pennsylvania. The counties of York, Dauphin, Schuylkill, and Northumberland each received 16 to 18 inches of precipitation.

Flood Damage

The major flood damage was concentrated in the urban centers in the Susquehanna Basin.

Wilkes-Barre

Because Wilkes-Barre had been flooded a number of times in the past, attempts had been made to control flooding. As a response to a flood crest of 33 feet of water on the north branch of the

Susquehanna River in the 1937 St. Patrick's Day flood, the U.S. Army Corps of Engineers built a dike with a maximum flood crest of 37 feet to protect Wilkes-Barre and adjoining Hanover Township. By 1943 an earthen levee 24,600 feet long and 160 feet of concrete wall had been completed. It was thought that this embankment would contain any possible flood of the future. After subsequent settling of the levee, in 1959 the U.S. Corps of Engineers added a wall some 2,230 feet long of steel-woven piles to the top of the levee crown to bring it above the probable maximum flood level. In addition, a system of fourteen flood-control lakes upstream from Wilkes-Barre was authorized, of which six were completed by 1971.

June 1972 Flood

The water of the Susquehanna began to rise on June 20, and by June 23 the Civil Defense Unit reported that the river level was between 33 and 34 feet at 6:00 A.M., the highest level since 1936. As a response, residents of Kingston and the areas of Wilkes-Barre outside the dike began to be evacuated. In order to protect the dikes and not block bridges, more than 10,000 volunteers began sandbagging.

By 10:30 A.M. the river had risen to 37.2 feet, and the River Forecast Center in Harrisburg was predicting a crest higher than 40 feet. At 11:10 A.M. the order was given for the orderly evacuation of Wilkes-Barre. The first dike broke at 1:12 P.M. at Forty Fort. Other dike breaks soon followed. By late afternoon over 100,000 people had been evacuated from Wilkes-Barre and surrounding areas. Schools, public buildings, and houses on high ground were soon jammed with refugees.

The crest of the flood occurred on June 24 at 40.91 feet. It required more than a week for the flood to subside, allowing people to return to their homes. The entire city was devastated. Besides the damage from the flooding, some gas mains had erupted, and many buildings burned to the water line. Many of the houses were so badly damaged that they had to be destroyed. Mud was everywhere, inside as well as outside buildings. The cemetery at Forty Fort had been eroded, and caskets and bodies had washed away. There was also some looting, and the National Guard was called to duty to protect the property. People throughout the East provided aid in the recovery efforts. Although official estimates are very general, the total property damage exceeded tens of millions of dollars, and recovery took years. Many people left the area permanently.

Sunbury

Sunbury is located at the confluence of the northern west branches of the Susquehanna River, and consequently it has been subject to repeated flooding. Because floods had invaded the city in 1936 and again in 1946, in 1948 the U.S. Army Corps of Engineers began constructing a system of levees and flood walls to protect the city. Some people objected to this system of flood control, for it greatly restricted the outdoor activities associated with the river front.

Although the river rose to a crest of 35.82 feet, 12 feet above normal flood level and more than a foot higher than the previous record crest of 34.61 feet in 1936, no flooding occurred in the city. A crew of volunteers manned the dike around the clock, sandbagging the possible openings and reinforcing places where leakage was expected. Five pumping stations, erected by the U.S. Army Corps of Engineers, discharged sanitary water and storm runoff water into the high water of the river.

Harrisburg

In the early days of the flood it was predicted that Harrisburg would escape the flood. On the morning of Thursday, June 22, the final issue of the *Harrisburg Patriot* stated, "There appears to be no immediate threat that the main channel of the Susquehanna, the Juniata, and West Branch will reach flood levels along the river basin." Rain continued to fall in torrents all day, however. The Susquehanna reached flood stage (12 feet) by noon on June 23, and the water continued to rise, reaching a level of 26 feet by midnight Thursday. In response, the governor of Pennsylvania and the mayor of Harrisburg called for the evacuation of 2,000 residents living along the water front.

The rivers invaded the new governor's mansion, and near the mansion a home caught fire from a break in a gas line. The rising water kept the firefighters from reaching the burning home. They fought the fire from the roofs of buildings, and before it could be controlled an entire row of houses burned to the ground.

The river finally crested in Harrisburg on Saturday, June 24, at 11:30 A.M. at a height of 30.33 feet, 3.5 feet higher than the 1936 flood. At the peak of the flood, almost half of the city was underwater. The city has been rebuilt on the floodplain and will in the future be subject to massive floods.

York

A number of cities that are not on the Susquehanna River were flooded because of the widespread rains. York was one of these.

York's flood protection was not always adequate. In 1942 the U.S. Army Corps of Engineers built the Rock Dam on the west branch of Colorama Creek. This flood control dam protected a portion of the city, but the smaller south branch of the Colorama Creek had no flood control. On June 23 the stream became a torrent, flooding the city. All bridges were impassable, and hundreds of people were evacuated. The Colorama crested at 26.4 feet, 2 feet above flood stage.

Although the flood was devastating, it would have been worse without flood control. It was thought that without the Rock Dam, the city would have had a greater inundation. Nevertheless, York's experience illustrates that a partial solution is inadequate for complete safety from flood. An integrated plan could possibly have saved the city.

Chemung River

The Chemung River, one of the northern tributaries of the Susquehanna, joins the latter at Athens, Pennsylvania, and passes westward through Bradford County before crossing the Pennsylvania–New York state line. The river flooded the Chemung area on June 22. At Chemung, New York, the crest reached 31.4 feet, more than 7 feet above the record crest of 23.97 feet in the 1946 flood.

The flood had a devastating effect on the Corning glass plant in Corning, New York. By Friday, June 23, the flood had inundated the entire city to a depth of about 5 feet, and then appeared to be subsiding. However, on Friday evening an unexplained surge of water, later referred to as "a flood within a flood," rushed over the city. A wave nearly 8 feet tall rushed through the city streets, sweeping everything before it. Although many people had previously been evacuated, the death toll from this single rush of water totaled 23 in the Corning–Painted Post area alone.

Other Areas

Although the major flooded areas were concentrated along the Susquehanna River, the entire state of Pennsylvania and portions of adjoining states underwent flooding. At Reading, on the Schuylkill River, the water filtration system and sewage disposal facilities were destroyed. Drinking water had to be rationed for weeks. Downingtown, Pottstown, and Norristown were flooded, and hundreds of families had to be evacuated. In contrast, flooding in Philadelphia was minimal. The wider Delaware River channel could handle the excess water.

Pittsburgh was flooded along its floodplain, with damages estimated at $45 million. However, the flood control dams—Kinzua, Tionesta, Mahoning Creek, Crooked Creek, Loyalhanna, and Youghiogheny—built after the devastating flood of 1936, were effective in greatly reducing the flood stage.

Other areas flooded included towns on the west branch of the Susquehanna and a few on the Juniata River.

Aftermath

The Hurricane Agnes floods demonstrated that the absolute control of flooding in a river system is not possible. When excessive precipitation occurs, the damage can be reduced but not eliminated. The cost of a flood disaster is difficult to estimate. In total, the Susquehanna floods caused more than 40 deaths. Thousands of families were homeless for months, and highways and bridges had more than $500 million of damage; property damage was in the range of billions of dollars; factories were closed for months, and some never reopened.

Tsunami Floods—Papua New Guinea Tsunami

Tsunamis are the world's most powerful waves. They are the product of undersea earthquakes normally found around the Pacific Rim, where powerful collisions of tectonic plates form highly seismic subduction zones. These earthquakes begin the movement of water that may extend for thousands of miles across the ocean. Between 1990 and 1999, 82 tsunamis were reported worldwide, a rate much higher than the average of 57 reported in previous decades. This increase in numbers is due not to an increase in the rate of tsunamis but to more reporting through improved global communication. Of the 82 tsunamis, 10 have taken more than 4,000 lives as mammoth waves washed over the shores. Some recent tsunamis are listed in Table 2.6 (see p. 61).

In recent decades about 86 percent of the tsunamis have been in the Pacific Ocean. Tsunamis have created disaster flooding in Nicaragua, New Guinea, Hawaii, Alaska, and many other places. It has long been believed that the western coast of the United States is relatively safe from the most disastrous tsunamis. Evidence now suggests that earthquakes could create large tsunamis every 200 to 300 years along the Cascadian subduction zone, an area along the Pacific Northwest's coast where a crustal plate carrying part of the Pacific Ocean is submerging under North America. As recently as April 1992, an earthquake with a magnitude of 7.1 on the Richter scale was generated at the southern end of this subduction zone, creating a small tsunami near Cape Mendocino, California.

The wave movement in a tsunami does not originate from the gravitational pull of the sun or the moon, but rather in an undersea earthquake or, less frequently, in a volcanic eruption, a meteorite impact, or an underwater landslide. With speeds exceeding 500 miles an hour in the deep ocean, a tsunami wave could easily keep pace with a Boeing 747. This underwater movement creates a sea-surface slope so gentle that the wave usually passes unnoticed in deep water.

A tsunami can speed silently and undetected across the ocean, then unexpectedly rise as destructively high waves in shallow coastal waters. A powerful tsunami can thus cause damage thousands of miles from its origin. The Hawaiian Islands are particularly vulnerable to tsunamis because of their mid-Pacific location. Since 1895 twelve tsunamis have struck Hawaii. In the most destructive of these, 159 people died in 1946 from an earthquake in Alaska, about 2,300 miles away.

In 1803 the Krakatoa volcano in Indonesia created the most devastating tsunami known. Within 100 miles of the explosion, 30,000 people died in the Sunda Strait. The waves reached a height of a twelve-story building as they crashed on the island shores.

On July 17, 1998, it was a quiet Friday evening on the northern New Guinea coast between the Sissano Lagoon and the Bismarck Sea coast. Without warning, at 6:49 P.M. an earthquake with a magnitude of 7.1 on the Richter scale occurred on the lagoon and suddenly deformed the ocean bottom. The normally flat sea bottom lurched upward, giving birth to a fearsome tsunami. Within minutes the sea rose above the shoreline as much as 90 feet. The initial wave quickly subsided, but within a few minutes a second wave 45 feet high rose, creating a rumble like that of a low-flying jet airplane. As the wave hit the shore, villages were swept into the sea, tossed into the mangrove forests, or battered into debris. Salt-water crocodiles and wild dogs preyed on the dead before rescue crews arrived. Over 2,300 villagers were drowned within 15 minutes.

Wind and Tidal Floods—Eastern Coast of England

Many severe and extensive floods result from the effects of strong storms that create tidal waves on shore. Shallow seas, such as on the shore of the North Sea, the Gulf of Mexico, and the Bay of Bengal, are particularly responsive to wind stress from high velocity winds. They are also surrounded by appreciable land areas near sea level, so high water levels can cause extensive flooding. Such high water levels are known as "storm surges."

The low-lying eastern coast of England has always been subject to flooding by abnormally high tides. As early as 1099, the Anglo-Saxons noted, "At Martinmas, the incoming tide reached up so strongly and did so much damage that none remembered the like before." Although tidal flooding continued through the ages, little research was done on them until the twentieth century.

In response to tidal flooding in London on January 7, 1928, in which 14 people drowned, researchers began to study tidal movements and waves. They found that tidal waves were caused not only by high winds but also by tides that traveled great distances. They found, for example, that high tides in the Thames estuary were often associated with winds that had created high tides in the Firth of Forth nine to ten hours earlier. The tide, as a storm surge, moved southeastward down the coast of Britain. In response to these findings, a rudimentary warning system was established.

One of the most disastrous of the English eastern coast tidal floods occurred on January 31, 1953. This event resulted from an unusually high spring tide combined with one of the strongest northern gales on record. High water exceeded 8 feet along the coast. More than 160,000 acres were flooded, 24,000 houses were damaged, and 300 people were drowned.

References

Benenson, B. "Insurance Finds New Takers," *Congressional Quarterly Weekly Reports* 51 (1993): 1861.

Bipartisan Task Force on Funding Disaster Relief. Federal Disaster Assistance. U.S. Senate 104-4. Washington, DC: U.S. Government Printing Office, 1995.

Changnon, Stanley A., ed. *The Great Flood of 1993: Causes, Impacts, and Responses.* Boulder: Westview Press, 1996.

Clark, C. *Planet Earth: Floods.* New York: Time-Life Books, 1982.

Federal Emergency Management Agency (FEMA). Interagency Hazard Mitigation Team Report. State Report, FEMA-994-OR-WI, FEMA-997-DR-IL, FEMA-998-NE, FEMA-1000-KS. Washington, DC: U.S. Government Printing Office, 1993.

General Accounting Office. *Flood Insurance: Financial Resources May Not Be Sufficient to Meet Future Capital Losses.* Letter Report, GAO/RCED-94-80. Washington, DC: U.S. Government Printing Office, 1994.

Goolsby, D. A., and W. A. Battaglin. "Occurrence, Distribution, or Transport of Agricultural Chemicals in Surface Water of the Midwestern United States." In D. A. Goolsby et al., eds., *Selected Papers on Agricultural Chemicals in Water Resources of the Midcontinental United States.* Open-File Report 93-418. Washington, DC: U.S. Geological Survey, 1993, 1–24.

Hall, B. C., and C. T. Wood. *Big Muddy: Down the Mississippi through America's Heartland.* New York: Penguin, 1992.

Interagency Floodplain Management Review Committee. *Sharing the Challenge: Floodplain Management into the Twenty-first Century.* Report to Floodplain Management Task Force, Washington, DC: U.S. Government Printing Office, 1994.

Kunreuther, H. "Managing Disaster Losses through Insurance." *Journal of Risk and Uncertainty* 12 (1996): 171–187.

Maisson, A. "The Great Flood of '93." *National Geographic* 185, no. 1 (1994): 42–81.

Moore, J. W., and D. P. Moore. *The Army Corps of Engineers and the Evolution of Federal Floodplain Management Policy.* Special Publication No. 20, Natural Hazard Research and Application Information Center, Institute of Behavioral Science. Boulder: University of Colorado, 1989.

Mrazik, B. R., and H. Appel Kinberg. "National Flood Insurance Program: Twenty Years of Progress toward Decreasing Nationwide Flood Losses." In *National Water Summary, 1988–89: Hydrological Events and Floods and Droughts.* U.S. Geological Survey Water Supply Paper 2370, 1991, pp. 133–145.

National Flood Damage Potential. 86th Cong., 1st sess. Washington, DC: U.S. Government Printing Office, 1959.

Parrett, C., N. B. Melcher, and R. W. James Jr. *Flood Discharge in the Upper Mississippi River Basin, 1993.* Circular 1120-A. Washington, DC: U.S. Geological Survey, 1993.

Salmon, J., and D. Hennington. *Prior Planning for Post-hurricane Reconstruction.* Report no. 88. Gainesville, FL: Florida Sea Grant College Program, 1987.

Task Force on Federal Flood Control Policy. *A Unified National Program for Managing Flood Losses.* Report no. 67-663. Washington, DC: U.S. Government Printing Office, 1966.

U.S. Army Corps of Engineers. *Floodplain Management Assessment of the Upper Mississippi River and Lower Missouri Rivers and Their Tributaries.* St. Louis, MO: U.S. Army Corps of Engineers, 1995.

U.S. Department of Agriculture. *USDA Emergency Assistance Paid to Flood States.* Washington, DC: USDA Office of the Chief Economist, July 8, 1994.

U.S. Senate, Committee on Public Works. A Program for Reducing the U.S. Water Resource Council. *Guidelines for Determining Flood Stage Frequency.* Bulletin 17B of the Hydrology Committee. Washington, DC: U.S. Government Printing Office, 1981.

Wahl, K. L., K. C. Vinny, and G. J. White. *Precipitation in the Upper Mississippi River Basin, January 1 through July 31, 1993.* Circular 1120-B. Washington, DC: U.S. Geological Survey, 1993.

White, G. F. *Changes in Urban Occupance of Flood Plains in the United States.* Research Paper no. 57. Chicago: Department of Geography, University of Chicago, 1958.

———. *Human Adjustment to Floods: A Geographic Approach to the Flood Problem in the United States.* Chicago: Department of Geography, University of Chicago, 1942.

Zaccharias, T. P. "Impact on Agricultural Products: Huge Financial Losses Lead to New Policies." In Stanley A. Changnon, ed., *The Great Flood of 1993: Causes, Impacts, and Responses.* Westview Press, 1996, chapter 7.

Chronology 2

The following tables together constitute a chronology of floods and the legislation passed to address them.

Table 2.1
Dates and Casualties of Selected Major World Floods

Date	Location	Deaths
1228	Holland	100,000
1642	China	300,000
1883, Aug. 27	Indonesia	36,000
1887	Huang He RIver, China	900,000
1889, May 31	Johnstown, PA	2,209
1900, Sept. 8	Galveston, TX	5,000
1903, June 15	Heppner, OR	325
1911	Chang Jiang River, China	100,000
1913, Mar. 25–27	Ohio and Indiana	732
1915, Aug. 17	Galveston, TX	275
1928, Mar. 13	Dam collapse, Saugus, CA	450
1928, Sept. 13	Lake Okeechobee, FL	2,000
1931, Aug.	Huang He River, China	3,700,000
1937, Jan. 22	Ohio and Mississippi Valleys	250
1939	Northern China	200,000
1947, Sept. 20	Honshu Island, Japan	1,900
1951, Aug.	Manchuria	1,800
1953, Jan. 31	Western Europe	2,000
1954, Aug. 17	Farahzad, Iran	2,000
1955, Oct. 7–12	India and Pakistan	1,700
1959, Nov. 1	Western Mexico	2,000
1959, Dec. 2	Fréjus, France	412
1960, Oct. 10	Bangladesh	6,000
1960, Oct. 31	Bangladesh	4,000
1962, Feb. 17	North Sea Coast, Germany	343
1962, Sept. 27	Barcelona, Spain	445
1963, Oct. 9	Dam collapse, Vaiont, Italy	1,800
1966, Nov. 3–4	Florence and Venice, Italy	113
1967, Jan. 18–24	Eastern Brazil	894
1967, Mar. 19	Rio de Janeiro, Brazil	436
1967, Nov. 26	Lisbon, Portugal	464
1968, Aug. 7–14	Gujarat State, India	1,000

Table 2.1 *continued*

Date	Location	Deaths
1968, Oct. 7	Northeastern India	780
1969, Jan. 18–26	Southern California	100
1969, Mar. 17	Mundau Valley, Alagoas, Brazil	218
1969, Aug. 20–22	Western Virginia	189
1969, Sept. 15	South Korea	250
1969, Oct. 1–8	Tunisia	500
1970, May 20	Central Romania	160
1970, July 22	Himalayas, India	500
1971, Feb. 26	Rio de Janeiro, Brazil	130
1972, Feb. 26	Buffalo Creek, WV	118
1972, June 9	Rapid City, SD	236
1972, Aug. 7	Luzon Island, Philippines	454
1972, Aug. 19–31	Pakistan	1,500
1974, Mar. 29	Tubarao, Brazil	1,000
1974, Aug. 12	Monty-Long, Bangladesh	2,500
1976, July 31	Big Thompson Canyon, CO	139
1976, Nov. 17	East Java, Indonesia	136
1977, July 19–20	Johnstown, PA	68
1978, June–Sept.	Northern India	1,200
1979, Jan.–Feb.	Brazil	204
1979, July 17	Lomblen Island, Indonesia	539
1979, Aug. 11	Morvi, India	15,000
1981, Apr.	Northern China	550
1981, July	Szechuan and Hupeh Provinces, China	1,300
1982, Jan. 23	Near Lima, Peru	600
1982, May 12	Guangdong, China	430
1982, Sept. 17–21	El Salvador and Guatemala	1,300+
1984, Aug.–Sept.	South Korea	200+
1987, Aug.–Sept.	Northern Bangladesh	1,000+
1988, Sept.	Northern India	1,000+
1993, July–Aug.	Midwest United States	48
1995, July	Hunan Province, China	1,200
1995, Aug. 19	Southwestern Morocco	136
1995, Dec. 25	KwaZulu Natal, South Africa	166
1996, Feb. 17	Biak Island, Indonesia	105
1996, April	Afghanistan	100+
1996, June–July	Southern China	315
1996, Aug. 7	Pyrenees Mountains, Spain	71
1997, July	Poland and Czech Republic	98
1997, Nov.	Bardera, Somalia	1,300+
1998, Jan.	Kenya	86
1998, Mar.	Southwestern Pakistan	300+
1998, July–Aug.	China	3,000+
1998, July–Sept.	Bangladesh	850
1998, July 17	Papua New Guinea	3,000
1998, Sept.	Guatemala	10,000+
1999, July–Aug.	East Coast, United States	50+

Source: National Weather Bureau.

Table 2.2
Deaths and Damages of U.S. Floods, 1903–1994

Year	Deaths	Property Damage ($ thousand unadjusted)	Property Damage ($ thousand adjusted to 1992 dollars)
1903	178	53	2,800
1904	0	7	350
1905	2	11	580
1906	1	0.4	20
1907	7	16	770
1908	11	10	530
1909	5	49	2,700
1910	0	21	1,100
1911	0	8	420
1912	2	78	4,300
1913	527	171	8,600
1914	180	18	1,000
1915	49	14	760
1916	118	26	1,000
1917	80	27	850
1918	0	8	200
1919	2	3	80
1920	42	25	490
1921	143	29	710
1922	215	52	1,500
1923	42	53	1,200
1924	27	17	400
1925	36	10	240
1926	16	23	570
1927	423	348	8,400
1928	15	45	1,100
1929	89	68	1,600
1930	14	16	400
1931	0	3	80
1932	11	10	330
1933	33	37	1,000
1934	88	10	260
1935	236	127	3,200
1936	142	283	6,900
1937	142	441	9,400
1938	180	101	2,100
1939	83	14	290
1940	60	40	840
1941	47	40	770
1942	68	99	1,800
1943	107	200	3,400
1944	33	101	1,700
1945	91	166	2,700
1946	28	71	1,400
1947	55	272	3,300
1948	82	230	2,500
1949	48	94	990

Table 2.2 *continued*

Year	Deaths	Property Damage ($ thousand unadjusted)	Property Damage ($ thousand adjusted to 1992 dollars)
1950	93	176	1,700
1951	51	1,029	9,400
1952	54	254	2,200
1953	40	122	1,020
1954	55	107	850
1955	302	995	7,500
1956	42	65	470
1957	82	360	2,500
1958	47	218	1,400
1959	25	141	890
1960	32	93	570
1961	52	154	910
1962	19	75	430
1963	39	178	990
1964	100	652	3,480
1965	119	788	4,100
1966	31	117	580
1967	34	375	1,700
1968	31	339	1,500
1969	297	903	3,600
1970	135	225	800
1971	74	288	900
1972	554	4,465	12,700
1973	148	1,894	5,000
1974	121	576	1,400
1975	107	1,373	3,100
1976	193	3,000	6,300
1977	210	1,300	2,500
1978	143	700	1,300
1979	121	3,500	5,800
1980	82	1,500	2,300
1981	84	1,000	1,400
1982	155	2,500	3,300
1983	200	4,000	4,900
1984	125	3,750	4,500
1985	70	500	600
1986	208	6,000	7,000
1987	88	1,500	1,700
1988	37	500	600
1989	70	1,100	1,200
1990	125	1,600	1,700
1991	63	1,700	1,800
1992	50	800	800
1993	109	16,370	—
1994	70	1,120	—

Note: Estimated annual deaths and damages (in current and constant 1992 dollars) related to floods in the United States, 1903–1994 (1993 and 1994 in current dollars only).
Source: National Weather Bureau.

Table 2.3
Selected U.S. River Floods

Allegheny (NY, PA)
Apr. 1806, Mar. 1865, June 1889, June 1892, Mar. 1905, Mar. 1907, Mar. 1910, Mar. 1913, July 1942, Apr. 1947

Arkansas (CO, KS, OK)
1826, June 1864, May 1867, June 1833, Oct. 1892, June 1904, June 1905, Oct. 1908, Apr. 1913, Aug. 1915, June and Aug. 1921, June 1923, Apr. 1927, July 1929, June 1935, May 1943, July 1948

Canadian (NM, TX)
Oct. 1904, Oct. 1923, Oct. 1930, June 1932, May and June 1935, June 1937, June 1938, Sept. 1941, July 1948

Clinch (VA, TN)
1862, Mar. 1886, Dec. 1901, Nov. 1906, Mar. 1917, Jan. 1918, Feb. 1923, Mar. 1929, Jan. 1932, Aug. 1940

Colorado (CO, UT, AZ)
1862, July 1884, Dec 1889, Feb. and June 1905, June 1909, July 1912, Jan 1916, June 1917, June 1918, May 1920, June 1921, May 1922, July 1927, Sept. 1939, June 1953

Colorado (TX)
July 1869, Apr. 1881, May 1908, Dec. 1913, May 1914, Sept. 1921, Apr. 1922, Oct. 1930, June 1935, Sept. 1936, July 1938, June 1939, June 1940, Sept. 1952

Columbia (OR, WA)
1849, 1862, 1876, May and June 1894, June 1913, May 1928, June 1988, Dec. 1997

Connecticut (VT, MA, CN)
1683, 1692, 1770, 1780, Mar. 1801, May 1814, Mar. 1843, May 1854, 1862, 1870, 1896, 1901, 1913, Nov. 1927, Mar. 1936, Sept. 1938

Cumberland (KY, TN)
1793, Mar. 1826, Jan. 1882, Mar. 1913, Jan. 1918, Dec. 1926, Jan. 1927, June 1928, Mar. 1929, Jan. 1946

Delaware (NY, NJ, PA)
1687, 1692, 1786, Jan. 1841, June 1862, Oct. 1869, Feb. 1896, Aug. and Oct. 1903, Mar. 1904, Mar. 1914, Aug. 1933, Mar. 1936, Aug. 1938, May 1942

Des Moines (IA)
June 1851, May 1903, May 1909, June 1918, Apr. 1933, June 1947

Eel (CA)
Jan. 1862, Feb. 1915, Mar. 1928, Jan. 1936, Feb. and Dec. 1937, Feb. 1940

French Broad (NC, TN)
Mar. 1867, May 1875, May 1901, Apr. 1902, Apr. 1903, July 1916, Mar. 1920, Aug. 1928, Aug. 1940

Gila (AZ)
Feb. 1891, Dec. 1906, Jan. 1916, Jan. 1923, Dec. 1923, Aug. 1931, Aug. 1934, Feb. 1937, Jan. 1941

Grand (Neosho) (KS, OK)
Sept. 1820, 1885, July 1904, Oct. 1908, June 1916, July 1922, Apr. 1926, Aug. 1927, Nov. 1928, July 1929, June 1938, Apr. 1941, May 1943, July 1948, July 1951

Table 2.3 *continued*

Guadalupe (TX)
July 1869, Dec. 1913, May 1914, Sept. 1919, Sept. 1921, July 1932, May 1929, May and June 1935, Apr. 1936, July 1936, July 1940, Sept. 1946, Apr. 1949, Sept. 1952

Gunnison (CO)
May 1884, June 1905, June 1909, May 1920, May 1930, May 1938

Hudson (NY)
Feb. 1857, Mar. 1913, Apr. 1922, Nov. 1927, Apr. 1928, Mar. 1936, Sept. 1938, Jan. 1949

Humboldt (NV)
May 1897, Apr. 1907, Mar. 1921, Feb. 1943, Apr. 1952

James (VA)
Aug. 1667, May 1771, Oct. 1870, Nov. 1877, Mar. 1913, Jan. 1935, Mar. 1936, Sept. 1944

Kanawha (WV)
Sept. 1861, Sept. 1878, May 1901, Mar. 1916, Mar. 1918, Nov. 1926, Jan. 1935, Aug. 1940

Kansas (KS)
1785, 1826, June 1844, 1858, 1867, June 1884, May 1903, June 1923, June 1935, July 1951

Kennebee (ME)
1770, May 1832, Apr. 1846, Oct. 1855, Oct. 1869, Oct. 1870, May 1887, Mar 1896, Dec. 1901, June 1917, May 1923, May 1929, Mar. 1936

Kentucky (KY)
1817, Mar. 1854, Feb. 1878, Feb. 1880, Mar. 1913, May 1927, Jan. 1939, July 1942

Lehigh (PA)
1675, Oct. 1786, June 1841, Feb. 1902, Oct. 1903, July 1935, Mar. 1936, May 1942

Los Angeles (CA)
Jan. 1815, 1825, Jan. 1862, Dec. 1886, Dec. 1889, Jan. 1916, Jan. 1934, Mar. 1938

Lytle (CA)
Feb. 1891, Jan. 1916, Feb. 1921, Feb. 1927, Mar. 1938

Malheur (OR)
Mar. 1894, Mar. 1910, Feb. 1925, Mar. 1932, Mar. 1952

Miami (OH)
Mar. 1805, Mar. 1847, Sept. 1866, Mar. 1898, Mar. 13, June 1924, Feb. 1929, Jan. 1952

Louisiana to Minnesota
1543, 1684, 1724, 1735, 1782, 1785, 1809, 1815, June 1844, June 1855, 1858, 1880, Apr. 1881, Mar. 1882, June 1883, May 1888, Apr. 1897, May 1903, June 1908, Apr. 1912, April 1913, Apr. 1916, Apr. 1922, May 1927, June 1929, May 1933, June 1935, Feb. 1937, May 1950, Apr. 1951, Apr. 1952, July and Aug. 1993

Table 2.3 *continued*

Missouri to Montana
June 1844, 1852, 1866, Apr. 1881, June 1884, June 1899, May 1903, June 1908, July 1909, June 1927, June 1929, Apr. 1930, June 1933, Apr. 1943, May 1947, June 1948, Mar. 1949, May 1950, July 1951, Apr. 1952, June to Sept. 1993

Muskingum (OH)
Apr. 1860, Feb. 1884, Mar. 1898, Mar. 1913, Aug. 1935, Jan. 1952

Ocmulgee (GA)
Jan. 1778, 1840, Nov. 1877, Mar. 1902, Dec. 1919, Jan. 1925, Feb. 1929, Mar. 1942, Nov. 1949

Ohio (OH)
1762, Mar. 1763, 1772, 1773, 1784, Apr. 1806, 1832, 1847, 1852, Mar. 1865, 1872, 1880, Feb. 1884, Mar. 1907, Mar. 1908, Mar. 1912, Mar. 1913, Mar. 1922, Mar. 1924, Oct. 1933, Mar. 1936, Jan. 1937, Mar. 1945, Mar. 1997

Osage (KS)
July 1844, July 1904, June 1915, Apr. 1927, June and Nov. 1928, June 1935, June 1938, Apr. and Oct. 1941, May 1943, July 1951

Ouachita (AR, LA)
May 1882, May 1923, May 1927, Mar. 1932, Feb. 1938, Mar. and Apr. 1945

Passaic (NJ)
Mar. 1902, July and Oct. 1903, Mar. 1904, Jan. 1905, Mar. 1936, June 1952

Pecos (NM, TX)
Mar. 1893, Oct. 1904, June 1905, Aug. 1916, Sept. 1919, Oct. 1930, Sept. 1932, July 1936, June 1937, May and Sept. 1941

Potomac (MD, WV, DC)
1870, Oct. 1877, June 1889, 1896, Feb. 1902, Jan. 1914, Mar. and May 1924, Mar. 1936, Apr. 1937, Oct. 1942, June 1949

Provo (UT)
May 1904, May 1907, June 1909, June 1911, May 1922, May 1952

Red (AR, TX, LA)
Aug. 1849, July 1876, June 1892, May 1908, Oct. 1923, Apr. 1927, May 1930, Feb. 1932, July 1933, June 1935, Feb. 1938, Apr. 1945, July 1951

Red of the North (ND, MN)
1776, May 1826, 1852, Apr. 1897, Apr. 1916, Mar. 1938, Apr. 1943, Apr. 1948, Apr. and May 1950

Rio Grande (CO, NM)
July 1828, June 1884, June 1902, June 1985, July 1906, Oct. 1911, July 1917, June 1927, June 1935, Sept. 1941, Apr. 1942, Aug. 1998

Table 2.3 *continued*

Rio Grande (TX)
Sept. 1904, June 1905, Aug. 1909, July 1912, Sept. 1919, June 1922, Sept. 1922, Sept. and Oct. 1932, June 1935, Apr. 1949

Sacramento (CA)
Jan. 1850, Jan. 1862, Feb. 1878, Feb. 1881, Mar. 1904, Mar. 1907, Mar. 1908, Feb. 1909, Jan. 1914, Mar. 1928, Jan. 1936, Dec. 1937, Feb. 1938, Feb. 1940, Feb. 1942, Dec. 1950, Mar. 1995

Salt (TX)
Feb. 1891, Mar. 1893, Nov. 1905, Jan. 1916, Feb. 1937, Mar. 1941

San Joaquin (CA)
Jan. 1862, Dec. 1867, 1890, Mar. 1907, Jan. 1917, Jan. 1914, June 1922, Jan. 1936, Dec. 1937, Mar. 1938, Nov. 1950

Savannah (GA)
1796, 1840, Sept. 1888, Aug. 1908, Feb. and Oct. 1929, Aug. 1940, June 1949

Schuylkill (PA)
July 1757, Jan. 1841, Sept. 1850, Oct. 1869, Mar. 1902, July 1935, May 1942

Smoky Hill (KS)
June 1895, May 1903, June 1909, June 1918, May 1921, May 1927, June 1938, Apr. 1943

Susquehanna (NY, PA)
1784, Oct. 1786, Feb. 1842, Mar. 1846, Mar. 1865, June 1889, May 1894, Dec. 1901, Mar. 1902, Mar. 1904, Apr. 1909, Oct. 1924, July 1935, Mar. 1936, Mar. and July 1948, Mar. 1949, June, 1972

Tombigbee (AL, MS)
Apr. 1892, Apr. 1900, May 1909, Mar. 1929, Mar. 1935, Mar. 1944, Jan. 1947, Feb. 1948, Jan. 1949, Apr. 1951

Tennessee (TN)
1793, Mar. 1867, Mar. 1875, Jan. 1882, Apr. 1886, Mar. 1897, May 1901, Mar. 1902, Mar. 1917, Dec. 1926, Jan. 1927, Mar. 1928, Feb. 1948

Truckee (CA, NV)
Apr. 1904, Mar. 1907, Jan. 1914, Dec. 1937, Nov. 1950

Wabash (IN, IL)
Sept. 1828, Jan. 1847, Aug. 1873, Feb. 1883, Mar. 1904, Mar. 1913, Sept. 1926, Jan. 1930, May 1943

Willamette (OR)
Dec. 1861, Jan. 1881, June 1894, Feb. 1890, Jan. 1903, Nov. 1909, Jan. 1923, Feb. 1927, Nov. 1942, Dec. 1945, Dec. 1946

Wisconsin (WI)
June 1881, Apr. 1888, July 1912, Apr. 1922, Mar. 1935, Sept. 1938, Aug. 1941, Mar. 1946

Yellowstone (MT)
June 1897, June 1918, June 1921, June 1938, June 1943, June 1944

Source: National Weather Bureau.

Table 2.4
Hurricanes, 1900–1999

Date	Hurricane Name	Location	Deaths
1900, Aug.–Sept.	N/A	Galveston, TX	6,000
1906, Sept. 19–24	N/A	Louisiana, Mississippi	350
1915, Sept. 29	N/A	Louisiana	500
1926, Oct. 20	N/A	Cuba	600
1928, Sept. 6–20	N/A	Southern Florida	1,836
1930, Sept. 3	N/A	Dominican Republic	2,000
1935, Aug. 29–Sept. 10	N/A	Caribbean, Southeastern United States	400+
1938, Sept. 21	N/A	New York, New England	600
1944, Sept. 9–16	N/A	North Carolina to New England	46
1954, Aug. 30	Carol	Northeastern United States	68
1954, Oct 5–18	Hazel	Eastern Canada and United States	347
1955, Aug 12–13	Connie	North and South Carolina, Virginia, Maryland	43
1955, Aug. 7–21	Diane	Eastern United States	400
1955, Sept. 19	Hilda	Mexico	200
1955, Sept. 22–28	Janey	Caribbean	500
1957, June 25–30	Audrey	Texas to Alabama	390
1960, Sept. 4–12	Donna,	Caribbean, Eastern United States	148
1961, Oct. 31	Hattie	British Honduras	400
1963, Oct. 4–8	Flora	Caribbean	6,000
1964, Oct. 4–7	Hilda	Louisiana, Mississippi, Georgia	38
1965, Sept. 7–12	Betsy	Florida, Mississippi, Louisiana	74
1966, June 4–10	Alma	Honduras, Southeastern United States	51
1966, Sept. 24–30	Inez	Caribbean, Florida, Mexico	293
1967, Sept. 5–23	Beulah	Caribbean, Mexico, Texas	54
1969, Aug 17–18	Camille	Mississippi, Louisiana	256
1970, July 30–Aug 5	Celia	Cuba, Florida, Texas	31
1970, Aug. 20–21	Dorothy	Martinique	42
1972, June 19–29	Agnes	Florida to New York	118
1974, Sept. 19–20	Fifi	Honduras	2,000
1975, Sept. 13–27	Eloise	Caribbean, Northeastern United States	71
1979, Aug. 30–Sept. 7	David	Caribbean, Eastern United States	1,100
1980, Aug. 4–11	Allen	Caribbean, Texas	272
1983, Aug. 18	Alicia	Southern Texas	17
1985, Oct 26–Nov 6	Juan	Southeastern United States	97
1992, Aug 24–26	Andrew	Southern Florida, Louisiana	14
1995, Sept. 4–6	Luis	Caribbean	14
1996, July 8–13	Bertha	Caribbean, Eastern United States	15
1996, Aug. 29–Sep 6	Fran	Caribbean	28
1996, Sept 9–10	Hortense	Caribbean	24
1997, Oct 8–10	Pauline	Southwestern Mexico	230
1998, Sep 21–23	Georges	Caribbean	600+
1999, July–Aug	Floyd	East Coast United States	50+

Table 2.5
Costliest East Coast United States Hurricanes 1900–1995

Rank	Hurricane	Year	Damage (U.S. $ Million)
1	Andrew	1992	28,620
2	Hugo	1989	7,910
3	Agnes	1972	6,930
4	Betsy	1965	6,875
5	Camille	1969	5,640
6	Diane	1955	4,516
7	Frederic	1979	3,933
8	New England	1938	3,864
9	Opal	1995	2,880
10	Alicia	1983	2,760
11	Carol	1954	2,549
12	Carla	1961	2,072
13	Donna	1960	1,962
14	Juan	1985	1,950
15	Celia	1970	1,694
16	Bob	1991	1,635
17	Elena	1985	1,625
18	Hazel	1954	1,554
19	Florida	1926	1,414
20	Texas	1915	1,264
21	Dora	1964	1,245
22	Eloise	1975	1,190
23	Gloria	1985	1,170
24	Northeast U.S.	1944	994
25	Beulah	1967	900
26	Texas	1900	760
27	Fla., La., Miss.	1947	757
28	Audrey	1957	748
29	Texas	1979	684
30	Cleo	1964	640

Note: Adjusted to 1994 dollars based on U.S. DOC Implicit Price Deflator for Construction.

Table 2.6
Recent Tsunamis

Flores Island, Indonesia
- December 12, 1992
- Maximum wave: 80 feet
- Fatalities: more than 1,000

Nicaragua
- September 2, 1992
- Maximum wave: 30 feet
- Fatalities: 170

Okushiri, Japan
- July 12, 1993
- Maximum wave: 63 feet
- Fatalities: 239

East Java, Indonesia
- June 2, 1994
- Maximum wave: 42 feet
- Fatalities: 238

Mindoro Island, Philippines
- November 14, 1994
- Maximum wave: 21 feet
- Fatalities: 49

Jalisco, Mexico
- October 9, 1995
- Maximum wave: 35 feet
- Fatalities: 1

Sulawesi Island, Indonesia
- January 1, 1996
- Maximum wave: 10 feet
- Fatalities: 9

Irian Jaya, Indonesia
- February 17, 1996
- Maximum wave: 46 feet
- Fatalities: 161

North Coast of Peru
- February 21, 1996
- Maximum wave: 15 feet
- Fatalities: 12

Sissano Lagoon, Papua New Guinea
- July 17, 1998
- Maximum wave: 45 feet
- Fatalities: more than 2,200

Table 2.7
Flood Legislation Dates

Flood Control Acts
- 1917, 1928, 1936, 1937, 1938, 1945, 1946, 1948, 1950, 1954, 1958, 1960, 1962, 1965, 1966, 1968, 1970

National Flood Insurance Acts
- 1952, 1956, 1968, 1989, 1994

Flood Prevention
- 1954

Disaster Relief and Emergency Assistance Acts
- 1936, 1937, 1966, 1969, 1970, 1973, 1974, 1980, 1988, 1990, 1993, 1994

Proclamation: Flood Relief
- 1936

Dam Acts
- 1906, 1972

River and Harbor Acts
- 1884, 1888, 1892, 1894, 1899, 1902, 1905, 1907, 1909, 1910, 1912, 1913, 1915, 1916, 1917, 1919, 1920, 1922, 1925, 1930, 1935, 1938, 1940, 1941, 1945, 1950, 1954, 1958, 1960, 1962, 1966, 1968, 1970, 1970 Act amended 1974, 1983, 1986, 1988, 1992

Water Quality Acts
- 1948, 1956, 1965, 1970

Water Resources
- 1958, 1974, 1976, 1978, 1986, 1988, 1990, 1992

Water Planning Act
- 1965

Wild and Scenic River Acts
- 1968, 1972, 1974, 1975, 1976, 1978, 1979, 1980, 1984, 1986, 1987, 1988, 1989, 1990, 1991, 1992, 1993, 1994

Directory of Organizations 3

Organizations dealing with floods have been established at all government levels, and a number of private associations have been formed as well. In the United States, the U.S. Army Corps of Engineers plays a dominant role in providing river structures that control floods. The following directory is arranged in three sections: federal agencies, private associations, and state agencies.

Federal Agencies

Environmental Protection Agency (EPA)
401 M Street SW
Washington, DC 20460
Phone: (202) 260-2090
Website: www.epa.gov

Description: Established in 1970 in the executive branch as an independent agency. It was created to provide coordinated and effective governmental action on behalf of the environment.

Purpose: The agency is designed to serve as the public's advocate for a livable environment.

Activities: The agency's water quality activities represent a coordinated effort to restore the nation's waters, including:

1. Development of national programs, technical policies, and regulations for water pollution control and water supply
2. General water protection
3. Marine and estuarine protection
4. Enforcement of standards
5. Water quality standards and effluent guidelines development
6. Technical direction, support, and evaluation of regional water activities
7. Technical assistance and technology transfer
8. Training in the field of water quality

Publications: Numerous publications.

Interagency Committee on Dam Safety (ICODS)
Program Development and Coordination Division
Mitigation Directorate
Federal Emergency Management Agency
500 C Street SW
Washington, DC 20472
Phone: (202) 646-2500
Website: www.fema.gov

Description: Established in 1980 at the request of the director of the Federal Emergency Management Agency.

The committee has one representative of each of the Departments of Agriculture, Defense, Energy, Interior, and Labor; FEMA; the Federal Energy Regulatory Commission; the Nuclear Regulatory Commission; the Tennessee Valley Authority; and the United States Section of the International Boundary Commission. The committee is chaired by members of the Federal Emergency Management Agency.

Purpose: ICODS functions under the Program Development and Coordination Division, Mitigation Directorate, Federal Emergency Management Agency as an interagency committee.

Activities: Coordinates policies for and gives guidance to federal agencies and departments participating in the National Dam Safety Program. President Jimmy Carter asked heads of each federal agency with responsibility for dam safety to adopt the Federal Guidelines for Dam Safety. The dam safety program was established on October 4, 1979, under President Carter's administration. The committee encourages maintenance of federal and state programs to enhance the safety of dams to protect human life and property. It disseminates information with agencies having common problems and responsibility for dam safety. It coordinates interagency activities and makes and discusses recommendations and policy issues that affect dam safety. The staff of the committee provides administrative and support services for its representatives. There are several subsidiary units.

Publications: Emergency Action Planning Guidelines for Dams; Federal Guidelines for Selecting and Accommodating Inflow Design Floods; Federal Guidelines for Earthquake Analyses and Design of Dams; Training Courses Related to Dam Safety; Glossary of Terms for Dam Safety; Federal Guidelines for Dam Safety.

National Weather Service (NWS)
National Oceans and Atmospheric Administration
U.S. Department of Commerce
Washington, DC 20230
Phone: (703) 260-0107
Website: www.nws.noaa.gov

Description: The National Weather Service is located in the National Oceans and Atmospheric Administration, which was formed in 1970 to include the National Weather Service, the National Ocean Survey, and the National Marine Fisheries Service.

Purpose: NWS provides daily forecasts and warnings for severe weather events such as hurricanes, tornadoes, winter storms, flooding, and tsunamis.

Activities: With its modernization program, NWS is able to maximize the use of advanced computer technology to capture, integrate, and analyze Doppler radar imagery and data from satellites and automated surface instruments, and to speed up the dissemination of its forecasts and warnings. This allows NWS to provide the public with more localized, timely, and accurate forecasts, increasing the lead time it has to prepare for severe weather events. NWS also provides services in support of aviation and marine activities, agriculture, forestry, and urban air quality control.

Publications: Weather maps.

U.S. Army Corps of Engineers (USACE)
Department of the Army

The Pentagon
Washington, DC 20310
Website: www.usace.army.mil

Description: The U.S. Army Corps of Engineers provides engineering, construction management, and environmental services in times of peace and war.

Purpose: The civil works program includes navigation, flood damage reduction, recreation, hydropower, environment regulations, and other missions.

Activities: The program includes construction of dams, flood control, environmental restoration, real estate acquisition in flood-prone areas, and management.

Publications: Numerous reports.

U.S. Committee on Irrigation and Drainage (USCID)
1616 17th Street, Suite 483
Denver, CO 80202
Phone: (303) 628-5430
Website: www.uscid.org/~uscid

Description: Founded 1952. Has 700 members and 2 staff and a budget of $75,000. Membership annual dues are $45 for individuals, $200 for institutions, $95 for libraries, and $450 for corporations. Members are engineers, scientists, and anyone interested. Holds triennial International Congress (September 1999, Granada, Spain).

Purpose: Works on irrigation, drainage, and flood control.

Activities: Promotes planning, design, construction, operation, and maintenance for irrigation, drainage, and flood control works. Keeps members informed of developments in water law and social issues affecting drainage and flood control. Affiliated with International Commission on Irrigation and Drainage.

Publications: A Guide to Acquiring a Computer System for the Management of Water Resources; Automation of Canal Irrigation Systems; Guidelines on the Construction of Horizontal Subsurface Drainage Systems; Newsletter, quarterly; *Bulletin,* semiannual; *Proceedings.*

U.S. Geological Survey (USGS)
Department of the Interior
12201 Sunrise Valley Drive
Reston, VA 20192

Phone: (800) 275-8747
Website: www.usgs.gov

Description: Established by the Organic Act of March 3, 1879. The USGS is directed to classify the public lands and to examine the geological structure, mineral resources, and products within and outside the national domain. In 1894 provision was made for gauging the streams and determining the water supply of the United States. In 1962 this authorization was expanded to include such examinations outside the public domain. Specific provision was made for topographic mapping and chemical and physical research through subsequent legislation. The USGS also is responsible for the management and conservation of the nation's biological resources and mineral information.

Purpose: The purpose of the USGS is to provide relevant, objective studies and information to help address issues and solve problems dealing with national resources, natural hazards, and their environmental effects on human and wildlife health.

Activities: USGS activities pertaining to water are:

1. Investigating natural hazards such as earthquakes, volcanoes, landslides, floods, and droughts
2. Maintaining an archive of land-remote sensing data for historical, scientific, and technical purposes, including long-term global environmental monitoring
3. Serving as the designated lead agency for the Federal Water Information Coordination Program

To attain these objectives the USGS collects and interprets data on the quality, quantity, and use of the nation's water resources.

As the nation's largest water, earth, and geological service and civilian mapping agency, the USGS works in cooperation with more than 2,000 organizations across the country to provide reliable, impartial, scientific information to resource managers, planners, and other customers. This information is gathered in every state by USGS scientists to minimize the loss of life and property from natural disasters, to contribute to the conservation and the sound economic and physical development of the nation's natural resources, and to enhance the quality of life by monitoring water, biological, energy, and mineral resources.

Publications: Special reports and studies.

Private Associations

American Lifesaving Emergency Response Team (ALERT)
National Association for Search and Rescue
4500 Southgate Place, Suite 100
Chantilly, PA 20151-1714
Phone: (703) 222-6277
Website: www.nasar.org

Description: Founded 1979. Has 60 members and 1 staff. Holds periodic meetings.

Purpose: To aid and rescue people caught in floods and other emergency situations.

Activities: Trains emergency personnel in flood and river rescue. Conducts training seminars to educate people in river and flood rescue. Exchanges techniques and information with interested agencies and responds to floods and other disasters. Maintains a 200-volume library of lifesaving materials. Has a placement service and charitable programs. Compiles statistics. Gives recognition award. Affiliated with the National Association for Search and Rescue.

Publications: None.

American Meteorological Society (AMS)
45 Beacon Street
Boston, MA 02108
Phone: (617) 227-2425
Website: www.ametsoc.org/ams

Description: Founded 1919. Has 11,000 members and 38 staff and a budget of $5.5 million. Has 81 local groups. Members are professional meteorologists, oceanographers, and hydrologists. Holds annual meeting.

Purpose: To disseminate information on the atmospheric and related oceanic and hydrospheric sciences.

Activities: Has scholarship programs, gives guidance service, career information, certification of meteorologists, approves competence in radio and television forecasting. Helps forecast tornadoes, hurricanes, and flash floods. Provides abstracting service. Prepares educational films, filmstrips, and slides. Has a reference library. Presents annual awards. Operates through many boards and committees.

Publications: AMS Newsletter, periodic; *Bulletin of the American Meteorological Society,* monthly; *Journal of Applied Meteorology,* monthly; *Journal of Atmospheric and Oceanic Technology,* bimonthly; *Journal of Climate,* monthly; *Journal of Physical Oceanography,* monthly; *Journal of the Atmospheric Sciences,* semimonthly; *Meteorological and Geoastrophysical Abstracts,* monthly; *Monographs; Monthly Weather Review; Weather and Forecasting,* quarterly; also conference reprints, glossary of meteorology, and books.

American Red Cross National Headquarters (ARC)
431 18th Street NW
Washington, DC 20006
Phone: (703) 248-4222
Website: www.redcross.org

Description: Founded 1881. Has staff of 28,323 and a budget of $1.5 billion. Has 2,658 chapters. Holds annual meeting.

Purpose: To give blood and assistance where needed.

Activities: Serves members of armed services, veterans, and their families; helps disaster victims; helps other Red Cross societies in emergencies. Provides blood, trains volunteers for chapters, hospitals, and community agencies. Performs international activities. Provides service opportunities for youth. Has 46 regional blood centers. Conducts research programs. Local chapters provide speakers. Presents Ann Magnussen award annually to an outstanding nurse. Gives Certificate of Merit, Good Neighbor Award, Harrman Award, Tiffany Award. Is affiliated with International Federation of Red Cross and Red Crescent Societies.

Publications: Annual Report and booklets.

Church World Service and Witness (CWSW)
475 Riverside Drive, Room 678
New York, NY 10115-0050
Phone: (212) 870-2257
Website: www.churchworldservice.org

Description: Founded in 1946. Has 33 members and 170 staff and a budget of $50 million. Is a division of the National Council of Churches of Christ in the United States. Holds semiannual CWSW Unit Committee board meeting. It is multinational.

Purpose: To provide relief to victims of disasters such as floods and famine.

Activities: Provides worldwide development and emergency aid to victims of floods, wars, etc. Promotes global education. Monitors human rights and international political issues. Sponsors immigration and refugee program. Affiliated with Church World Services.

Publications: CWS Up-Date, biweekly; *Notebook,* monthly; *One Great Hour of Sharing Materials,* annual; *Regional Newsletter,* periodic; *Annual Report.* Also prepares promotional materials, films, posters, folders, and fact sheets.

Friends Disaster Service (FDS)
241 Keenan Road
Peninsula, OH 44264
Phone: (330) 650-4975

Description: Founded in 1974. Members are people who want to help others. Quaker oriented. Holds annual meeting that includes fund-raiser.

Purpose: To assist people in need.

Activities: Provides help in cleanup and restoration activities to areas devastated by natural disasters. Priority is given to elderly, low-income, uninsured, and disabled people. Cooperates with other relief agencies.

Publications: Newsletter, periodic.

Mennonite Central Committee (MCC)
10 South 12th Street
PO Box 500
Akron, PA 17501-0500
Phone: (717) 859-3889

Description: Founded in 1920. Has 37 members and a budget of $39 million. Has 9 regional groups. Holds annual meeting in February.

Purpose: To perform disaster relief services.

Activities: This is the relief and service agency of North American Mennonite and Brethren in Christ churches. Participates in programs of agriculture, education, economic development, medicine, self-help relief, and disaster services. Some 900 workers serve in 50 countries in Africa, Asia, Europe, and South, Central, and North America. Has reference library with archival material. Works through many special departments.

Publications: Conciliation Quarterly; Crafts of the World, periodic; *Dialogue on Disabilities,* quarterly; *Jottings,* monthly; *MCC Contact,* quarterly; *Mennonite Central Committee—Intercom,* bimonthly; *Newsletter; Peace Office Newsletter,* bimonthly; *Washington Memo,* bimonthly; and *Women's Concerns Report,* bimonthly.

Mennonite Disaster Service (MDS)
10 South 12th Street
PO Box 500
Akron, PA 17501-0500
Phone: (717) 859-3889

Description: Founded in 1950. Has 4 staff. Has 5 regional groups and 50 local groups. Holds annual conference in February.

Purpose: To assist those in need during a disaster.

Activities: Coordinates responses to disasters for the Mennonite churches. Local units respond and help to clean up, repair, and rebuild in time of disasters. If the need is too great for their community, other units of the service give help. Also gives blood for local clinics and helps rebuild homes in ghettos and rural poverty areas.

Publications: Newsletter, quarterly.

National Association for Search and Rescue (NASAR)
4500 Southgate Place, Suite 100
Chantilly, VA 20151
Phone: (703) 222-6277
Website: www.nasar.org

Description: Founded in 1974. Has 3,500 members and 7 staff and a budget of $3 million. Membership annual dues are $69 for individuals, $170 for organizations, and $250 for corporations. Is multinational. Members are directors or coordinators of state and regional rescue services, medical and fire rescue personnel, and organizations or associations involved in rescue services. Holds an Annual Response Conference, educational conferences, and a trade show.

Purpose: To promote and develop rescue and disaster capabilities.

Activities: Acts as liaison of state, federal, local, and private rescue groups. Conducts training programs and promotes standardization of procedures. Sponsors survival education programs to help people cope with disaster situations. Has reference library containing 600 books and articles on rescue and disasters. Gives annual recognition award to individuals or groups who contributed most to rescue field.

Publications: Briefings, quarterly; *Response,* quarterly.

National Association of Catastrophe Adjusters (NACA)
PO Box 740217
Dallas, TX 75354-0217

Description: Founded in 1979. Has 500 members and 1 staff. Annual membership dues are $100 for regular, associate, or associate business. Holds annual meeting and seminar exhibits, always in January.

Purpose: To assist people faced with disasters.

Activities: Insurance catastrophe claims adjusters assist people who have faced a disaster such as flood, wind, hail, or earthquake. Promotes welfare of members. Maintains high ethical standards. Conducts continuing education classes in all lines of losses.

Publications: National Association of Catastrophe Adjusters, Inc., annual; *Membership Directory,* annual.

National Association of Flood and Stormwater Management Agencies (NAFSMA)
1401 Eye Street NW, Suite 900
Washington, DC 20005
Website: www.nafsma.org

Description: Founded 1977. Has 60 members and 4 staff. Members are state, county, and local people interested in flood control. Holds annual meeting, workshop, and conference.

Purpose: To reduce or eliminate flooding.

Activities: State, county, and local government members work to reduce or eliminate flooding and provide for improved stormwater management. They also work for conservation of watersheds and water resources management. NAFSMA works through committees. Formerly was the National Association of Urban Flood Management Agencies, but changed its name in 1988.

Publications: Legislative Report, periodic; *Technical Bulletin,* periodic; *Newsletter,* monthly.

Natural Hazards Research and Applications Information Center (NHRAIC)
University of Colorado

Campus Box 482
Boulder, CO 80309-0482
Phone: (303) 492-6818
Website: www.colorado.edu/hazards

Description: Founded 1977. Staff of 10. Nonmembership. Holds meeting in July in Boulder, Colorado, as a workshop on hazards research and application.

Purpose: To serve as a clearinghouse for information on natural disasters.

Activities: Helps develop workshops on natural disasters. Collects information on natural disasters and their mitigation and disseminates this information to those interested. Conducts research on natural hazards problems. Funds program for researchers doing field work after a disaster. Addresses natural disaster issues. Has reference library of 12,000 holdings on economic, social, and behavioral aspects of natural hazards.

Publications: Environment and Behavior Monograph Series, periodic; *Natural Hazards Observer,* bimonthly; *Natural Hazards Working Paper Series,* periodic; *Quick Response Research Reports Series,* periodic; *Special Publication Series,* periodic; *Topical Bibliographies Series,* periodic; *Newsletter;* legislative news, project reports, and schedule of events.

U.S. Committee on Large Dams (USCOLD)
1616 17th Street, Suite 483
Denver, CO 80202
Phone: (303) 628-5430
Website: www2.privatei.com/~uscold/

Description: Founded in 1928. Has 1,150 members and 2 staff and a budget of $100,000. Membership annual dues are $60 for individuals and $450 for organizations. Members are interested in the design and construction of dams. Holds triennial international conference and congress and holds annual meeting and lecture.

Purpose: To advance the safe construction of dams to prevent flooding from breaks.

Activities: Participates in the activities of the International Commission of Large Dams, which provides a forum for discussion, tours, and publication of technical reports dealing with water resources. Presents monetary USCOLD scholarship annually.

Publications: ICOLD Congress Transactions, triennial; *ICOLD Symposium Transactions,* biennial; books; bulletins; *Membership Directory; Newsletter,* 3 per year.

State Agencies

Oregon Water Resources Congress (WRC)
1201 Court St. NE
Salem, OR 97301
Phone: (503) 363-0121
Website: www.owrc@owrc.org

Description: Founded 1971. Has 300 members and a budget of $109,000. Has 7 regional groups. Members are people interested in water control and land development. Holds annual conference in May with exhibits.

Purpose: To promote improvement of rivers and harbors to prevent floods.

Activities: Develops navigation, irrigation, flood control, and utilization of rivers, lakes, harbors, and water resources. Presents annual Water Leaders of the Century Award. Operates through several committees and sections. Formed by merger of the National Rivers and Harbors Congress and the Water Resources Association.

Publications: Hotline, periodic; *Platform,* every 5–6 years; *Water Resources Congress—Washington Report,* bimonthly; brochures.

Passaic River Coalition (PRC)
246 Madisonville Road
Basking Ridge, NJ 07920
Phone: (908) 766-7550

Description: Founded in 1971. Has 2,500 members and 7 staff and a budget of $225,000. Annual membership dues are $15 for individuals. There are 60 regional groups, 30 state groups, and 25 local groups. Members are concerned about the Passaic River. Holds its annual meeting at Basking Ridge, N.J., in June as well as another meeting in the fall.

Purpose: Concerned with the Passaic River Watershed, which provides water to 3.5 million people and flood control.

Activities: Seeks to resolve problems of the river system such as pollution, flood control, and urban decay. Does research in land use, water quality, flood control, and historic preservation. Sponsors environmental education. Provides assistance and education to interested people and groups. Receives grants for special studies and projects. Employs college interns to provide them with professional experience. Has speakers' bureau. Compiles statistics. Has a 9,000-volume reference library. Gives annual award of achievement for outstanding contribution to the improvement of the Passaic River Watershed. Operates through several committees.

Publications: Citizen Alerts; Groundwater Monitor, quarterly; *Passaic River Restoration Newsletter,* quarterly; *Passaic River Review,* biennial; *Vibes from the Libe,* annual; *Watershed News,* bimonthly; pamphlets, reports, and inventory.

States also have water resource agencies that consider all aspects of water problems, including floods: Arizona Department of Water Resources; Colorado Water Conservation Board; Illinois State Water Survey; University of Massachusetts Water Resources Research Center; Wright Water Engineers, Inc.; and Wyoming Disaster and Civil Defense.

References

Encyclopedia of Associations, 33d ed., vol. 1. Detroit: Gale Research, 1998.

Encyclopedia of Associations: International Organizations, 32d ed. Detroit: Gale Research, 1998.

Encyclopedia of Governmental Advisory Organizations, 12th ed. Detroit: Gale Research, 1998.

The United States Government Manual, 1998/99. Washington, DC: U.S. Government Printing Office, 1998.

Laws and Regulations

The development of modern flood control legislation began in 1917. Since then many flood control acts have been passed, and most of these have been revised numerous times. Most significant, however, were the Flood Control Acts of 1936, 1938, and 1944 establishing the fundamental regulations for administering the modern flood control programs.

Along with the need for basic flood control, Congress recognized that the destruction from floods was so great that federal aid was needed to support private insurance companies. Hence federal laws have been passed to provide federal insurance to protect property in flood-prone areas. In addition, Congress normally provides direct federal aid to devastated flood areas.

Flood Control Acts

Flood Control Act of 1917 (Levee Act)

Mar. 1, 1917, ch. 144, 39 Stat. 948
Mar. 4, 1923, ch. 277, 42 Stat. 1505
Aug. 2, 1946, ch. 753, Title 1, 121, 60 Stat. 822

Purpose

The purpose of this act was "to provide for the control of floods of the Mississippi River and of the Sacramento River, California, and for other purposes."

Flood Control Areas

The work on the Mississippi River was limited to the area south of the Ohio River mouth and was to be directed by the secretary of war according to the plans of the Mississippi River Commission with the approval of the U.S. Chief of Engineers. The act had the dual purpose of controlling floods and providing for the general improvement of the river. The act also provided for a survey of the Atchafalaya Outlet in order to determine the cost of protecting the basin from the floodwaters of the Mississippi River either by its divorcement from the Mississippi River or by other means. The act also indicated that no federal money was to be expended until assurance had been secured that the local authorities contributed at least one-half of the total expenditures for such construction and repair.

In the Sacramento River, the act called not only for flood control but also for the removal of debris and for continued navigational improvements of the river.

Surveys and Improvements

Besides the specific provisions for improvement of the Mississippi and Sacramento Rivers, in a general provision the act provided for surveys to improve rivers and harbors. Each survey of a river had to include a comprehensive study of the watershed in regard to the following:

1. The extent and character of the area to be affected by the proposed improvement
2. The provable effect on any navigable water or waterway
3. The possible economical development and utilization of water power

Flood Control Act of 1928

See Mississippi River Flood Control Act

Flood Control Act of 1936

June 22, 1936, ch. 688, 1 to 4, 8, 9, Stat. 1570, 1571, 1596
Apr. 27, 1937, ch. 134, 50 Stat. 95
July 19, 1937, ch. 511, 1, 50 Stat. 518
Aug. 28, 1937, ch. 877, 4, 50 Stat. 877
June 28, 1938, ch. 795, 1, 52 Stat. 1215
Aug. 18, 1941, ch. 377, 1, 55 Stat. 638
Aug. 4, 1954, ch. 656, 7, 68 Stat. 688

Establishment of a National Policy

This act recognized the need for a national flood control policy in the United States. It was based on Congress's findings that destructive river floods disrupt orderly human processes and cause loss of life and property, including the erosion of the land, and also interrupts the channels of commerce between states. Hence Congress declared that the control of floods on navigable rivers and their tributaries was a proper activity of the federal government in cooperation with the states and their subdivisions and localities. Furthermore, the investigation and improvement of rivers and other waterways, including watersheds, for flood control purposes were in the interests of the nation's general welfare. The act indicated that the federal government should improve, or participate in, the improvement of navigable waters or their tributaries, including their watershed, for flood control purposes if the benefits to the people of the area would exceed the estimated costs, and if their lives and social security would otherwise be adversely affected.

Implementation

The act indicated that federal investigations and improvements of rivers and other waterways for flood control and allied purposes would be under the jurisdiction of the War Department and the supervision of the U.S. Army Chief of Engineers. The federal role in investigations of watersheds, including measures of runoff, water flow retardation, and soil erosion prevention, would be carried out by the Department of Agriculture.

Before any project was implemented, the states, political subdivisions, and localities had to give assurance to the secretary of war that they would (1) provide without cost to the United States all bonds, easements, and rights-of-way necessary for the construction of the project, (2) hold the United States free from damages due to construction work, and (3) maintain and operate all the works after completion in accordance with regulations prescribed by the secretary of war, provided that (1) the dam was constructed without delay after the dam site had been secured, (2) when expenditures for land and other items by the states or other agencies for any individual project exceeded the estimated construction cost, the local agency concerned would be reimbursed one-half of its excess expenditures over the original estimated production cost, (3) the secretary of war would determine the proportion of the present estimated cost of the land, right-of-way, and easement, that each state or local agency should contribute in consideration for the benefits to be received by each agency, and (4) if 75 percent of the project lay outside of the state, the above provisions would not apply.

Flood Control Compacts

Any two or more states could enter into compacts or agreements in connection with any project or operation authorized by the act for flood control or for the prevention of damage to life or property by reason of floods. Each compact had to have the consent and ratification of Congress, except where all expenditures were provided by the Department of War.

Flood Control Projects

The act provided that the following projects be completed: Lake Champlain Basin; Merrimack River; Connecticut River Basin; southern New York and eastern Pennsylvania; Susquehanna River Basin; Potomac River Basin; Tar River; Savannah River; Escambia River Basin; Mississippi River; Pearl River; Homochitto River; Buffalo River; Big Black River; Red River Basin; Quachita River Basin; Arkansas River Basin; White River Basin; Upper Mississippi River; Red River of the North Basin; Minnesota River; Illinois and Des Plaines River Basin; Sangamon River Basin; Kankakee River Basin; Rock River Basin; Ohio River Basin; Wabash River; Cumberland River; Missouri River Basin; Kansas River; Cheyenne River; Yellowstone River; Little Missouri River; Milk River; Los Angeles and San Gabriel River; Santa Ana River; Eel River; Columbia River Basin; Willamette River; Umatilla River; Lewis River; Cowlitz River; Stillaguamish River; Puyallup River; Skagit River.

Flood Control Act of 1937

Aug. 28, 1937, ch. 877, 2 to 4, 6, 50 Stat. 877, 880
Aug. 11, 1939, ch. 699, 1, 53 Stat. 1414

Aug. 18, 1941, ch. 377, 9, 55 Stat. 650
July 24, 1946, ch. 596, 13, 60 Stat. 641
Jan. 19, 1948, ch. 2, 1, 62 Stat. 4
Sept. 3, 1954, ch. 1264, Title II, 208, 68 Stat. 1266
Mar. 7, 1974, Pub. L. 93-251, Title I, 26 88 Stat. 20
Nov. 17, 1986, Pub. L. 99-662, Title IX, 915(6), 100 Stat. 4191

Flood Control

This act amended the Flood Control Act of 1936. It included the following new provisions:

1. The construction of levees, flood walls, and drainage structures for the protection of cities and towns in the Ohio River Basin, the projects to be selected by the chief of engineers with the approval of the secretary of war.
2. The secretary of war was also authorized for flood control programs, the removal of accumulated snags and other debris, and the cleaning of channels in navigable streams.
3. The secretary of agriculture was authorized to make preliminary examinations and surveys for runoff and water flow retardation and soil-erosion prevention of watersheds.
4. The secretary of agriculture was also to provide improvements for the enactment of state and local laws imposing suitable permanent restrictions on the use of flood-prone lands and to provide for runoff and water flow retardation and soil-erosion prevention studies.
5. The act extended the 1936 act, which provided for the support of flood control surveys. Approximately 100 rivers were added to the 1936 list.

Flood Control Act of 1938

June 28, 1938, ch. 795, 1 to 9, 52 Stat. 1215, 1216, 1220, 1223, 1225, 1226
Aug. 11, 1939, ch. 699, 5, 53 Stat. 1415
Aug. 18, 1941, ch. 377, 8, 55 Stat. 650
Dec. 22, 1944, ch. 665, 15, 58 Stat. 907
May 17, 1950, ch. 188, Title II, 216, 64 Stat. 184
Sept. 3, 1954, ch. 1264, Title II, 207, 68 Stat. 1266
Aug. 4, 1977, Pub. L. 95-91, Title III, 301(b), 91 Stat. 577

New Projects

The 1938 act amended the 1937 act, adding nineteen river basins for flood control projects in the nation.

Flood Control Act of 1941

Aug. 18, 1941, ch. 377, 55 Stat. 638, 639, 642, 644, 648, 650, 651
July 24, 1946, ch. 596, 5, 12, 60 Stat. 642, 652
June 30, 1948, ch. 771, Title II, 206, 62 Stat. 1182
May 17, 1950, ch. 188, Title II, 210, 64 Stat. 183
Oct. 31, 1951, ch. 654, 3(b), 65 Stat. 708
June 16, 1953, ch. 114, 67 Stat. 61
Sept. 3, 1954, ch. 1264, Title II, 206, 68 Stat. 1266
June 28, 1955, ch. 194, 69 Stat. 186
Oct. 23, 1962, Pub. L. 87-874, Title II, 206, 76 Stat. 1194
Mar. 7, 1974, Pub. L. 93-251, Title I, 82, 88 Stat. 34
June 20, 1977, Pub. L. 95-51, 2, 91 Stat. 233
May 27, 1987, Pub. L. 100-45, 9, 101 Stat. 323

The 1941 act amended the 1938 act. Thirty-one river basins were specifically selected for:

1. Improvement of navigation
2. Flood control
3. National security aspects
4. Stabilization of employment in the region
5. Development of electricity for the region

Flood Control Act of 1944

Dec. 22, 1944, ch. 665, 58 Stat. 887

The 1944 Flood Control Act extended previous flood control acts and navigational projects in the nation's river basins.

> In connection with the exercise of jurisdiction over the rivers of the nation through the construction of works of improvement, for navigation or flood control, as herein authorized, it is declared to be the policy of the Congress to recognize the interests and rights of the States in determining the development of the watersheds within their borders and likewise their interests and rights in water utilization and control, as herein authorized to

preserve and protect to the fullest possible extent established and potential uses, for all purposes, of the waters of the Nation's rivers; to facilitate the consideration of projects on a basis of comprehensive and coordinated development; and to limit the authorization and construction of navigation works to those in which a substantial benefit to navigation will be realized therefrom and which can be operated consistently with appropriate and economic use of the waters of such rivers by other users.

Flood Control

This act listed forty-nine river basins and rivers for improvement for the benefit of navigation and the control of destructive floodwaters. Since this legislation was enacted in wartime, improvement of the rivers and their basins not only was considered to be in the interest of national security but also would add an adequate reservoir of useful public works for the postwar construction program. The act also provided that penstocks (flood gates) and other facilities were to be adapted for possible future use in the development of hydraulic power.

Flood Control Act of 1946

July 24, 1946, ch. 596, 60 Stat. 641
Oct. 30, 1951, ch. 636, 65 Stat. 693
Mar. 7, 1974, Pub. L. 93-251, Title I, 7, 88 Stat. 20
Nov. 17, 1986, Pub. L. 99-662, Title VIII, 818, Title IX, 915(c), 100 Stat. 4170, 4191
Nov. 28, 1990, Pub. L. 101-640, Title I, 102(Y), 104 Stat. 4617

Twenty-two basins were specifically selected as well as thirty-eight individual streams and rivers for flood control projects.

Flood Control Act of 1948

June 30, 1948, ch. 771, Title II, 62 Stat. 1175 (33-701c, note 701 n. 701o, 701s, 701t)
July 11, 1956, ch. 558, 70 Stat. 522 (33-701s)
Oct. 23, 1962, Pub. L. 87-874, Title II, 205, 75 Stat. 1194 (33-701s)
Mar. 7, 1974, Pub. L. 93-251, Title I, 61, 88 Stat. 29 (33-701s)
Dec. 29, 1981, Pub. L. 97-140, 2(a), 95 Stat. 1717 (33-701s)
Nov. 17, 1986, Pub. L. 99-662, Title IX, 915(a), 100 Stat. 4191. (33-701s)

Title II lists fifteen river basins, twelve rivers, and four areas for flood control. Title II is cited as the Flood Control Act of 1948.

Flood Control Act of 1950

May 17, 1950, ch. 188, Titles I and II, 64 Stat. 170
June 26, 1955, ch. 194, 69 Stat. 186

Title II lists more than seventy river basin projects for flood control and other improvements.

Flood Control Act of 1954

Title II, Sept. 3, 1954, Pub. L. 780, ch. 1264, 68 Stat. 1248
June 28, 1955, ch. 194, 69 Stat. 186

This act adds twenty-nine river basins to the nation's flood control project.

Flood Control Act of 1958

Pub. L. 85-500, Title II, 208, July 3, 1958, 72 Stat. 319

This act lists thirty-four rivers and river basins for improvements of navigation and control of destructive floodwaters.

Flood Control Act of 1960

Pub. L. 86-645, Title II, July 14, 1960, 74 Stat. 488
Pub. L. 87-874, Title II, 208, Oct. 23, 1962, 75 Stat. 1196
Pub. L. 89-298, Title II, 220, Oct. 27, 1965, 79 Stat. 1089
Pub. L. 89-789, Title II, 206, 208, Nov. 7, 1966, 80 Stat. 1422, 1423
Pub. L. 91-611, Title II, 225, Dec. 31, 1970, 84 Stat. 1832
Pub. L. 93-251, Title I, 13, 64, March 7, 1974, 88 Stat. 17, 30
Pub. L. 101-640, Title III, 321, 104 Stat. 4643

Title II provides funds to improve the flood control measures in thirty river basins.

Flood Control Act of 1962

Pub. L. 87-874, Title II, Oct. 23, 1962, 76 Stat. 1180
Pub. L. 91-611, Title II, 234, Dec. 31, 1970, 84 Stat. 1833
Pub. L. 100-387, Title IV, 417, Aug. 11, 1988, 102 Stat. 959

Title II provides public work for the improvement of flood control conditions in thirty-eight rivers and their basins.

Flood Control Act of 1965

Pub. L. 89-298, Title II, Oct. 27, 1965, 79 Stat. 1073
Pub. L. 94-587, Title I, 131, Oct. 22, 1976, 90 Stat. 2928
Pub. L. 97-128, Dec. 29, 1981, 95 Stat. 1681
Pub. L. 97-295, 6(b), Oct. 12, 1982, 96 Stat. 1314
Pub. L. 103-437, 15(d), Nov. 2, 1994, 108 Stat. 4592

Title II, Flood Control, lists thirty-five specific projects, ten general projects, two comprehensive projects, and the revision of several earlier projects.

Flood Control Act of 1966

Pub. L. 89-789, Title II, Nov. 7, 1966, 80 Stat. 1418
Pub. L. 99-662, Title XI, 1107, Nov. 17, 1986, 100 Stat. 4229

By 1966 Congress recognized that flood control alone could not prevent the flooding of floodplains. As a response, Congress began its initial efforts to control how floodplains could be used.

In the 1966 Flood Control Act, Congress concluded that:

> In recognition of the increasing use and development of the flood plains of the rivers of the United States and the need for information on flood hazards to serve as a guide to such development, and as a basis for avoiding future flood hazards by regulation of use by states and political divisions thereof, and to assure that Federal departments and agencies may take proper cognizance of flood hazards, the Secretary of the Army, through the Chief of Engineers, is authorized to compile and disseminate information on floods and flood damages, including identification of areas subject to inundation by floods of various magnitudes and frequencies, and general criteria for guidance of Federal and non-Federal agencies in the use of flood plains; and to provide advice to other Federal agencies and local interests for their use in planning to ameliorate the flood hazards.

Seventeen new river basin projects were authorized in the act.

Flood Control Act of 1968

Pub. L. 90-483, Title II, Aug. 13, 1968, 82 Stat. 739
Pub. L. 99-662, Title IX, 913, Nov. 17, 1986, 100 Stat. 1490
Pub. L. 100-676, 12, Nov. 17, 1988, 102 Stat. 4025
Pub. L. 103-66, Title V, 5001(a), Aug. 10, 1993, 107 Stat. 378

The act lists thirty river basins that are to be improved for navigation and flood control.

Flood Control Act of 1970

Pub. L. 91-611, Title II, Dec. 31, 1970, 84 Stat. 1824
Pub. L. 93-222, 4, Dec. 23, 1971, 85 Stat. 799
Pub. L. 99-662, Title IX, 912(a), Title XI, 1107(b), Nov. 17, 1986, 100 Stat. 4189, 4230

The act lists fifteen rivers and their basins for improvement of navigation and the control of destructive floodwaters.

Flood Prevention

Watershed Protection and Flood Prevention Act of 1954

Pub. L. 566, Aug. 4, 1954, Chapter 656, 68 Stat. 666.

Congressional Funding

This law is based on Congress finding that erosion, floodwater, and sediment damages in the watersheds of the rivers and streams of the United States cause loss of life and danger to property. This constitutes a menace to national welfare. Congress needs to cooperate with states and their political subdivisions, soil or water conservation districts, flood prevention or central districts, and other local public agencies for the purpose of preventing such damages and to further the conservation, development, utilization, and disposal of water and thereby preserving and protecting the nation's land and water resources.

Development of Projects

The secretary of agriculture is authorized, upon application from a state agency:

1. To conduct such investigations and surveys as may be necessary to prepare plans for works or improvement
2. To make such studies as may be necessary for determining the physical and economic soundness of plans for works of improvement, including a determination as to whether benefits exceed costs
3. To cooperate and enter into agreements with and to furnish financial and other assistance to local organizations, provided that, for the land-treatment measures, the federal assistance shall not exceed the rate of assistance for similar practices under existing national programs
4. To obtain the cooperation and assistance of other federal agencies in carrying out the purpose of this act

Requirements for Implementation

The secretary of agriculture, in order to provide federal assistance for the installation of works, shall require local organizations:

1. To acquire without cost to the federal government such land, easement, or rights-of-way that are needed in connection with works of improvement assisted by the federal government
2. To assume such proportionate share of the cost of installing any work of improvement involving federal assistance as determined by the secretary of agriculture in consideration of anticipated benefits from such improvement, provided that no part of the construction cost for purposes other than flood prevention and features related thereto shall be borne by the federal government under this act
3. To make arrangements, satisfactory to the secretary of agriculture, for defraying costs of operating and maintaining such works of improvement
4. To acquire, or provide assurance that landowners have acquired, such water rights, pursuant to state land, as may be needed in the installation and operation of the work or improvement
5. To obtain agreements to carry out recommended soil

> conservation measures and proper farm plans from owners of not less than 50 percent of the land situated in the drainage areas above each retention reservoir to be installed with federal assistance

Flood Insurance

Federal Flood Insurance Act of 1956

Pub. L. 1016, Aug. 7, 1956, 70 Stat. 1078

This act established the federal flood insurance program for the nation. Congress found:

> In the case of reoccurring natural disasters, including reoccurring floods, insurance protection against individual and public loss is not always practically available through private or public sources. With specific reference to insurance against flood loss, the Congress finds that insurance against certain losses resulting from this peril is not so available. Since preventive and protective means and structures against the effects of these disasters can never wholly anticipate the geographic incidence and infinite variety of the destructive aspects of these forces, the Congress finds that the safeguards of insurance are a necessary adjunct of preventive and protective means and structures.
>
> Inasmuch as these disasters impact interstate and foreign commerce, hamper national defense, and cause widespread distress and hardships adversely affecting the general welfare, without regard to State boundary lines, and in the absence of insurance, protection from private or public sources, the Congress ought to provide for such protection in the case of floods, and study the feasibility and need for similar programs in the case of other forms of natural disasters against which insurance protection is not generally or practically available in all geographical areas.

Purpose

The purpose of this act is to authorize the establishment of a program of federal insurance and reinsurance against still other natural disaster perils to the extent that such insurance or reinsurance is not available on reasonable terms and conditions from the public or private sources.

The act is also designed to encourage private insurance covering the extent of the risks above the limits presented in the act and to provide federal reinsurance to the extent desirable and necessary to carry out this purpose.

In addition, the act authorizes the establishment of a program of loans, and a program combining insurance and loans, to assist flood victims who have entered into contracts with the administration under the act.

Administration

To assist in carrying out the functions, powers, and duties vested in this act, a commission may be appointed. The administration is authorized to establish insurance and reinsurance against loss resulting from damage to or destruction of real or personal property, including that owned by a state or local government, due to a flood.

The administration is also authorized to enter into contract with any person who has a subsequent loss resulting from damage to or destruction of real property due to floods. The administration:

1. Will guarantee any public or private financing institution against loss of principal and interest with respect to any loans.
2. Will make a loan directly to a person if a loan to finance a flood loss is not available from an institution on reasonable terms.

The act also gives the administration the authority to establish a program combining insurance and loans in order to provide the greatest variety and amount of protection against loss to the greatest numbers of affected persons.

Insurance rates are to be established by the administration and altered from time to time as financial conditions justify.

National Flood Insurance Act of 1968

Pub. L. 90-448, Title XIII, Aug. 1, 1968, 82 Stat. 572

This act strengthened the national flood insurance program. Congress based its changes on the following:

1. From time to time flood disasters have created personal hardships and economic distress that have required unforeseeable disaster relief measures and have placed an increasing burden on the nation's resources.
2. Despite the installation of preventive and protective works and the adoption of other public programs designed to reduce losses caused by flood damage, those methods have not been sufficient to protect adequately against growing exposure to future flood losses.
3. As a matter of national policy, a reasonable method of sharing the risk of flood losses is through a program of flood insurance that can complement and encourage preventive and protective measures.
4. If such a program is initiated and carried out gradually, it can be expanded as knowledge is gained and experience is appraised, thus eventually making flood insurance coverage available on reasonable terms and conditions to persons who need such protection.
5. Many factors have made it uneconomical for the private insurance industry alone to make flood insurance available to those in need of such protection, on reasonable terms and conditions.
6. A program of flood insurance with large-scale participation of the federal government and carried out to the maximum extent practical to the private insurance industry is feasible and can be initiated.
7. In addition, a program of flood insurance can promote public interest by providing appropriate protection against the perils of flood losses and encourage sound land use by minimizing exposure to flood losses.
8. The objective of a flood insurance program shall be integrally related to a unified national program for flood plain management.

Purpose

The purpose of this act is:

1. To authorize a flood insurance program by means of which flood insurance, over a period of time, can be made available on a nationwide basis through the cooperative effort of the federal government and the private insurance industry

2. To provide flexibility in the program so that such flood insurance may be based on workable methods of pooling risks, minimizing costs, and distributing burdens equitably among those who will be protected by flood insurance and the general public
3. To encourage state and local governments to make appropriate land use and adjustments to constrict the development of land that is exposed to flood damage and to minimize damage caused by flood losses
4. To guide the development of proposed future constrictions, where practicable, away from locations that are threatened by flood hazards
5. To encourage lending and credit institutions, as a matter of national policy, to assist in furthering the objectives of the flood insurance program
6. To assure that any federal assistance provided under the program will be related closely to all flood-related programs and activities of the federal government
7. To authorize continuing studies of flood hazards in order to provide for a constant reappraisal of the flood insurance program and its office or land use requirements

The act was implemented under four chapters.

Chapter I: The National Flood Insurance Program

The secretary of housing and urban development was authorized to establish a national flood insurance program that enables interested persons to purchase insurance against loss resulting from physical damage or loss of real property arising from any flood in the United States.

Scope of the Program and Priorities

Priority was given to residential properties designed for the occupancy of one to four families and for business properties owned or leased and operated by small business concerns.

If studies reveal the need for flood insurance, the flood insurance program may be extended, if feasible, to other residential property, other business property, agricultural properties, properties occupied by private nonprofit organizations, and properties owned by state and local governments and their agencies.

The flood insurance program was to be available only to states and areas that had (1) shown a positive interest in recurring flood insurance coverage under the flood insurance program, and

(2) given satisfactory assurance that by June 30, 1970, permanent land use and control measures had been adopted by the state or area, according to U.S. standards, and that the application and enforcement of such measures would begin as soon as technical information on floodways and on controlling flood elevation was available.

Nature and Limitation of Insurance Coverage

Criteria were established to provide regulations for the general terms and conditions of insurability that were applicable to properties eligible for flood insurance. These included:

1. The types, classes, and locations of properties which shall be eligible for flood insurance
2. The nature and limits of loss or damage in areas (or subdivisions) that may be covered by such insurance
3. The classification, limitations, and rejection of any risks that may be advisable
4. Appropriate minimum premium
5. Appropriate loss deductibles
6. Any other terms and conditions relating to insurance coverage or exclusion that may be necessary to carry out the program

Estimates of Premium Rates

The act requires that, from time to time, the rate for flood insurance coverage be determined. The risk premium rates for flood insurance are to be based on the consideration of the risk involved and accepted actuarial principles, and include (1) the applicable operating costs and allowances provided in the established schedules, and (2) any administrative expenses for carrying out the flood insurance program.

Establishment of Chargeable Premium Rates

The rates established by the secretary of the Department of Human and Urban Development would, insofar as practicable, be:

1. Based on a consideration of the respective risks involved, including differences in risks due to land use measures, flood proofing, flood forecasting, and similar measures
2. Adequate, on the basis of accepted actuarial principles, to provide reserves for anticipated losses, or, if less than such amounts, consistent with the objective

of making flood insurance available, where necessary, at reasonable rates so as to encourage prospective insureds to purchase such insurance
3. Stated so as to reflect the basis for such rates

National Flood Insurance Fund

To carry out the flood insurance program, the National Flood Insurance Fund was established with $250 million. This fund was available, without fiscal year limitation, for (1) making payments, (2) paying reinsurance claims under the excess loss reinsurance coverage, (3) paying administrative expenses, (4) other expenses, and (5) reinvestment of increased premiums.

Dissemination of Flood Insurance Information

Information is to be made available from time to time, to the public and to state and local agencies as to (1) the flood insurance program, its coverage and objectives, and (2) established and chargeable flood insurance premium rates, including the basis for and differences between such rates.

Prohibition against Certain Duplication of Benefits

Notwithstanding the provisions of any other law, federal disaster assistance was made available to any person:

1. For the physical loss, destruction or damage of real or personal property to the extent that such loss, destruction, or damage is covered by a valid claim which may be adjusted and paid under flood insurance made available under the authority of the act
2. Except in the situation provided for the physical loss, destruction, or damage of real or personal property to the extent that such loss, destruction, or damage could have been covered by a valid claim under flood insurance that had been made available under the authority of the act

Properties in Violation of State of Local Law

No flood insurance coverage shall be provided by this act for any property that has been declared by the state or local authority to be in violation of regulations that are intended to discourage or otherwise restrict land development or occupancy in flood-prone areas.

A Flood Insurance Advisory Committee is to provide necessary information to control the issuance of flood insurance.

Chapter II: Organization and Administration of the Flood Insurance Program

Industry Flood Insurance Pool

The act requires the federal government to encourage private insurance companies to form pools of companies for the purpose of assuming, on such terms as agreed upon, financial responsibility, along with the federal government, a reasonable position of responsibility for the payment of claims for losses under the flood insurance program.

Agreements with Flood Insurance Pool

The agreement of the federal government with the private insurance pool shall specify:

1. The terms and conditions under which risk capital will be available for the adjustment and payment of claims
2. The terms and conditions under which the pool shall participate in premiums received and profits and losses realized or sustained
3. Maximum amount of profits
4. Terms of operating costs
5. Terms of premiums/equalization payments

In addition, such agreements include that:

1. No insurance company will be excluded if they meet the prescribed conditions
2. The insurance companies will take all measures necessary to provide continuity of flood insurance coverage by the pool
3. All insurance companies and agents will be permitted to cooperate with the pool as fiscal agents, or otherwise, on a risk-sharing basis, to the maximum extent

Chapter III: Coordination of Flood Insurance with Land Management Programs in Flood-Prone Areas

Identification of Flood-Prone Areas

The federal government, through the Departments of Housing and Urban Development, Interior, Agriculture, Commerce, the Tennessee Valley Authority, and other federal agencies and through state and local areas, have the responsibility:

1. To identify and publish information with respect to all floodplain areas, including coastal areas in the United States, that have special flood hazards
2. To establish flood risk zones in all such areas and to make estimates with respect to the rates of probable flood-caused losses for the various flood and risk zones, within fifteen years

Criteria for Land Management and Use

Studies are to be conducted as to (1) management and use of flood-prone areas, (2) flood control, (3) flood zoning regulations, and (4) flood damage prevention. Such studies will include:

1. Laws and regulations or ordinances relating to encroachments and obstructions on stream channels and flooding
2. The orderly development and use of flood plains of rivers or streams
3. Flooding fines
4. Floodplain zoning, building codes, building permits, subdivisions, or other restrictions

On the basis of such studies, measures will be passed:

1. To contract the development of land that is exposed to flood damage
2. To guide the development of proposed construction away from flood hazards
3. To assist in reducing damage due to floods
4. To improve long-range management

Purchase of Certain Insured Properties

The act provides for the purchase of properties in flood-risk areas.

National Flood Insurance Program Act of 1989

Pub. L. 101-137, Nov. 3, 1989, 103 Stat. 824

This act amended the 1968 Flood Insurance Act as follows:

Establish or update flood-risk zone data in all such areas, and make estimates with respect to the rates of probable flood caused loss for the various flood-risk zones for each of these areas.

A study was also to be conducted as to the extent to which private insurance could be used to provide flood insurance coverage.

The director of the Federal Emergency Management Agency was to conduct a study to determine the impact of a relative sea level rise on the flood insurance rate. This study was also to project the economic losses associated with the estimated sea level rise and to aggregate such data for the United States as a whole and by region. The director was to report to Congress within one year.

National Flood Insurance Reform Act of 1994

Pub. L. 103-325, Title V, Sept. 23, 1994, 108 Stat. 2255 to 2287

This act amended the 1989 act.

Disaster Relief

Flood Disaster Protection Act of 1973

Pub. L. 93-234, Dec. 31, 1973, 87 Stat. 975
Pub. L. 94-50, Title III, 303, July 2, 1975, 89 Stat. 256
Pub. L. 94-198, Dec. 31, 1975, 89 Stat. 1116
Pub. L. 94-375, 14(a), Aug. 3, 1976, 90 Stat. 1075
Pub. L. 95-128, Title VII, 703, Oct. 12, 1977, 91 Stat. 1144
Pub. L. 98-181, Title IV, 451c, Nov. 30, 1983, 97 Stat. 1229
Pub. L. 98-479, Title II, 204(j), Oct. 17, 1984, 98 Stat. 2233
Pub. L. 100-707, Title I, 109(t), Nov. 23, 1988, 102 Stat. 4710
Pub. L. 103-325, Title V, Subtitle A, 511, Subtitle B, 522 to 526, 531, Subtitle F, 582(c), Sept. 23, 1994, 108 Stat. 2255, 2258, 2259, 2260, 2262, 2267, 2287

This act was to expand the National Flood Insurance Program by substantially increasing the limits of coverage and the total amount of insurance authorized and by requiring known flood-prone communities to participate in the program.

Congressional Findings

The act was based on the following congressional findings:

1. Annual losses throughout the nation from floods and mudslides are increasing at an alarming rate, largely as a result of the accelerating development of, and concentration of, population in areas of flood and mudslide hazards.
2. The availability of federal loans, grants, guarantees, insurance, and other forms of financial assistance is often a determining factor in land use and in the location and construction of public and private industrial, commercial, and residential facilities.
3. Property acquired or constructed with grants or other federal assistance may be exposed to risk or loss through floods, thus frustrating the purpose for which such assistance was extended.
4. Federal instrumentalities insure or otherwise provide financial protection to banking and credit institutions whose assets include a substantial number of mortgage loans, and often indebtedness secured by property exposed to loss and damage from floods and mudslides.
5. The nation cannot afford the tragic losses of life caused annually by flood occurrences, nor the increasing property losses suffered by flood victims, most of whom are still inadequately compensated despite the provisions of costly disaster relief benefits.
6. It is in the public interest for persons already living in flood-prone areas to have both an opportunity to purchase flood insurance and access to more adequate limits of coverage, so that they will be indemnified for their losses in the event of future flood disasters.

The act's purpose is:

1. To substantially increase the limits of coverage authorized under the National Flood Insurance Program
2. To provide for the expeditious identification of flood-prone areas and the dissemination of information on them
3. To require state or local communities, as a condition of future federal financial assistance, to participate in the

flood insurance program and to adopt adequate flood-plain ordinances with effective enforcement provisions consistent with federal standards to reduce or avoid future flood losses

4. To require the purchase of flood insurance by property owners who are being assisted by federal programs or by federally supervised, regulated, or insured agencies or institutions in the acquisition or improvement of land facilities located or to be located in identified areas having special flood hazards

Financial Considerations

Title I provides specific information on the increased limits of coverage, requirements to purchase flood insurance, establishment of changeable rates, financing of programs to cover losses from erosion and undermining of shorelines, appeals, and flood insurance premium equalization payments.

Title II is devoted to disaster mitigation requirements. It includes effect of nonparticipation in flood insurance programs, repeal of disaster assistance penalty, accelerated identification of flood-risk zones, authority to issue regulations, consultation with local officials, permission of national banks to invest in agricultural credit corporations, and the flexible interest rate authority for mobile home loans.

Robert T. Stafford Disaster Relief and Emergency Assistance Act of 1974

Pub. L. 93-288, May 22, 1974, Title I through Title VIII, 88 Stat. 143

Pub. L. 95-51, 1, June 20, 1977, 91 Stat. 233

Pub. L. 96-446, Oct. 13, 1980, 94 Stat. 1893

Pub. L. 96-568, 2, Dec. 22, 1980, 94 Stat. 3334

Pub. L. 100-707, Title I, 102(a), 103 (a) to (d), (f), 104 to 107 (a), 108, Nov. 23, 1988, 102 Stat. 4689 to 4707

Pub. L. 101-591, 5, Nov. 16, 1990, 104 Stat. 2936

Pub. L. 102-247, Title II, 205, Feb. 24, 1992, 106 Stat. 38

Pub. L. 103-181, 2, 3, Dec. 3, 1993, 107 Stat. 2054

Pub. L. 103-337, Title XXXIV, 3411, 3412b, Oct. 5, 1994, 108 Stat. 3100, 3111

This act defines a major disaster as any hurricane, tornado, storm, flood, high water, wind-driven water, tidal wave, tsunami, earthquake, volcanic eruption, landslide, mudslide, snowstorm, drought, fire, explosion, or other catastrophe in any part of the United States which, in the determination of the president, causes damage of sufficient severity and magnitude to warrant major disaster assistance under this act, above and beyond emergency services by the federal government, to supplement the efforts and available resources of the states, local government, and disaster relief organizations in alleviating the damage, loss, hardship, or suffering caused thereby.

Congressional Findings

Congress found it necessary to enact this law because disasters often cause loss of life, human suffering, loss of income, and property loss and damage, and because disasters often disrupt the normal functioning of government and communities and adversely affect individuals and families with great severity.

Functions of the Act

This act is designed to assist the efforts of the states in expediting the provision of aid, assistance, and emergency services, and the reconstruction and rehabilitation of devastated areas by:

1. Revising and broadening the scope of existing disaster relief programs
2. Encouraging the development of comprehensive disaster preparedness and assistance plans, program capabilities, and organizations by the states and local governments
3. Achieving greater coordination and responsiveness to disasters
4. Encouraging individuals, states, and local governments to protect themselves by obtaining insurance coverage to supplement or replace government assistance
5. Encouraging hazard mitigation measures to reduce losses from disasters, including development of land use and constructive regulations
6. Providing federal assistance for both public and private losses sustained in disasters
7. Providing a long-range economic recovery program for major disaster areas

Title II: Disaster Preparedness Assistance

The president is authorized to establish a program of disaster preparedness that utilizes the services of all appropriate agencies, including the Defense Civil Preparedness Agency, to include:

1. Preparation of disaster preparedness plans for mitigation, emergency warning operations, rehabilitation, and recovery
2. Training and exercises
3. Postdisaster critiques and evaluation
4. Annual series of programs
5. Coordination of federal, state, and local government programs
6. Application of science and technology
7. Research

Any state desiring assistance must create an agency to plan and administer such a disaster preparedness program. The state must submit to the president a plan that

1. Sets forth a comprehensive and detailed state program for preparation against, and assistance following, emergencies and major disasters
2. Includes provisions for appointment and training of appropriate staffs, formulation of necessary regulations, procedures and conduct of required exercises

The act also requires that the federal agencies be prepared to issue warnings of disasters to state and local governments. Not only federal agencies but also private and commercial communication systems will be used.

Title III: Disaster Assistance Administration

The act provides for the appointment of a Disaster Assistance Administration. Immediately upon declaration of a major disaster, the president is to appoint federal coordinating offices. In order to aid the disaster areas, the office shall:

1. Make an initial appraisal of the types of relief most urgently needed
2. Establish such field offices as are deemed necessary
3. Coordinate the administrative rulings, including public and private organizations such as the Red Cross,

the Mennonite Disaster Service, the Salvation Army, and so on

4. Take any other actions necessary to aid disaster victims

Title IV: Federal Disaster Assistance Programs

This act authorizes the president to have any federal agency repair, reconstruct, restore, or replace any facility owned by the United States that is damaged or destroyed by any major disaster. The act also authorizes the president to provide to any individual unemployed as a result of a major disaster such benefit assistance as he deems appropriate while the individual is unemployed. The president is also authorized to make grants to states for the purpose of meeting disaster-related necessary expenses or needs, though only on the condition that 25 percent of such a cost is paid to such individual or family from funds made available by a state. If low-income households are unable to purchase adequate amounts of nutritious food, the act authorizes the president to distribute, through the secretary of agriculture and other agencies, coupon allotments to such households pursuant to the provision of the Food Stamp Act of 1964. The president is also authorized to assure that adequate stocks of food will be ready and conveniently available for emergency mass feeding and distribution in any area of the United States that suffers a disaster or emergency. No person, otherwise eligible for any kind of replacement housing payment under the Uniform Relocation Assistance and Real Property Acquisition Policies Act of 1970 shall be denied such eligibility as a result of being unable, because of a major disaster, to meet the occupancy requirements set by such act; if low-income families are unable to secure legal services adequate to meet their needs as a consequence of a major disaster, the president is to assure that such programs are conducted with the advice and assistance of appropriate federal agencies and state and local bar associations. The president also has the responsibility to provide professional counseling services, including financial assistance to state and local agencies or private mental health organizations to provide such services or training of disaster workers, to victims of major disasters in order to relieve mental health problems caused or aggravated by such major disasters or its aftermath. The president is also authorized to make loans to any local government that may suffer a substantial loss of tax or other revenue and has demonstrated a need, with the amount of the loan being based on need.

There are a number of entitlement factors affected by major disasters:

1. Emergency communications: Establish temporary communication systems and make such communications available to state and local governments and others
2. Emergency public transportation: Provide temporary public transportation services in an area affected by a major disaster to meet emergency needs and to provide transportation for governmental offices, supply centers, stores, post offices, schools, major employment centers, and other needed places

Title V: Economic Recovery for Disaster Areas

This Title provided assistance for economic recovery after the period of emergency aid and replacement of essential facilities and services had been completed of any major disaster area that had suffered a dislocation of the economy of sufficient severity to require:

1. Assistance in planning for development to replace that lost in the major disaster
2. Continued coordination of assistance available under federal-aid programs
3. Continued assistance toward the restoration of the employment base

To implement this title, a Recovery Planning Council was to be appointed to review programs for a recovery investment plan. Funds could be used:

1. To make loans for the acquisition or development of and improvement of land for public works, public service, and development of facility usage, including acquisition of parks and open spaces
2. To make supplementary grants to increase the federal share for projects for which funds are reserved

The title also provided that:

1. Grants and loans may be made to any state, local government, or private or public nonprofit organization
2. No supplementary grant will increase the federal share greater than 90 percent
3. Loans under this act shall bear an interest rate determined by the secretary of the treasury

4. Financial assistance under this title shall not be extended to assist establishments to relocate from one area to another or to assist sale contracts

Other Disaster Relief Acts

Disaster Loan Act of 1936
Apr. 17, 1936, ch. 234, 1, 4, 49 Stat. 1232
Disaster Loan Corporation Act of 1937
Feb. 1, 1937, ch. 10, 50 Stat. 19
Disaster Relief Act of 1966
Pub. L. 89-769, Nov. 6, 1968, 80 Stat. 1316–1321
Disaster Relief Act of 1969
Pub. L. 91-79, Oct. 1, 1965, 83 Stat. 125
Disaster Relief Act of 1970
Pub. L. 91-606, Dec. 31, 1970, 84 Stat. 1744
Pub. L. 92-209, Dec. 16, 1971, 85 Stat. 743
Uniform Relocation Assistance and Real Property Acquisition Policies Act of 1970
Pub. L. 91-646, Jan. 2, 1971, 84 Stat. 1894
Pub. L. 100-17, Title IV, 402–417, Apr. 2, 1987, 101 Stat. 246 to 256
Pub. L. 102-240, Title I, Part A, 1055, Dec. 18, 1991, 105 Stat. 2002
Disaster Relief Act Amendment of 1980
Pub. L. 96-568, 1, 2, Dec. 22, 1980, 94 Stat. 3334
Disaster Assistance Act of 1988
Pub. L. 100-387, Aug. 11, 1988, 102 Stat. 124
Pub. L. 101-82, Title V, 503, Title VI, 602, Aug. 14, 1989, 103 Stat. 586, 587
Pub. L. 101-239, Title I, 1004(a), Dec. 19, 1989, 103 Stat. 586, 587
Pub. L. 101-624, Title XV, 1541, Nov. 28, 1990, 104 Stat. 3691
Pub. L. 102-237, Title VI, 602(b), Dec. 12, 1991, 105 Stat. 1999
Disaster Relief and Emergency Assistance Amendments of 1988
Pub. L. 100-707, Title I, Nov. 23, 1988, 102 Stat. 4689 to 4711
Disaster Assistance Act of 1989
Pub. L. 101-82, Aug. 14, 1989, 103 Stat. 564
Pub. L. 101-134, 1, Oct. 30, 1989, 103 Stat. 780
Pub. L. 101-220, 9, Dec. 1989, 103 Stat. 1882
Pub. L. 101-624, Title XXII, 2231, 2232, 2235, Nov. 28, 1990, 104 Stat. 3958, 3959
Pub. L. 102-237, Title VI, 602(a), Dec. 12, 1991, 105 Stat. 1878

Proclamation: Contribution to American Red Cross for Flood Relief by the President of the United States of America

President Franklin D. Roosevelt, on March 19, 1936, presented this proclamation to the American people.

> Flood waters raging throughout eleven states have driven 200,000 people from their homes, with every indication that this number may be materially increased within the next twenty-four hours. In this grave emergency, the homeless are turning to our great national relief agency, the American Red Cross, for food, clothing, shelter, and medical care.
>
> To enable the Red Cross to meet this immediate obligation and to continue to carry the burden of caring for those unfortunate men, women, and children until their homes are restored and they can return to normal living conditions, it is necessary that a minimum relief fund of three million dollars be raised as promptly as possible.
>
> As President of the United States and as President of the American Red Cross, I am, therefore, urging our people to contribute promptly and most generously so that sufficient funds may be available for the relief of these thousands of our homeless fellow citizens. I am confident that in the face of this great need, your response will be as immediate and as generous as has always been the case when the Red Cross has acted as your agent in the relief of human suffering.

Dam Acts

National Dam Inspection Program Act of 1972

Pub. L. 92-367, Aug. 8, 1972, 86 Stat. 506

Deaths and property damage resulting from the failure of a number of dams prompted Congress to pass legislation to inspect dams to ensure safety.

Program

The secretary of the army, acting as soon as possible through the chief of engineers, was to carry out a national program of inspection of dams that were 25 feet or more in height from the natural bed of the stream and had an impounding capacity at maximum storage of 50 acre feet of water or more.

Purpose

The purpose of the program was to protect human life and property. All dams in the United States were to be inspected except those under the jurisdiction of:

1. The Bureau of Reclamation
2. The Tennessee Valley Authority
3. The International Boundary and Water Commission
4. The Federal Power Commission
5. Dams inspected within 12 months prior to this act
6. Dams determined not to pose any threat to human life and property

In determining whether a dam constituted a danger to human life or property, the inspector must take into consideration the possibility that endangerment might occur to overtopping, seepage, settlement, erosion, sediment, cracking, earth movement, earthquakes, failure of bulkheads, flashboards, gates or conduits, or other conditions.

The secretary of the army must report to the governor of the state the condition of all dams inspected. If hazardous conditions are found, advice will be given to the governor as to remedial measures necessary to mitigate any hazardous conditions.

Dam Safety Act of 1986

Pub. L. 99-662, Title XII, 1206, Nov. 17, 1986, 100 Stat. 4264

This act amended the National Dam Inspection Act of 1972.

In order to assure greater safety, the act specifies that each inspection program include the following:

1. Prior to construction of any dam, plans are to be reviewed to provide reasonable assurance of the dam's safety and integrity over its intended life.
2. A procedure will be developed to assure that dams will

be constructed and operated in a safe and reasonable manner.

3. A procedure will be developed to inspect each dam within a state at least every five years, and every three years when a dam breakage could cause loss of life.
4. A procedure will be developed for more detailed and frequent safety inspections when warranted.
5. The state will be given the authority to require changes or modifications in a dam, or in its operation, in order to assure the dam's safety.
6. Each state is expected to develop a system of emergency procedures that would be used in the event of a dam failure or an imminent dam failure. Each state is also expected to identify the dams whose failure could reasonably be expected to endanger human life, the maximum area that would be inundated in the event of a dam failure, and the necessary public facilities that would be affected by such inundation.
7. The state is expected to have the authority to assure repairs or other changes needed to maintain the integrity of the dam.
8. The state is expected to have authority and necessary emergency funds to assure immediate repair or other changes to, or removal of, a dam in order to protect human life and property, and if the dam's owner does not take appropriate action, the state must act expeditiously.

The act also provided for a program of research, in cooperation with the National Bureau of Standards, in order to develop improved techniques and equipment for rapid and effective dam inspection, together with devices for the continued monitoring of dams for safety purposes.

Dam Act of 1906

June 21, 1906, ch. 3508, 34 Stat. 386

Specific River Acts

Mississippi River Flood Control Act of 1928

May 15, 1928, ch. 569, 45 Stat. 534

June 19, 1930, ch. 542, 46 Stat. 787
June 15, 1936, ch. 548, 49 Stat. 1508
Nov. 30, 1945, ch. 496, 59 Stat. 587

Purpose

The purpose of this act was primarily the control of floods on the Mississippi River and its tributaries.

Flood Control

The project was to control floods of the Mississippi River in its alluvial valley near Cape Girardeau, Missouri. Before any construction could begin, the act required that surveys be completed to ascertain the best method to secure flood control in addition to levees. All flood control work also had to be built to protect adjacent lands. Furthermore, all floodways, spillways, or diversion channels were to provide protection to the same degree as levees. The concept of local contributions as written into past acts was maintained in this act.

Damage Liability

The act indicated that the United States was not liable for any damage from floods or floodwaters at any place. If, however, surveys revealed that levees could not protect against floods, the United States was to acquire ownership of the land subjected to floods. The United States was to provide flowage rights for additional floodwaters that passed by reason of diversions from the main channel of the Mississippi River.

This act amended the 1917 act, which provided for control of floods of the Mississippi River and of the Sacramento River in California.

Development of the Coosa River, Alabama and Georgia Act of 1954

Pub. L. 436, June 28, 1954, 68 Stat. 309

This legislation was enacted in connection with the comprehensive program for the development of the water resources of the Coosa River and its tributaries. It was to be implemented under the provision of the River and Harbor Act of 1945.

Purpose

The act provided for a comprehensive plan for the development of the Coosa River for the use or benefit of interstate commerce, for the improvement and utilization of water-power development, and for other beneficial public uses, including recreational purposes.

The dams constructed were to provide a substantively continuous series of pools and were to include basic provisions for the future economical construction of navigation facilities. Further development required that there be the maximum flood control storage that was economically feasible with respect to past flood records, but in no event should flood control storage be less than that required to compensate for the effect of valley storage displaced by the proposed reservoir, or less in quantity and effectiveness than the amount of flood control storage that could feasibly be provided by the currently authorized federal multiple-purpose project at Howell Mill Shoals, constructed to elevation 490 with surcharge storage to elevation 495.

The dams could be built in sequence on the condition that the dam or dams providing for maximum flood control benefits would be constructed first, under a different order of construction, and approved by the secretary of the army.

De Luz Reservoir, California Act of 1954

Pub. L. 547, July 28, 1954, 68 Stat. 575

This act was passed to deliver water to the Fallbrook Public Utility District and to provide water to Camp Joseph H. Pendleton, U.S. Army Base.

The secretary of the army, through the chief of engineers, in accordance with the Flood Control Act of 1944, is authorized to utilize for purposes of flood control such portions of the capacity of the De Luz Reservoir as may be available.

Colorado River Storage Project Act of 1956

Pub. L. 485, April 11, 1956, ch. 203, 70 Stat. 105
Pub. L. 87-433, June 13, 1962, 18, 76 Stat. 102
Pub. L. 88-568, Sept. 2, 1964, 1, 78 Stat. 852
Pub. L. 90-537, Sept. 30, 1968, Title V, 205(d), 88 Stat. 273
Pub. L. 93-320, June 24, 1974, Title II, 205(d), 88 Stat. 273
Pub. L. 96-470, Oct. 19, 1980, Title I, 108(c), 94 Stat. 2239

Pub. L. 98-569, Oct. 30, 1984, 5, 98 Stat. 2939

This act authorizes the secretary of the interior to construct, operate, and maintain the Colorado River Storage Project.

Purpose

The principal purpose of this act was to initiate the comprehensive development of the water resources of the Upper Colorado River Basin, for the purpose of regulating the flow of the Colorado River, storing water for beneficial consumptive uses, making it possible for the states of the Upper Basin to utilize, consistently with the provisions of the Colorado River Compact and the Upper Colorado River Basin Compacts, providing for the reclamation of arid and semiarid land, for the control of floods, and for the generation of hydroelectric power.

Development

The act authorized the construction of a number of new dams. The benefits of the dams were expected to exceed the costs. It was the intent of Congress that no new dams or reservoirs would be in any national park or monument. If the cost of irrigation to Navajos exceeded their ability to pay, the debt would be forgiven.

The hydroelectric power plants and transmission lines to be constructed, operated, and maintained by this act were to operate in conjunction with other federal power plants, present and potential, so as to produce the greatest practicable amount of power and energy that could be sold at firm power and energy rates. The development of hydroelectric plants by this act was not to interfere with the operation of the Colorado River Compact, the Upper Colorado River Basin Compact, the Boulder Canyon Project Act, the Boulder Canyon Project Adjustment Act, and any other contract lawfully entered into under such Compacts and Acts.

Revenue

Revenues in the Basin Fund in excess of operating needs were to be paid annually to the general fund of the Treasury for:

1. The costs of each unit that are allocated to power production
2. The costs of each unit that are allocated to municipal water supply production

3. Interest on the unauthorized balance of the investment in the power and water supply features of each unit
4. The costs of each storage unit that are allocated to irrigation

Colorado River Flooding Protection Act of 1986

Pub. L. 99-450, Oct. 8, 1986, 100 Stat. 1129
Pub. L. 103-437, 16(a) (4), Nov. 2, 1994, 108 Stat. 4594

The purpose of the act is to establish a federally declared flooding for the Colorado River below Davis Dam.

Congress found that:

1. There are multiple purposes established by law for the dams and other control structures administered by the secretary of the interior on the Colorado River.
2. The maintenance of the Colorado River Floodway established in this act is essential to accomplish these multiple purposes.
3. Developments within the Floodway are and will continue to be vulnerable to damaging flows such as the property damage that occurred in 1983 and may occur in the future.
4. Certain federal programs that subsidize or permit development within the Floodway threaten human life, health, property, and natural resources.
5. There is a need for coordinated federal, state, and local action to limit Floodway development.

In response, Congress declared that the purposes of this act are:

1. To establish the Colorado River Floodway, so as to provide benefits to river users and to minimize the loss of life, protect health and safety, and minimize damage to property and natural resources by restricting further federal expenditures and financial assistance, except public health funds, which have the effect of encouraging development within the Colorado River Floodway
2. To establish a task force to advise the secretary of the

interior and the Congress on establishment of the Floodway and on managing existing and future development without the Floodway, including the appropriateness of compensation in specified cases of extraordinary hardship

Development of Floodway

Federal expenditures or financial assistance may include:

1. The building of any dam, channel, or levee for the purpose of flood control, water conservation, power, or water quality
2. Other remedial or corrective actions, including but not limited to drainage facilities essential to assist in controlling adjacent high groundwater conditions caused by flood flows
3. The maintenance, replacement, reconstruction, repair, and expansion of public or tribally owned or operated roads, structures (including bridges), or facilities
4. Adjustment of the boundaries of the Floodway to account for changes in flows caused, directly or indirectly, by roads or structures

Other projects approved by this act for the development of the Floodway included:

1. Projects for the study, management, protection, and enhancement of fish and wildlife resources and habitats
2. Establishment, operation, and maintenance of air and water navigation aids
3. Scientific research, including aeronautical, atmospheric, space, geologic, marine, fish, and wildlife
4. Assistance for emergency actions essential to the saving of lives and the protection of property and the public health and safety
5. Assistance for public health purposes, such as mosquito abatement programs
6. Nonstructural projects for riverbank stabilization that are designed to enhance or restore natural stabilization systems
7. Recreational developments such as regional parks, golf courses, docks, and boat launching ramps

8. Compatible agricultural uses that do not involve permanent crops and include only a minimal amount of permanent facilities in the Floodway

Land Control

No lease of land is permitted by this act within the Colorado River Floodway that is owned by the United States unless the lease is consistent, as determined by the secretary of the interior, with the operations and maintenance of the Colorado River Floodway.

River and Harbor Acts

The River and Harbor Acts have the basic purpose of improving navigation of vessels. Indirectly, the improvement of navigable rivers has a positive effect on controlling floodwaters. The U.S. Army Corps of Engineers is the agency that improves the navigation of rivers. The act was passed in 1884 and has been amended many times.

River Harbor Act of 1884
- July 5, 1884, ch. 229, 1, 4, 23 Stat. 147
- Mar. 3, 1909, ch. 264, 6, 35 Stat. 818
- Aug. 30, 1954, ch. 1076, 1(15), 68 Stat. 967

River and Harbor Act of 1888
- Aug. 11, 1888, ch. 860, 1 to 4, 6 to 8, 11, 25 Stat. 419 to 423, 425
- June 13, 1902, ch. 1079, 1, 32 Stat. 340, 367
- Mar. 2, 1907, ch. 2509, 1, 34 Stat. 1102
- Mar. 3, 1909, ch. 264, 3, 35 Stat. 817
- Aug. 30, 1954, ch. 1076, 1(15), 68 Stat. 967
- Apr. 26, 1978, Pub. L. 95-269, 1, 92 Stat. 218

River and Harbor Act of 1892
- July 13, 1892, ch. 158, 5, 27 Stat. 111

River and Harbor Act of 1894
- Aug. 18, 1894, ch. 299, 28 Stat. 356, 360, 362
- June 13, 1902, ch. 1079, 11, 32 Stat. 374
- Aug. 8, 1917, ch. 49, 7, 40 Stat. 266

River and Harbor Act of 1899
- Mar. 3, 1899, ch. 425, 1, 7, 9 to 20, 30 Stat. 1148, 1150 to 1155
- Feb. 20, 1900, ch. 23, 2, 3, 31 Stat. 32
- June 13, 1902, ch. 1079, 12, 32 Stat. 32
- June 25, 1948, ch. 646, 39, 62 Stat. 992

Oct. 15, 1982, Pub. L. 97-322, Title 1, 107(b), 108(b), 96 Stat. 1582
Jan. 12, 1983, Pub. L. 97-449, 2(f), 96 Stat. 2440
River and Harbor Act of 1902
June 13, 1902, ch. 1079, 1, 3, 5, 6, 9 to 12, 32 Stat. 340, 367, 371 to 375
Feb. 10, 1932, ch. 26, 47 Stat. 42 (33, 541)
Oct. 31, 1951, ch. 654, 4(4), 60 Stat. 709
River and Harbor Act of 1905
Mar. 3, 1905, ch. 1482, 4, 6, 33 Stat. 1147, 1148
River and Harbor Act of 1907
Mar. 2, 1907, ch. 2509, 1, 5, 34 Stat. 1102, 1110, 1119
River and Harbor Act of 1909
Mar. 3, 1909, ch. 264, 3, 5, 6, 35 Stat. 817, 818
River and Harbor Act of 1910
June 25, 1910, ch. 382, 1, 3, 4, 36 Stat. 658, 669, 676
Mar. 1, 1917, ch. 144, 4, 39 Stat. 951
June 5, 1920, ch. 252, 9, 41 Stat. 1015
River and Harbor Act of 1912
July 25, 1912, ch. 253, 1, 8, 9, 12, 13, 37 Stat. 206, 218, 222, 223, 233, 234
July 3, 1930, ch. 847, 3, 46 Stat. 946
Oct. 17, 1940, ch. 895, 3, 54 Stat. 1200
River and Harbor Act of 1913
Mar. 4, 1913, ch. 144, 1, 3, 4, 37 Stat. 803, 816, 825, 826
Nov. 2, 1994, Pub. L. 103-437, 12(b), 108 Stat. 4590
River and Harbor Act of 1915
Mar. 4, 1915, ch. 142, 3 to 5, 7, 13, 38 Stat. 1052, 1053, 1055
Jan. 12, 1983, Pub. L. 97-449, 2(d), (1), 96 Stat. 2440
River and Harbor Act of 1916
July 27, 1916, ch. 260, 1, 3, 39 Stat. 393, 396, 399, 402, 411
River and Harbor Act of 1917
Aug. 8, 1917, ch. 49, 1, 5, 7, 9, 13, 15 to 17, 40 Stat. 252, 266 to 268
River and Harbor Act of 1919
Mar. 2, 1919, ch. 95, 1 to 4, 8, 40 Stat. 1286, 1287, 1290
Apr. 26, 1976, Pub. L. 95-269, 2, 92 Stat. 219
River and Harbor Act of 1920
June 5, 1920, ch. 252, 2, 9, 41 Stat. 1010, 1015
River and Harbor Act of 1922
Sept. 22, 1922, ch. 427, 5, 6, 9 to 11, 13, 42 Stat. 1042, 1043, 1047
River and Harbor Act of 1925
Mar. 3, 1925, ch. 467, 5, 7, 10, 11, 43 Stat. 1191, 1197

River and Harbor Act of 1930
July 3, 1930, ch. 847, 2, 3, 6, 8, 12, 46, Stat. 945–949
May 17, 1950, ch. 168, Title I, 105, 64 Stat. 168
July 14, 1960, Pub. L. 86-645, Title I, 103, 74 Stat. 484
Dec. 31, 1970, Pub. L. 91-611, Title I, 104, 84 Stat. 1819
River and Harbor Act of 1935
Aug. 30, 1935, ch. 831, 1, 5, 7 to 10, 49 Stat. 1028, 1048
River and Harbor Act of 1938
June 20, 1938, ch. 535, 1, 2, 4, 5, 10, 12, 52 Stat. 802, 804, 805, 808
River and Harbor Act of 1940
Oct. 17, 1940, ch. 895, 3, 54 Stat. 1200
River and Harbor Act of 1941
See Flood Control Act of 1941
River and Harbor Act of 1945
Mar. 2, 1945, ch. 19, 59, Stat. 10
River and Harbor Act of 1948
June 30, 1948, ch. 771, Title I, 62 Stat. 1172
Oct. 27, 1965, Pub. L. 89-298, Title III, 306, 79 Stat. 1094
Mar. 7, 1974, Pub. L. 93-251, Title I, 93, 88 Stat. 39
River and Harbor Act of 1950
May 17, 1950, ch. 188, Title I, 64 Stat. 163
River and Harbor Act of 1954
Sept. 3, 1954, ch. 1264, Title I, 68 Stat. 1248
Aug. 9, 1955, ch. 674, 69 Stat. 612
River and Harbor Act of 1958
Pub. L. 85-500, Title I, 104, 105, 111, July 3, 1958, 72 Stat. 300, 303
Pub. L. 89-298, Title III, 302, 309, Oct. 27, 1965, 79 Stat. 1092, 1094
Pub. L. 98-63, Title I, 101, July 30, 1983, 97 Stat. 313
Pub. L. 99-662, Title IX, 941, Title XI, 1104, Nov. 17, 1986, 100 Stat. 4199, 4228
River and Harbor Act of 1960
Pub. L. 86-645, Title I, July 14, 1960, 74 Stat. 480
Pub. L. 89-298, Title III, 310(a), Oct. 27, 1965, 79 Stat. 1095
Pub. L. 91-611, Title I, 112(a), Dec. 31, 1970, 24 Stat. 1821
Pub. L. 94-587, Title I, 133(a), Oct. 22, 1976, 90 Stat. 2928
Pub. L. 90-662, Title IX, 915(d), Nov. 17, 1986, 100 Stat. 4191
River and Harbor Act of 1962
Pub. L. 87-874, Title I, Oct. 23, 1962, 76 Stat. 1173
River and Harbor Act of 1965
Pub. L. 89-298, Title III, Oct. 27, 1965, 79 Stat. 1089

River and Harbor Act of 1966
Pub. L. 89-789, Title I, Nov. 7, 1966, 80 Stat. 1405
River and Harbor Act of 1968
Pub. L. 90-483, Title I, Aug. 13, 1968 82 Stat. 731 (33, 59c-1.59g to 59i, 426i, 562a)
Pub. L. 99-662, Title IX, 915(f), 940, Nov. 17, 1986, 100 Stat. 4191, 4199
River and Harbor Act of 1970
Pub. L. 91-611, Title I, Dec. 31, 1970, 84 Stat. 1818
Pub. L. 93-251, Title I, 23, Mar. 7, 1974, 88 Stat. 20
Pub. L. 98-181, Title I, 1306, Nov. 30, 1983, 97 Stat. 1293
Pub. L. 99-662, Title VIII, 817, Nov. 17, 1986, 100 Stat. 4170
Pub. L. 100-676, 24, Nov. 17, 1988, 102 Stat. 4027
Pub. L. 102-580, Title I, 102(4), Oct. 31, 1992, 106 Stat. 4809

Bibliography 5

Because floods have occurred throughout history, the body of literature on them is voluminous. It has been prepared by governmental agencies, professional societies, individual scientists, and popular writers. Consequently, the works listed in this bibliography range from scientific and technical studies to popular accounts. This chapter thus provides a wide perspective on floods. Bibliographies and handbooks are listed first, followed by annotated entries on books, journal articles, and a list of selected journals that publish articles on floods. The final section provides listings of professional papers and water research reports treating floods by government agencies.

Books

Bibliographies

Ferguson, Bruce K. *Urban Stormwater Management Bibliography.* Public Administration Series, Bibl. no. P2795. Monticello, IL: Vance Bibliographies, 1989, 15 pp.

Landman, Georgina B., and T. W. Ihloff. *The*

Legal Aspects of Flood Plain Zoning and Management: An Annotated Bibliography. Exchange Bibl. no. 1093. Chicago, IL: Council of Planning Librarians, 1976, 26 pp.

Moe, Christine E. *Environmental Impacts of Spillway Openings and Flooding in the Lower Mississippi River.* Public Administration Series, Bibl. no. 376. Monticello, IL: Vance Bibliographies, 1979, 17 pp.

———. *Rio Grande Flood Control and Drainage.* Public Administration Series, Bibl. no. P769. Monticello, IL: Vance Bibliographies, 1981, 27 pp.

Weathers, John W., ed. *Flood Damage Prevention: An Indexed Bibliography,* 8th ed. Knoxville, TN: Tennessee Valley Authority and Water Resources Research Center, University of Tennessee, 1976, 61 pp.

Handbooks

U.S. Federal Emergency Management Agency. *Preparing for Hurricanes and Coastal Flooding: A Handbook for Local Officials.* Washington, DC: 1983, 136 pp.

U.S. Water Resources Council. *Floodplain Management Handbook.* Washington, DC: GPO, 1981, 69 pp.

General

Baker, Victor R., R. Craig Kochel, and Peter C. Patton, eds. *Flood Geomorphology.* New York: John Wiley & Sons, 1988, 503 pp. ISBN 0-471-62558-2.

Numerous writers contributed to this huge volume. Flood geomorphology is the study of the role of floods in shaping the landscape. Geomorphologists analyze the causes of floods, flood processes, and changes in flood-related processes. The book is divided into five parts. Part one considers external controls; part two deals with flood erosional and depositional processes; part three explores the interaction of climate, landscapes, and floods; part four describes flood phenomena; and part five provides examples of the interaction of floods with human activity on land. The book is well illustrated with tables, figures, and pictures. Each article has many references, and a sizable index enables the reader to find information easily.

Cooke, Roger, Max Mendel, and Han Vrijling, eds. *Engineering Probabilistic Design and Maintenance for Flood Protection.*

Boston: Kluwer Academic Publishers, 1997, 213 pp. ISBN 0-7923-4399-9.

Many authors contributed to this volume, which is the proceedings of the First Conference on Engineering Probability in Flood Defense, organized by the Department of Mathematics and Information of the Delft University of Technology and the Department of Industrial Engineering and Operations Research of the University of California at Berkeley, held June 1–2, 1995, in Delft, the Netherlands. The conference took place when major floods were occurring in the Netherlands and in California, in the winter of 1994–1995. The papers here show how probabilistic techniques have helped to solve problems in the area of flood defense. Solutions to problems as complex as flood defense require expertise from many disciplines. This collection illustrates a mathematical approach to flood defense. Each paper has an abstract and references for further reading.

Fagan, Brian. *Floods, Famines, and Emperors: El Niño and the Fate of Civilization*. New York: Basic Books, 1999, 284 pp. ISBN 0-465-01120-9.

This book, written with emotion and feeling, describes the effects of El Niño through the ages. Although this weather phenomenon has always been with us, its great influence on civilization is only now being recognized.

The volume is divided into three parts. Part one describes how El Niño was first identified and the progress scientists have made in defining its role in the global weather machine. For the first time, the existence of climatic anomalies in one part of the world have been identified in other world areas. This means that for the first time there are scientific data and tools to discern the climatic history of human civilization. To illustrate, it is now recognized that there is strong correlation between unusual climatic shifts and unusual historical events. For example, the fall of the Old Kingdom in Ancient Egypt coincided with the severe droughts that ravaged the Nile Valley in 2180 B.C.; those droughts, in turn, were triggered ultimately by interactions between the atmosphere and the ocean on the other side of the world.

Part two of the book revolves around the basic question of how climatic events affect the course of civilization. For example, how do droughts, famines, and floods affect a people's faith in the institutions of their society and the legitimacy of their rulers? Part three discusses the relationships between carrying capacity of the land and population density. El Niño's causing droughts at one time and floods at another affects human endeavors worldwide. Thus, productivity of the land and population density must be viewed from a global perspective.

This book has a few figures, an index, and notes and sources for each chapter.

Flippo, Herbert N., Jr. *Floods in Pennsylvania.* Series: Water Resources Bulletin No. 13, Harrisburg, PA: Department of Environmental Resources, Office of Resource Management; and Washington, DC: U.S. Geological Survey, 1977, 59 pp.

To design floodway structures and offer proper management of lands that are prone to flooding, floods must be studied and understood. This volume presents methods for estimating flood discharges on unregulated streams with no ungauged sites. Ten regression models show magnitude and frequency on urbanized and unregulated streams in Pennsylvania. The volume has figures, tables, and plates as illustrations, plus four appendixes.

Ghosh, S. N. *Flood Control and Drainage Engineering,* 2d ed. Brookfield, VT: A. A. Balkema Publishers, 1997, 295 pp. ISBN 90-6191-481-7.

This book can be used as a textbook for both undergraduate and graduate students, and engineers can use it as a reference text. Chapters 1 through 3 deal with flood problems and flood control structures. Chapters 4 and 5 discuss spillways and design planning and operation of reservoirs. Chapter 6 deals with flood protection measures. Chapter 7 discusses forecasting and warning of impending floods. Chapter 8 explains the cost benefit of flood control projects. Chapters 9 and 10 deal with drainage of flooded areas. Two new chapters have been added to this second edition; one deals with water-logging and salinity, and the final chapter discusses remote sensing technology for flood control. This book employs a mathematical approach to flooding and control and is illustrated with many figures. Selected references and a selected bibliography are found at the end of the volume.

Hoyt, William, and Walter B. Langbein. *Floods.* Princeton, NJ: Princeton University Press, 1955, 469 pp.

Even though this is not a recent book, it is full of pertinent information on floods. It is recognized that floods are as much a part of the landscape as hills and valleys and must be dealt with. The book discusses why there are flood problems and gives the history of floods and damages caused by them. It shows how water can be controlled by dams, dikes, reservoirs, and so on. The federal flood control program began about 1850 when flood protection was applied to the lower Mississippi River, and it has continued to expand and improve since then. The volume has photos, figures, and tables as illustrations as well as a list of references.

Jacobson, Robert B., ed. *Geomorphic Studies of the Stream and Flood of November 3–5, 1985, in the Upper Potomac and Cheat River Basins in West Virginia and Virginia.* U.S. Geological Survey Bulletin 1981. Denver: U.S. Geological Survey, 1993, 96 pp.

This is a multidisciplinary study of the geomorphic effects of a severe storm that occurred in the Appalachian Mountains in West Virginia and Virginia. After an introductory chapter, the remaining four chapters discuss the meteorology of the storm, landslides that occurred, depositional aspects of the flood on the Cheat River and the Black Fork in West Virginia, and flood hydrology and the geomorphic impact on valley floors. This was the largest flood recorded in the South Branch Potomac River Basin. Chapters have bibliographic references, figures, and photos. There is a map in the back pocket showing the area studied.

Jordan, P. R., and L. J. Combs, eds. *Summary of Floods in the United States during 1990 and 1991. U.S. Geological Survey Water Supply Paper* 2474. Washington, DC: GPO, 1996, 257 pp. ISBN 0-607-86217-3.

This volume describes 50 severe, unusual, and widespread floods in 28 of the 50 states in 1990 and 1991. Flooding was more widespread in 1990 than 1991. The most destructive and widespread flooding occurred in Oklahoma, Texas, Arkansas, and Louisiana, causing many deaths and billions of dollars in damages. Articles have maps showing the areas flooded. Data are provided so that the reader can compare the floods of this period with previous floods. There is a summary of the floods of 1990–1991 and many figures and tables. Bibliographic references are found throughout the book, and a glossary and an index are included.

Mayer, L., and D. Nash, eds. *Catastrophic Flooding.* Boston: Allen & Unwin, 1987, 410 pp. ISBN 0-04-551142-X.

This is a collection of papers presented at the Eighteenth Annual Geomorphology "Binghamton" Symposium on Catastrophic

Flooding at Miami University, September 26–27, 1987. The term catastrophic flooding applies to devastating floods or floods that cause changes in stream channel characteristics. Such floods are caused by unusual climate conditions and/or failure of dams. Special attention is given in this volume to the causes and effects of catastrophic flooding and to how the sediment in these circumstances differs from the deposits of a normal stream. The frequency of catastrophic floods was also investigated. Each chapter includes bibliographic references and figures as illustrations.

Milne, Antony. *Floodshock: The Drowning of Planet Earth.* Gloucester, England: Alan Sutton, 1986, 176 pp. ISBN 0-86299-270-2.

This interesting volume begins with the story of the world's most famous flood—Noah's flood. Chinese history also starts with a similar great flood. Floods affect more people than any other disaster except droughts, and the death toll from a serious flood is much higher than those of other disasters. A study by the Universities of Toronto and Colorado in 1969 compared natural disasters over a twenty-year period and showed that flood-related events headed the list of fifteen categories. Tsunamis often follow an earthquake, resulting in many deaths. The chapter "Drowning of America" details the devastation of the Mississippi, Kansas, Missouri, Connecticut, Ohio, Conemaugh, and other rivers. The chapter "The Flood Engineers" tells the story of the Johnstown Dam disaster of May 1889, the worst flood in American history. It explains why dams collapse and what can be done to prevent this from happening. The book has excellent flood photographs and includes a bibliography for further reading.

Mount, Jeffrey F. *California Rivers and Streams: The Conflict between Fluvial Process and Land Use.* Berkeley: University of California Press, 1995, 359 pp. ISBN 0-520-20192-2.

This volume looks at how rivers work and how land use practices interact with river processes. Rivers affect the lives of all Californians, and little attention is paid to them until they begin to flood—and then they leave a mark wherever the flood occurs. The book is divided into two parts. Part one explains how rivers work, discussing such topics as water in motion, sediment transport and deposition, river discharge, river network, and the climate and geology of California rivers. Part two has chapters discussing the past 200 years of California rivers, mining and logging pertaining to the rivers, food production, flood frequency, damming the rivers, and the future of the rivers. The book provides many figures as illustrations, and the chapters contain lists of relevant readings.

National Research Council, Committee on Techniques for Estimating Probabilities of Extreme Floods. *Estimating Probabilities of Extreme Floods: Methods and Recommended Research.* Washington, DC: National Academy Press, 1988, 141 pp. ISBN 0-309-03791-3.

This book discusses rare floods and probabilities of when they can occur. The study of such floods is critical, because they kill people and destroy property, and trying to prevent them is extremely costly. This report is devoted to methods of estimating the probabilities of rare floods, ways to improve existing methods, and ways to develop new methods for probability estimation of rare floods that occur less than once in 100 years. The Committee on Techniques for Estimating Probabilities of Extreme Floods was appointed by the Water Science and Technology Board. The book has many tables and figures as well as a list of references.

Singh, Vijay P., ed. *Hydrology of Disasters.* Volume 24 in the Water Science and Technology Library. Boston: Kluwer Academic Publishers, 1996, 442 pp. ISBN 0-7923-4092-2.

Disasters are caused by environmental extremes. Some disasters are short-lived, whereas others exist for a long term. Various types of natural disasters are discussed in this book, consisting of 13 chapters. Of interest here are chapters four and five, which deal with floods. Floods occur every year, causing loss of life and property, thus requiring big investments in flood engineering projects to help prevent floods. Flood frequency has to be studied to know the peak flows in order to work on the overall design of the engineering projects. Dams have essential benefits such as water supply, flood control, irrigation, recreation, and hydropower. However, catastrophic floods occur when a dam breaks causing death and destruction of property. This was brought to people's attention in the 1970s with the failure of the Buffalo Creek Coal-Waste Dam in West Virginia in 1972, the Teton Dam in Idaho in 1976, the Laurel Run Dam in Johnstown, Pennsylvania, in 1977, and the Kelly Barnes Dam in Georgia in 1977. These chapters have figures, mathematical tables, and excellent bibliographic references.

Thomas, Lowell. *Hungry Waters: The Story of the Great Flood.* Chicago, IL: John C. Winston Company, 1937, 321 pp.

This volume covers the great flood of 1937 that hit such places as Cincinnati, Ohio; Indianapolis and Evansville, Indiana; Portsmouth, Ohio; Wheeling, West Virginia; Louisville, Frankfort, and Paducah, Kentucky; Cairo, Illinois; Memphis, Tennessee; and New Orleans, Louisiana. The author also gives accounts of famous floods such as the Johnstown flood of 1889 that killed over 2,200 people and caused over $10,000,000 in property damage. Plans for flood control and prevention are discussed. This book is illustrated with many flood pictures and maps of the Lower Mississippi and Ohio Basin. An interesting chapter gives dates of floods in America, beginning with the Mississippi River flood of 1543 and concluding with the Ohio River flood of 1937. Another interesting chapter details the part played by the Red Cross.

Flood Hazard Management

Brookes, Andrew. *Channelized Rivers: Perspectives for Environmental Management.* A Wiley-Interscience Publication. New York: John Wiley & Sons, 1988, 326 pp. ISBN 0-471-91979-9.

Many people were involved for eight years in research and management of rivers to produce this book. The book is divided into five parts. Part one presents the history and the importance of river channelization to help prevent floods. Part two discusses the legislation in effect on channelization. Part three discusses the physical and biological results of river channelization, and part four offers recommendations for mitigating adverse effects or restoring natural characteristics to channels. Part five discusses in detail the need for further research on river channelization. The book was written especially for civil engineers, geomorphologists, biologists, hydrologists, and conservationists as well as for general river managers. The book includes bibliographic references and many figures and tables as well as an author index, a geographical index, and a subject index.

Handmer, John, ed. *Flood Hazard Management: British and International Perspectives.* Exeter, England: Short Run Press Ltd., 1987, 297 pp. ISBN 0-86094-208-2.

This volume is the result of research and policy development activity at the Middlesex Polytechnic Flood Hazard Research Center. The difference between flood control management and flood hazard research as treated in the United States and Britain is shown. Gilbert White's approach to flood control and problems is mentioned and contrasted with the British method. In this book Scotland and Northern Ireland are excluded, and only urban and coastal flooding is considered. The book has six parts. Part one discusses British urban flood hazard; part two discusses flood-related institutions and policies; part three looks at ways to implement both local and international land use policies; part four lists hazard response; part five gives appraisal and risks for the project; and part six provides an overview and lessons learned by Britain. Figures, tables, and references are found throughout the text.

Saul, A. J., ed. *Floods and Flood Management.* Fuel Mechanics and Its Applications Series. Boston: Kluwer Academic Publishers, 1992, 543 pp. ISBN 0-7923-2078-6.

This volume presents the proceedings of the Third International Conference on Floods and Flood Management, held in Florence, Italy, in 1992. It was attended by international engineers, scientists, managers, and researchers to disseminate information and new developments in the technology of flood management. Of special interest are papers on flood forecasting and warning, risk hazard and damage assessment, a section dealing with flood defense systems, and a section containing papers on spillways and control structures. There are many figures and tables used as illustrations, and each paper includes bibliographic references and conclusions.

Flood Forecasting

Dracup, John A., Edmond D. H. Cheng, Joanne M. Nigg, and Thomas A. Schroeder. *The New Year's Eve Flood on Oahu, Hawaii, December 31, 1987–January 1, 1988.* Series: Natural Disaster Studies. Washington, DC: National Academy Press, 1991, 72 pp. ISBN 0-309-04433-2.

This is Volume 1 in the Natural Disaster Studies prepared for the Committee on Natural Disasters. Torrential rains fell over the southeastern part of Oahu, causing major flooding and several million dollars in damages. Unfortunately, flood prediction warning systems were unable to predict this flood. The purpose of this book is to improve flood control and flood forecasting facilities.

This small volume should be of interest to hydrologists, meteorologists, floodplain managers, and people who respond to disasters. Oahu needed to increase the rain gauge capacity to preclude overflows, and it needed a higher monitoring frequency of telemetered rain gauges. In addition to the failure of flood control facilities, the flood occurred because the soil was already saturated when the heavy rains came. In addition, sediment and debris already filled debris basins, thus directing streams away from their normal channels. This volume has many pictures, figures, and tables as illustrations and includes bibliographic references.

Singh, Vijay P., ed. *Flood Hydrology.* Boston: D. Reidel Publishing Company, 1987, 429 pp. ISBN 90-277-2574-1.

This volume contains the Proceedings of the International Symposium on Flood Frequency and Risk Analysis held May 14–17, 1986, at Louisiana State University in Baton Rouge. The purpose of this meeting was to assess the current state of the art of flood frequency and risk analysis. This book contains papers on several specific subjects such as hydrology of floods, streamflow simulation, streamflow forecasting, coastal and urban flooding, flood management, and flood control programs. Papers have figures to illustrate and bibliographic references. There is a subject index as well as an author index.

Tidal Floods

Peregrine, D. H., ed. *Floods Due to High Winds and Tides.* The Institute of Mathematics and Its Applications Conference Series. New York: Academic Press, 1981, 106 pp. ISBN 01-12-551820-X.

This volume presents the Proceedings of the Conference on Floods Due to High Winds and Tides held at the University of Bristol on January 9, 1980, arranged by the Environmental Mathematics Group of the Institute of Mathematics and Its Applications. Some of the most extensive floods are caused by severe wind storms carrying high tides on shallow seas. Shallow seas (the North Sea, the Gulf of Mexico, and the Bay of Bengal) are more responsive to wind stress from high winds than is deep water. They are surrounded by land at or below sea level, so high water, known as "storm surges," causes flooding. Flood warning systems as well as defenses against floods are discussed. Flooding caused by strong and high winds is also discussed. The papers in this volume tend to be mathematically oriented. The book includes figures, photos, and bibliographic references.

Flash Floods

American Meteorological Society. *Second Conference on Flash Floods*. Boston: American Meteorological Society, 1980, 258 pp.

This volume includes nonrefereed papers that were presented at the Second Conference on Flash Floods, held in Atlanta, Georgia, on March 18, 1980. The book begins with papers discussing case studies of recent flash floods followed by human response and help available to victims of flash floods. Papers in the next sections deal with climatology and satellite and radar applications. The last group of papers examines forecasting techniques and warning systems. Papers have references and figures. An author index is found at the front of the volume.

Conference on Flash Floods: Hydrometeorological Aspects. Boston: American Meteorological Society, 1978, 200 pp.

The papers in this volume were presented at the Conference on Flash Floods: Hydrometeorological Aspects, May 2–3, 1978, in Los Angeles, California. The papers were divided into six different categories. Session 1 included papers covering meteorological aspects such as the meteorology of Hawaiian flash floods, the environment of flash flood storms, and Midwestern flash flood storms. Session 2 included papers on meteorological observations on such subjects as rain estimation in the Big Thompson Canyon and Johnstown floods, severe rainstorms, and use of radar to predict local flash floods. Session 3 covered hydrometeorology, including Alaska's flash flood events, flash flood warning systems, and predicting flash flood peak flows. Section 4 included papers on hydrology. The papers in session 5 presented case studies, and session 6 was devoted entirely to the Johnstown flash flood of July 19–20, 1977. Each paper provides a list of references. The volume is well illustrated with figures, including pictures.

Davis, Lee. *Natural Disaster: From the Black Plague to the Eruption of Mt. Pinatubo*. New York: Facts on File, 1991, 321 pp. ISBN 0-8160-2034-5.

Scientists can study the heights of bodies of water over a period of time and then predict fairly accurately whether a flood is going to occur. Flash floods cannot be predicted, but warning signs can be found along highways where flash floods do occur after a rainstorm. If you live near a river or a sea, you will have a flood sooner or later. So the question is, Why do people build along rivers and why do cities develop along rivers? It is done for food and commerce. Alluvial soils built up from floods are rich and produce great crops for food. The composition of the soil contributes to the fact that water may run off if the soil is sand or gravel and water is absorbed if the soil is clay or fine. There is no runoff. Consequently, when water builds up, human inhabitants have made dikes and dams to divert it. When a dam breaks, a horrendous flood occurs, such as the Johnstown flood in 1889. A table shows the world's worst recorded floods, and another provides a chronology. Many other disasters such as avalanches, earthquakes, famines and droughts, epidemics, cyclones, hurricanes, ice and snowstorms, tornadoes, typhoons, volcanic eruptions, and storms are discussed. A selected bibliography is included.

Kansas City Flash Flood of September 12–13, 1977: A Report to the Administrator. National Disaster Survey Report 77-2. Rockville, MD: National Oceanic and Atmospheric Administration, National Weather Service, 1977, 49 pp.

This study of the Kansas City flash flood of September 12–13, 1977, was done by a survey team. They studied the broadcast media, civil defense, law enforcement, and individual user reaction and published their findings in this report. Twenty-four people were killed and property damage exceeded $90 million, even though people had been warned of a flash flood because a large rainfall was followed by a second major downpour. The broadcast media did an excellent job of warning, but many people did not take the warning seriously. Many of the deaths were associated with automobiles. The survey team offers numerous recommendations to prevent such a disaster again. This small volume has many figures as illustrations.

Dams

Adams, John A., Jr. *Damming the Colorado: The Rise of the Lower Colorado River Authority, 1933–1939.* The Centennial Series of the Association of Former Students, Texas A&M University, No. 35. College Station, TX: Texas A&M University Press, 1990, 161 pp. ISBN 0-89096-426-2.

The history of the development of the Colorado River in the 1930s is one of the reclamation, conservation, and hydroelectric projects of the New Deal in the West. Water development was a part of the conservation movement. Presidents Theodore Roosevelt, Howard Taft, and Woodrow Wilson advocated protection of water resources in the public domain through water regulation and legislation and cooperation with public agencies. The West offered great possibilities for industrial development and the electric industry, and since rivers and streams were in the public domain, the evolution of water resources was greatly influenced. Control and development of the Colorado River with dams, reservoirs, and hydroelectric power stations helped eliminate vast flood damage. The Lower Colorado River Authority (LCRA) was regarded as the Texas Little TVA. Tables as well as illustrations depicting flood and dam construction are found throughout the book, and chapter notes and bibliographic references can be found at the end of the book.

Lawson, Michael L. *Dammed Indians: The Pick-Sloan Plan and the Missouri River Sioux, 1944–1980.* Norman: University of Oklahoma Press, 1982, 261 pp. ISBN 0-8061-1657-9.

The author chronicles the events, personalities, and agencies involved in the massive restructuring of the Missouri River in the Pick-Sloan Plan. This river is sacred to the Sioux Indians, so this plan was the most destructive act inflicted on any tribe in the United States. The Indians lost old homesteads when land was taken for reservoirs and dams that flooded thousands of acres of Sioux land. This study shows that the damages suffered by the Missouri River Sioux tribe were much greater than the benefits received. Many lessons were learned from the Pick-Sloan experience. The tribes experienced difficulty in obtaining funds due them, and the rights of Native Americans and their land and resources continue to be eroded. The book has notes for each chapter as well as a bibliography and an index.

Flood Damage

Deadly Waters. Charleston, SC: Historic Publications, 1994, 82 pp. ISBN 1-882526-O3-1.

This small volume depicts the damage done by the 1994 Tropical Storm Alberto. The damage done and lives lost in the flood are described for three states—Alabama, Georgia, and Florida. Elba,

Alabama, was hit especially hard by the flood of 1994 when the Chattahoochee River peaked at 121 feet and joined the Choctawhatchee and Pea Rivers to flood 320,000 acres in muddy water. In Albany, Georgia, the Flint River crested at 44.1 feet where flood stage is 20 feet. The flood forced 20,000 residents from their homes. Caskets were unearthed from cemeteries. In Florida, it was Caryville, near Tallahassee, that was hardest hit. Residents were evacuated from their homes. Relief given by the National Guard, Salvation Army, Humane Society, American Red Cross, and others is discussed. The book is well illustrated with pictures showing damage done by the flood.

Flood Frequency

Singh, Vijay P., ed. *Hydrologic Frequency Modeling.* Boston: D. Reidel Publishing Company, 1987, 645 pp. ISBN 90-277-2572-1.

This volume contains the Proceedings of the International Symposium on Flood Frequency and Risk Analysis held May 14–17, 1986, at Louisiana State University in Baton Rouge. The purpose of this meeting was to assess the current state of the art of flood frequency and risk analysis. This volume contains papers on several specific subjects such as flood frequency analysis, flood frequency models, mixed distributions, rainfall frequency analysis, entropy in flood frequency analysis, parameter estimation, flood frequency models, and multivariate stochastic models. There are figures and mathematical explanations used as illustration. There is both a subject and an author index.

———. *Regional Flood Frequency Analysis.* Boston: D. Reidel Publishing Company, 1987, 400 pp. ISBN 90-277-2575-6.

This volume contains the Proceedings of the International Symposium held May 14–17, 1986, at Louisiana State University in Baton Rouge. The purpose of this meeting was to assess the state of the art of flood frequency and risk analysis. This volume contains papers on several specific subjects such as regional frequency analysis, regional frequency for ungauged watersheds, regional frequency, comparison of regional frequency methods, and paleohydrologic flood analysis. The book is illustrated with many tables and figures and includes bibliographic references. There is both a subject and an author index.

Flood Reservoirs

Floods and Reservoir Safety, 3d ed. London: Thomas Telford Publications for the Institution of Civil Engineers, 1996, 63 pp. ISBN 0-7277-2503-3.

In 1990 the Working Party on Floods and Reservoir Safety was given the task of updating the 1978 Engineering Guide on Floods and Reservoir Safety. W. J. Carlyle chaired the group, which included engineers and hydrologists from Britain, Ireland, and France. M. F. Kennard replaced Carlyle as chair in 1995 to complete the revision. Topics such as floods and waves protection standards, derivation of reservoir design flood inflow, reservoir flood routing, wave surcharge and dam freeboard, floods during dam construction and improvement, and overtopping of embankment dams are discussed. The book contains two appendixes, a glossary, a key references list, and a bibliography.

Hall, M. J., D. L. Hockin, and J. B. Ellis. *Design of Flood Storage Reservoirs.* Oxford, England: CIRIA (Construction Industry Research and Information Service), 1993, 187 pp. ISBN 0-7506-1057-3.

This book supersedes CIRIA Technical Note TN 100, which was used as a guide to methods for runoff estimation from urbanized areas and for the design of flood storage reservoirs used in surface water drainage in the development of new towns. This new edition was produced under CIRIA Research Project RP393. It reviews the original draft with present comments, reviews the literature, looks at areas for updating, and seeks information on operational aspects. The study was conducted in collaboration with the Institute of Hydrology. This book is really concerned with the problems of engineering design to provide adequate flood protection for urbanized areas. The book contains two appendixes and a list of references as well as a list of books for further reading.

Specific Floods

United States—General

Clark, Champ, and the Editors of Time-Life Books. *Flood: Planet Earth.* Alexandria, VA: Time-Life Books, 1982, 176 pp. ISBN 0-8094-4308-2.

This interesting volume deals with major floods all over the world, with special emphasis given to the United States. For instance, there is an excellent section on taming the mighty Mississippi River, providing the history of floods caused by this river along with photos for various years and discussions of ways used to stop the flooding. Another interesting chapter addresses flash floods caused by torrential rains or resulting from specific dam breaks. Flash floods are extremely dangerous and cause a great deal of damage, for they cannot be predicted. The volume is illustrated with many colored photos and includes a list of bibliographic references.

Mississippi Basin Flood of 1993

Changnon, Stanley, ed. *The Great Flood of 1993: Causes, Impacts, and Responses.* Boulder: Westview Press, 1996, 321 pp. ISBN 0-8133-2619-2.

The many contributors to this volume illuminate the social and economic impacts of the 1993 flood as well as the response made by volunteers, forecasters, and private and public institutions. Chapter 1 provides an overview of the flood. Chapters 2 through 6 describe physical aspects of the flood and its effects on the environment. Chapters 7 through 11 discuss the social, economic, and policy impacts. Chapter 12 summarizes the political, physical, and socioeconomic impacts of the flood. The last chapter summarizes what was learned from the 1993 flood, what can be done to prevent floods, and how floods can be dealt with if they do occur. The chapters have references, figures, and pictures of the flood.

Goldstein, Norm, and Geoff Haynes, eds. *The Flood of '93: America's Greatest Natural Disaster.* By the Associated Press. New York: Wieser & Wieser, 1993, 128 pp. ISBN 0-312-10795-1.

This is a picture book telling the story of the nine states flooded by the Mississippi River in 1993. The failure of levees, sandbag emergency construction, rescuing people and pets, and cleaning up after the flood are all covered. A map shows the states that were hardest hit and the counties that received federal disaster aid.

Governor's Workshop on the Great Flood of 1993: Long-Term Approaches to the Management of the Mississippi and Illinois Rivers Including Lessons Learned and Information Gaps. ILENR/RE-94/08. Springfield, IL: Illinois Department of Energy and Natural Resources, 1994, 80 pp.

This workshop, attended by about 150 people (listed in appendix II), addressed the flood's causes and its impacts. The great flood of 1993, which caused more than a billion dollars in damage, was considered the most devastating flood in modern U.S. history and the worst disaster in Illinois history. The workshop participants looked at ways to forecast floods, the management of floods, and geologic factors related to the 1993 flood. Environmental effects of the 1993 flood were also studied. Appendix I consists of reports filed by group moderators and monitors. This is an interesting volume describing the reaction to the 1993 flood.

Pielke, Roger A., Jr. *Midwest Flood of 1993: Weather, Climate, and Societal Impacts.* Boulder: National Center for Atmospheric Research, 1996, 159 pp.

This report reviews what is known about the societal problems wrought by large-scale floods in the United States as well as problems such as damage to property, ecosystems, and people. It also contributes to ways to deal more effectively with floods and how people respond to floods. The report addresses the Midwest flood of 1993, summarizing the damages caused and the lessons learned for future use. The book has four appendixes, and the chapters have bibliographic references.

Schalk, Gregg K., and Robert B. Jacobson. *Scour, Sedimentation, and Sediment Characteristics at Six Levee-Break Sites in Missouri from the 1993 Missouri River Flood.* Water Resources Investigation Report 97-4110. Denver: U.S. Geological Survey in cooperation with Missouri Department of Natural Resources at Rolla, Missouri, 1997, 72 pp.

This small volume describes the scour and characteristics of the sediment caused by six levee breaks on the Missouri River during the 1993 flood. It also describes the effects of the levee breaks in the soil and land-use resources on the Missouri River floodplain. The flow hydraulics at special levee breaks and the role of levee-break complexes in the routing of sediment were evaluated in the study. Most of the levees along the Missouri River that protected farmland in Missouri either failed or overflowed during the 1993 flood. References cited and tables used to illustrate the volume are listed.

Wegner, Michael, Lyle Boone, and Tim Cochran, eds. *Iowa's Lost Summer: The Flood of 1993.* Des Moines: Iowa State University

Press and Des Moines Register and Tribune Company, 1993, 108 pp. ISBN 0-8138-1809-5.

This beautifully illustrated picture volume was dedicated to Steven M. West, a National Guard soldier from Ogden, Iowa, who was electrocuted on July 16, 1993, while performing duties during the flood, and to several others who lost their lives during flood-related traffic accidents. The 1993 flood was the worst natural disaster in Iowa's history. The book illustrates how everyone cooperated to help flood victims. It tells the story of the devastation that occurred when all the rivers overflowed. The last page is a summary of events of the flood of 1993, beginning March 27 and ending August 29.

Big Thompson Flood

Gruntfest, Eve C., ed. *What We Have Learned Since the Big Thompson Flood.* Proceedings of the Tenth Anniversary Conference, July 17–19, 1986. Boulder: Natural Hazards Research and Application Information Center, 1987, 271 pp.

This volume is divided into six parts. Part one provides an overview of the Big Thompson flood, covering such topics as recovery effort, the state's role in identifying bodies, and the operation of a temporary morgue. Part two covers mitigation issues such as the flood damage reduction program, the National Flood Insurance Program, dam failure hazards, the Colorado Flood Hazard Mitigation Program, and impacts of the flood. Part three discusses progress in forecasting, and part four considers warning systems and responses. Part five compares the Big Thompson flood with the 1982 Estes Park dam-break flood and discusses geomorphology and hydrology research. Part six provides a summary of recommendations made at the symposium. There are four appendixes, one of which is an extensive bibliography. Figures and photos are found throughout the book.

Pennsylvania

Busch, W. F., and L. C. Shaw. *Floods in Pennsylvania: Frequency and Magnitude.* Open-File Report. Prepared in Cooperation with Commonwealth of Pennsylvania, Department of Forests and Waters, Harrisburg, PA. Washington, DC: U.S. Geological Survey, 1960, 231 pp.

This report details a way to determine the magnitude of floods occurring with frequencies up to 50 years for Pennsylvania streams not regulated and streams that have a drainage basin smaller than 10 square miles. On the major streams—the Schuylkill, Delaware, Susquehanna, and Chemung Rivers—the magnitude of floods can be determined for frequencies up to 100 years. For people living along streams, industries, waterworks, and so on, it is of great importance to be familiar with the frequency and magnitude of floods. This knowledge is also valuable in building bridges, railroads, highways, levees, and sewage disposal. The book consists of tables for each of the major river basins, a physiographic map of Pennsylvania, a map of river basins, and a map showing average precipitation for the period of 1931–1955. There are two maps showing the frequency and the magnitude of floods in Pennsylvania.

Mills, R. Adam. *Hydrologic Data of the June 1972 Flood in Pennsylvania.* Series: Water Resources Bulletin No. 9. Harrisburg, PA: Department of Environmental Resources; and Washington, DC: U.S. Geological Survey, 1974, 97 pp.

This volume describes the impact that the 1972 flood, the most devastating ever recorded in the area, had on central Pennsylvania. The flood was caused by the tropical storm Agnes, which began in the Gulf of Mexico and flooded the Susquehanna River Basin. This book provides the meteorological summary of the storm, flood peaks, flood hydrographs, and flood profiles. The book is well illustrated with figures and tables.

Shank, William H. *Great Floods of Pennsylvania: A Two-Century History,* 2d ed. York, PA: American Canal and Transportation Center, 1972, 90 pp. ISBN 0-933788-38-X.

The first edition of this book, published in 1968, received little attention, for it was thought that the flood of 1936 was the biggest of all time. After the great flood of 1972, however, a new edition was needed. This small volume describes the topography and major drainage basins and the causes of floods. An interesting chapter discusses the frequency of floods in Pennsylvania and is followed by a chapter on the nineteenth-century floods, including the 1841 and 1889 floods. The Johnstown flood has a chapter of its own and is followed by a chapter on the floods of 1936 that hit Harrisburg, Williamsport, Sunbury, Johnstown, and Pittsburgh (it was Pittsburgh's worst flood). A chapter is devoted to the 1955 flood on the Delaware River, followed by a chapter on the 1972 flood, a most devastating flood. The final chapter is devoted to flood forecasting. The book is well illustrated with pictures.

Mississippi River, 1982–1983

Stone, Roy B., and R. H. Bingham. *Floods of December 1982 to May 1983 in the Central and Southern Mississippi River and the Gulf of Mexico Basins. U.S. Geological Survey Water Supply Paper* 2362. Washington, DC: U.S. Geological Survey, 1991, 96 pp.

The authors discuss the four major floods that occurred in the central and southern Mississippi River Basin from December 1982 to May 1983. They examine the conditions prior to the floods, rainfall amounts, the frequency of floods in the area, and, finally, the effects of the floods. States affected were Illinois, Missouri, Arkansas, Mississippi, and Louisiana. It is estimated that the damages exceeded $200 million for the December floods. The book has 36 figures, 21 tables, and 1 map illustrating flooded sites.

Acadiana, Louisiana

Conrad, Glenn R., and Carl A. Brasseaux. *Crevasse: The 1927 Flood in Acadiana.* Lafayette, LA: The Center for Louisiana Studies, University of Southwest Louisiana, 1994, 125 pp. ISBN 0-940984-88-1.

This is a detailed story of the 1927 flood in Acadiana and of how it affected people in the region. This book is the result of a lecture given on the flood and interviews with people who survived and were able to provide family albums and archival collections for the many pictures. People who endured the flood like to relate their experiences and the rehabilitation they faced. The first part of the book is text with many maps and figures and is followed by page after page of photographs provided by people of the area.

Journal Articles and Government Documents

Floods in General

Baker, V. R., et al. "Application of Geological Information to Arizona Flood Hazard Assessment." *Proceedings of the International Symposium on Hydraulics/Hydrology of Arid Lands and the National Conference on Hydraulic Engineering, San Diego, CA,* 1990, pp. 621–626.

Balocki, J. B., and S. J. Burges. "Relationships Between n-Day Flood Volumes for Infrequent Large Floods." *Journal of Water Resources Planning and Management* 120 (November-December 1994): 794–818.

Bradley, B. D. "After Record Flooding, South Starts Cleanup." *Engineering News-Record* 233 (July 18, 1994): 8.

Bravo, R., D. A. Dow, and J. R. Rogers. "Parameter Determination for the Muskingum-Cunge Flood Routing Method." *Water Resources Bulletin* 30 (September-October 1994): 891–898.

Breeding, S. D. "Texas Floods of 1940." *U.S. Geological Survey Water Supply Paper* 1046 (1948): 1–91.

Curole, Windell A. "Flood Threat Response in South Louisiana." *Proceedings of the Eighth Symposium on Coastal and Ocean Management, Part 2, New Orleans, LA* 1993, pp. 2252–2255.

Darnell, T. "After the Deluge Communities Wade Through." *American City and County* 105 (April 1990): 24.

D'Aulaire, P. O., and E. D'Aulaire. "Lost Beneath the City [L. Reese Trapped in Storm Drain in Houston]." *Reader's Digest* 137 (July 1990): 113–118.

"Drought—or Flood? How California Prepares." *Western Water* (January-February 1986): 4–10.

Eckhoff, D. W. "A Flood in the Desert." *Civil Engineering (American Society of Civil Engineers)* 57 (March 1987): 40–43.

Explaining the Flood Risk. Series: EP (Washington, DC), 1110--2--8, Washington, DC: U.S. Army Corps of Engineers, 1992, 31 pp.

Follansbee, R., and J. B. Spiegel. "Flood on Republican and Kansas Rivers, May and June 1935." *U.S. Geological Survey Water Supply Paper* 796 (1937): 21–52.

Freund, Arthur. "Fast-Track Electrical Rebuilding after Flood Disaster." *ECEM: Electrical Construction and Maintenance* 87 (August 1988): 74–79.

Geake, E. "A Little Flood Goes a Long Way." *New Scientist* 141 (January 8, 1994): 17.

Green, C. H., et al. "The Risks from Flooding: Which Risks and Whose Perception?" *Disasters* (London) 15 (September 1991): 227–236.

"The Hidden Danger": Low-Water Crossing. Series: NOAA/PA, 96074. Silver Spring, MD: National Weather Service Office of Hydrology, 1994, 4 pp.

Jarvis, C. S., et al. "Floods in the United States." *U.S. Geological Survey Water Supply Paper* 771 (1936): 1–497.

Jennings, Marshall E., and Richard Paulson. "Summary of Floods and Droughts in the United States." *Proceedings of the National*

Conference on Hydraulic Engineering, Colorado Springs, CO, 1988, pp. 813–818.

Julien, P. Y., and G. J. Klaassen. "Sand-Dune Geometry of Large Rivers during Floods." *Journal of Hydraulic Engineering* 121 (September 1995): 657–663.

Keith, L. "Flooding Mobilizes Georgia Hams." *QST* 75 (September 1994): 90–91.

Keller, E. A., and M. H. Capelli. "Ventura River Flood of February 1992: A Lesson Ignored?" *Water Resources Bulletin* 28 (September-October 1992): 813–832.

McMullen, L. D. "Surviving the Flood: Teamwork Pays Off in Des Moines." *American Water Works Association Journal* 86 (January 1994): 68–72.

Mroz, P. J. "The Fragile Planet: Drought and Flood—Two Faces of One Coin." *Bulletin of the American Meteorology Society* 74 (December 1993): 2398–2399.

Myslewski, D. J. "Rain of Terror." *QST* 62 (January 1978): 50–52.

O'Connor, J. E., et al. "A 4,500-Year Record of Large Floods on the Colorado River in the Grand Canyon, Arizona." *Journal of Geology* 102 (January 1994): 1–9.

Ouarda, Taha B. M. J., and Fahim Ashkar. "Bootstrap-Based Intercomparison of Regional Flood Estimation Procedures." *Proceedings of the International Conference on Hydropower, Part 3, San Francisco, CA,* 1995, pp. 2466–2475.

Pearce, F. "The Rivers That Won't Be Tamed." *New Scientist* 130 (April 13, 1991): 38–41.

Plazak, D. J. "Flood Control Benefits Revisited." *Journal of Water Resources Planning and Management* 112 (April 1986): 265–276.

Reel, D. V., and L. S. Bond. "Flooding in the Desert: Taking Control." *Public Works* 119 (December 1989): 29–30+.

Reinke, A. F. "Wabash River Flood at Vincennes." *Public Works* 75 (December 1944): 11–12+.

"River Washes Out Landfill." *Engineering News-Record* 230 (February 8, 1993): 17–18.

Robbins, C. H., and W. D. Canaan. "Stormwater Infrastructure Inventory and Application." *Public Works* 127 (February 1996): 40–42.

Sandoval, D. "Recyclers Recover from Summer Flood." *Recycling Today (Ohio)* 31 (September 1993): 76+.

Silverman, Robin, and Linda Magness. "I Survived the Flood." *Ladies' Home Journal* 114 (April 1998): 30, 32, 37.

Southard, Rodney E. *Base (100-Year) Flood Elevations for Selected*

Sites in Montgomery County, Missouri. Rolla, MO: State Emergency Management Agency; and Denver, CO: U.S. Geological Survey, 1998, 17 pp.

Stackhouse, J. L. "After the Rains Came." *Public Works* 96 (October 1965): 94–96.

Strauser, Claude N., James T. Lovelace, and Dave Busse. "Great Flood of 1994 the Disaster That Did Not Happen." *Proceedings of the First International Conference on Water Resources, Part 2, San Antonio, TX,* 1995, pp. 952–955.

"Suit Cites Unnecessary Flood." *Engineering News-Record* 226 (January 14, 1991): 24–25.

Turcotte, D. L. "Fractal Theory and the Estimation of Extreme Floods." *Journal of Research of the National Institute of Standards and Technology* 99 (July-August 1994): 377–389.

Umbrell, E. R. "Clear-Water Contraction Scour under Bridges in Pressure Flow." *Journal of Hydraulic Engineering* 124 (February 1998): 236–240.

"When It Rains Salt [River] Pours." *Engineering News-Record* 230 (January 18, 1993): 12.

Wise, L. L. "Is Los Angeles Ready for a Flood?" *Engineering News* 156 (May 17, 1956): 40–42+.

Flash Floods

Berling, R. L. "Disaster Response to Flash Floods." *American Society of Civil Engineers Proceedings* 104 (November 1978): 35–44.

Blood, Wesley H., and John Humphrey. "Design Cloudburst and Flash Flood Methodology for the Western Mohave Desert, California." *Proceedings of the International Symposium on Hydraulics/Hydrology of Arid Lands and the National Conference on Hydraulic Engineering, San Diego, CA,* 1990, pp. 561–566.

Chang, Tiao J., and Hong Y. Sun. "Investigation of Potential Flash Floods in the Scioto River Basin." *Proceedings of the First International Conference on Water Resources, Part 1, San Antonio, TX,* 1995, pp. 294–301.

Costa, John E. "Hydraulics and Basin Morphometry of the Largest Flash Floods in the Conterminous United States." *Journal of Hydrology* 93 (September 15, 1987): 313–338.

Dick, G. S., et al. "Controls on Flash Flood Magnitude and Hydrograph Shape: Upper Blue Hills Badlands, Utah." *Geology* 25 (January 1997): 45–48.

Hales, J. E., Jr. "Kansas City Flash Flood of 12 September 1977." *American Meteorological Society Bulletin* 59 (June 1978): 706–710.

Hjalmarson, H. W. "Flash Flood in Tanque Verde Creek, Tucson, Arizona." *Journal of Hydraulic Engineering* 110 (December 1984): 1841–1852; discussion, 113 (March 1987): 413–418.

Holle, R. L., and S. P. Bennett. "Lightning Ground Flashes Associated with Summer 1990 Flash Floods and Streamflow in Tucson, Arizona: An Exploratory Study." *Monthly Weather Review* 125 (July 1997): 1526–1536.

Loganathan, G. V., et al. "Flash Flood Forecasting." *Proceedings of the Twenty-fourth Annual Water Resources Planning and Management Conference, Houston, TX,* 1997, pp. 94–99.

Lucchitta, I., and N. Suneson. "Flash Flood in Arizona: Observations and Their Application to the Identification of Flash-Flood Deposits in the Geologic Record." *Geology* 9 (September 1981): 414–418.

Maddox, R. A., et al. "Meteorological Characteristics of Flash Flood Events over the Western United States." *Monthly Weather Review* 108 (November 1980): 1866–1877.

Never Say Never. Washington, DC: Federal Emergency Management Agency, 1996. 4 pp.

"Prediction and Mitigation of Flash Floods: A Policy Statement of the American Meteorological Society." *Bulletin of the American Meteorological Society* 74 (August 1993): 1586–1587.

Reid, I., et al. "Prediction of Bed-Load Transport by Desert Flash Floods." *Journal of Hydraulic Engineering* 122 (March 1996): 170–173.

Ribble, George. "Scodie Canyon [CA] Flash Floods of 1984." *Proceedings of the National Conference on Hydraulic Engineering, Colorado Springs, CO,* 1988, pp. 258–263.

Schultz, L. W. "The Central Kansas Flash Floods of June 1981." *Bulletin of the American Meteorological Society* 65 (March 1984): 228–234.

Stewart, Kevin G. "Effecting Timely Responses to Urban Flash Floods." *Proceedings of the Third Water Resources Operations Management Workshop, Fort Collins, CO,* 1988, pp. 759–771.

Sweeney, Timothy L. "Flash Flood Hydrologic Forecast Model AD-VIS." *Proceedings of the Third Water Resources Operations Management Workshop, Fort Collins, CO,* 1988, pp. 683–692.

Woolley, R. R. "Cloudburst Floods in Utah, 1850–1938." *U.S. Geological Survey Water Supply Paper* 994 (1946): 1–128.

Flood Control

General

"Aftermath of Agnes." *American Gas Association Monthly* 54 (October 1972): 17–18.

Ashkar, F., et al. "Separation of Skewness: Reality of Regional Artifact." *Journal of Hydraulic Engineers* 118 (March 1992): 460–475; discussion, 119 (April 1993): 535–540.

Avakyan, A. B., and A. A. Polyushkin: "Flood Control Experience in the USA." *Hydrotechnical Construction* 23 (July 1989): 53–58.

Borah, D. K. "Scour-Depth Prediction under Armoring Conditions." *Journal of Hydraulic Engineering* 115 (October 1989): 1421–1425; discussion, 117 (August 1991): 1082–1088.

Brown, E. L. "Lake Okeechobee Project Combining Flood Protection and Navigation." *Civil Engineering* 5 (December 1935): 780–783.

Burian, S. J., et al. "Historical Development of Wet-Weather Flow Management." *Journal of Water Resources Planning and Management* 125 (January-February 1999): 3–13.

Chariton, Anthony J. "Elmhurst Quarry Flood-Control Projects." *Proceedings of the Twenty-first Annual Conference on Water Policy and Management: Solving the Problems, Denver, CO,* 1994, pp. 107–110.

Charles, M. "ASCE to White House: Improve Flood Controls." *Civil Engineering (American Society of Civil Engineers)* 4 (August 1994): 96.

Chitale, S. V. "Comparison of Width and Friction Factor Predictors and Implications." *Journal of Hydraulic Engineering* 21 (May 1995): 432–436.

Classen, A. G. *Practical Aspects of Flood Control and Reclamation of Overflowed Lands.* Austin, TX: Reclamation Department, 1935, 80 pp.

Davis, Douglas R. "The Only Way to Manage a Desert: Utah's Liability Immunity for Flood Control." *Journal of Energy Law and Policy* 8 (1987): 95–118.

Davis, E. I. "Development of a Flood-Control Plan for Houston, Tex." *American Society of Civil Engineers Proceedings* 78 (December 1952): 1–19.

Easterbrook, Gregg. "'Deep Tunnel': How Our Money Flows into Chicago's Sewers: The World According to TARP [Critical of the Tunnel Reservoir Plan, Intended to Control Flooding and Water Pollution and Rehabilitate Chicago's Urban Canal Systems]." *Washington Monthly* 11 (November 1979): 30–36.

Evans, H. S. "Lessons in Flood Control from New York State." *Roads and Bridges* 87 (November 1949): 75–77+.

Filippone, Ella F., and Joseph W. Walsh. "The Flood Control Saga in the Passaic River Basin." *Population and Environment* 11 (Summer 1990): 285–298.

Fischer, K. J., M. D. Harvey, and E. F. Sing. "Geomorphic and Sedimentologic Evaluation of a Proposed Flood Control Project, Truckee River, Reno, Nevada." *Proceedings of the National Conference, Part 2 on Hydraulic Engineering, San Diego, CA,* 1990, pp. 820–825.

Fisher, E. A., and P. A. Covas. "Genesee River Flood Control at Rochester, NY." *Civil Engineering* 9 (May 1939): 305–308.

"Flood Management." *Compressed Air* 100 (April-May 1995): 20–28.

Foley, D. A. "Flood Control Doesn't Have to Be Ugly." *Civil Engineering (American Society of Civil Engineers)* 65 (November 1995): 50–53.

Ford, D. T. "Interactive Nonstructural Flood-Control Planning." *American Society of Civil Engineers Proceedings* 107 (October 1981): 351–363; discussion, *Journal of Water Resources Planning and Management* 109 (January 1983): 117–118.

Gavett, Kerry L., Michael J. Fiore, and Eric J. Meyer. "Evaluation of the Impact of Recent Flooding on the Operation of a Groundwater Extraction and Treatment System at a Superfund Site." *Proceedings of the National Conference on Environmental Engineering, Boulder, CO,* 1994, pp. 764–771.

Gee, H. C. "Hydraulic Problems of Local Interests under the Central and Southern Florida Project." *American Society of Civil Engineers Proceedings* 79 (July 1953): 1–8.

Gilligan, Carolyn. "Funding Regional Flood Control Improvements in Fort Bend County, Texas." *Proceedings of the Twenty-fourth Annual Water Resources Planning and Management Conference, Houston, TX,* 1997, pp. 643–653.

Hodson, C. "Bridge Replacement Spearheads Mammoth Flood Control Project." *Highway and Heavy Construction* 134 (November 1991): 34–37.

Horn, Dennis R. "Prioritizing Flood Control Planning Needs." *Journal of Water Resources Planning and Management* 113 (March 1987): 283–292.

Kerr, J. "Catchy Culverts." *Civil Engineering (American Society of Civil Engineers)* 67 (May 1997): 59–61.

Kisinger, K. A., et al. "Abandoned Quarry Will Provide Flood Control." *Public Works* 123 (December 1992): 60–61.

Kittraldge, Mark G. "Quantitative CO_2—Flood Monitoring Denver Unit, Wasson (San Andres) Field." *SPE Formation Evaluation* 8 (December 1993): 299–305.

Lawlor, W. F. "Flood Control in the Middle Mississippi." *American Society of Civil Engineers Proceedings* 81 (September 1955): 1–9.

Lentz, A. T. "Free Flood Control by Utilities on Wisconsin Rivers." *Public Utilities* 50 (December 4, 1952): 843–849.

Little, C. K. "Flood Control for the Mississippi Yazoo Delta." *American Society of Civil Engineers Proceedings* 83 (May 1957): 1–7.

Lloyd, David W., and Charles A. McKnight. "Case Study of the Goldsmith Gulch Flood Control Project [in Denver, Colorado]." *Proceedings of the Twenty-fourth Annual Water Resources Planning and Management Conference, Houston, TX,* 1997, pp. 25–30.

Lovan, Hayley, Jennifer Eckert, Scott E. Stonestreet, and Colette Diede. "Flood Control and Habitat Preservation in the Mojave River Victorville, California." *Proceedings of the First International Conference on Water Resources, Part 2, San Antonio, TX,* 1955, pp. 1556–1560.

Luetje, E. H. "Basin's Biggest Plant to Pump against Floods." *Engineering News* 145 (October 12, 1950): 48.

McMillen, R. F. "Flood-Prone Subdivision Gets Relief." *Public Works* 124 (July 1993): 45–46.

Murphy, W. M., and C. W. Geelan. "Hurricane Flood Protection for Texas City, Texas." *American Society of Civil Engineers Proceedings* 93 (May 1967): 157–179; discussion, 93 (November 1967): 265–266; reply, 94 (August 1968): 358–359.

Newson, M. D., and D. Sear. "The Role of Geomorphology in Monitoring and Managing River Sediment Systems." *Water and Environmental Management Journal* 12 (February 1998): 18–24.

Platt, Rutherford H. "Metropolitan Flood Loss Reduction through Regional Special Districts." *Journal of the American Planning Association* 52 (Autumn 1986): 467–479.

Post, N. M., and H. B. Stussman. "Inflatable Rubber Makes Comeback." *Engineering News-Record* 223 (September 14, 1989): 30–31.

"River Washes Out Landfill." *Engineering News-Record* 230 (February 8, 1993): 17–18.

Rosta, P. "Spare Tires Stand against Flood." *Engineering News-Record* 240 (April 20, 1998): 22–23.

Schull, H. W., Jr. "Pumps to Tame Florida Floods." *Engineering News* 152 (April 22, 1954): 36–37.

Shields, F. Douglas, Jr., and Charles M. Cooper. "Riparian Wetlands and Flood Stages." *Proceedings of the ASCE National Conference on Hydraulic Engineering, Buffalo, NY,* 1994, pp. 351–355.

Smith, J. H. "Small Watershed Project Eliminates Flood Hazards." *Public Works* 94 (December 1963): 103–104.

Steinberg, T. "'That World's Fair Feeling': Control of Water in Twentieth-Century America." *Technology and Culture* 34 (April 1993): 401–409.

"Symposium on the International Decade for Natural Disaster Reduction, Nashville, Tenn., January 23–28, 1994." *Bulletin of the American Meteorological Society* 75 (January 1994): 83–94.

Valenti, M. "Computerized Flood Control." *Mechanical Engineering* 114 (February 1992): 124.

Veatch, N. T., et al. "Flood Protection in the Kansas River Basin." *American Water Works Association Journal* 45 (July 1953): 685–693.

Webb, B. "Pipeline Supports Save Pipelines from Flood-Induced Ruptures." *Pipeline and Gas Journal* 222 (March 1995): 66–69.

Wetmore, Thomas E. "Flooding Controlled by Bridge Relocation." *Public Works* 121 (June 1990): 86–87.

White, G. F. "A Perspective on Reducing Losses from Natural Hazards." *Bulletin of the American Meteorology Society* 75 (July 1994): 1237–1240.

Design

Bottin, Robert R., Jr. "Design for Flood Control, Wave Protection, and Prevention of Shoaling, Rogue River, Oregon." Technical Report, HL-82-18. Vicksburg, MI: U.S. Army Engineer Waterways Experiment Station, June 1983, 61 pp.

Bourquard, E. H. "Hydraulic and Structural Design Changes: Handling Floods on Mill Creek and the Allegheny River at Coudersport, PA." *Engineering News* 152 (May 20, 1954): 38–40.

Bowen, J. D., et al. "Storm Drain Design: Diffusive Flood Routing for PCs." *Journal of Hydraulic Engineering* 115 (August 1989): 1135–1150.

Curtis, D. C. "Fault-Tolerant Design for Data Acquisition and Flood Forecast Systems." *Public Works* 119 (April 1988): 38–40.

Dawdy, D. R., and D. P. Lattenmaier. "Initiative for Risk-Based Flood Design." *Journal of Hydraulic Engineering* 113 (August 1987): 1041–1051; discussion, 115 (March 1989): 416–422.

Debo, T. N., and G. N. Small. "Hydrologic Calibration: The Forgotten Aspect of Drainage Design." *Public Works* 120 (February 1989): 58–59.

"Erosion Control Matting Helps Prevent Flooding." *Public Works* 123 (August 1992): 136.

Foley, Deborah A., and Ferris W. Chamberlin. "Integrating Community Needs with Engineering Design." *Proceedings of the Twenty-second Annual Conference on Integrated Water Resources Planning for the Twenty-first Century, Cambridge, MA,* 1995, pp. 759–762.

French, Richard H. "Design of Flood Protection for Transportation Alignments on Alluvial Fans." *Journal of Irrigation and Drainage Engineering* 118 (March-April, 1992): 320–330.

Gay, George E., Ernest W. Clement, and Stanford W. Lynch. "Review of the Design, Construction, and Operation of the Lake Carolyn Flood Control Pump Station." *Proceedings of the ASCE Seventeenth Annual National Conference, Fort Worth, TX,* 1990, pp. 686–691.

Leise, R. J. "Building On-site Storm Water Detention Facilities." *Water/Engineering and Management* 138 (June 1991): 26–27.

Lewis, G. L. "Jury Verdict: Frequency Versus Risk-Based Culvert Design." *Journal of Water Resources Planning and Management* 118 (March-April 1992): 166–184.

Maynord, S. T. "Gabion-Mattress Channel-Protection Design." *Journal of Hydraulic Engineers* 121 (July 1995): 519–522.

McCuen, R. H., and T. V. Hromadka. "Flood Skew in Hydrologic Design on Ungaged Watersheds." *Journal of Irrigation and Drainage Engineering* 114 (May 1988): 301–310.

Ormsbee, L. E., et al. "Design of Dual-purpose Detention Systems Using Dynamic Programming." *Journal of Water Resources Planning and Management* 113 (July 1987): 471–484.

Rogers, W. F., and Vijay P. Singh. "Evaluating Flood Retarding Structures." *Advances in Water Resources* 9 (December 1986): 236–244.

Salem, E. B., and C. T. Haan. "Impact of Parameter Uncertainty on the Design of Small Flood Water Retarding Structures." *Applied Engineering in Agriculture* 7 (January 1991): 86–90.

Steeves, M., and C. Chapman. "Public Accepts Stormwater Control Plan [Mobile, Alabama]." *Water/Engineering and Management* 135 (April 1988): 22–24.

Sutko, Timothy E., and Syndi Flippin. "Design Storms and Sizing of Flood Control Facilities." *Proceedings of the International Symposium on Hydraulics/Hydrology of Arid Lands and National*

Conference on Hydraulic Engineering, San Diego, CA, 1990, pp. 154–159.

Taylor, Scott M. "National Survey of Design and Maintenance Practices of Flood Control Systems in the United States." *Proceedings of the First International Conference on Water Resources, Part 2, San Antonio, TX,* 1995, pp. 1466–1470.

Titmarsh, G. W., et al. "Celebration Procedures for Rational and USSCS Design Flood Methods." *Journal of Hydraulic Engineering* 121 (January 1995): 61–70; discussion, 122 (March 1996): 176–177.

Tseng, Minz T., Earl E. Eiker, and Darryl W. Davis. "Risk and Uncertainty in Flood Damage Reduction Project Design." *Proceedings of the National Conference on Hydraulic Engineering, San Francisco, CA,* 1993, pp. 2104–2109.

Wallis, J. R., and E. F. Wood. "Relative Accuracy of Log Pearson III Procedures." *Journal of Hydraulic Engineering* 111 (July 1985): 1043–1056; discussion, 113 (September 1987): 1205–1214.

Whipple, W., et al. "Implementing Dual-purpose Stormwater Detention Programs." *Journal of Water Resources Planning and Management* 113 (November 1987): 779–792.

Williams, P. B. "Rethinking Flood-Control Channel Design." *Civil Engineering (American Society of Civil Engineers)* 60 (January 1990): 57–59, discussion, 60 (May 1990): 40+.

Yanmaz, A. M., and F. Coskun. "Hydrological Aspects of Bridge Design: Case Study." *Journal of Irrigation and Drainage Engineering* 121 (November-December 1995): 411–418.

Zwanenberg, J. G. "Massive Sea Gates Cure Centuries-Old Flooding Problem." *Hydraulics and Pneumatics* 41 (April 1988): 62+; 41 (June 1988): 60–62.

Levees

Brandes, William F., and Bruce A. Tschantz. "Flood Impact and Management of Levees in Tennessee." *Proceedings of the National Water Conference Specialty Conference, Newark, DE,* 1989, pp. 242–248.

"Breached Levee Had Help [Massive Flooding Caused by Sabotage]." *Engineering News-Record* 233 (November 14, 1994): 13–14.

Christenson, J. A. "A Workable Compromise on Flood Control." *Civil Engineering (American Society of Civil Engineers)* 64 (September 1994): 6.

Denning, James. "When the Levee Breaks." *Civil Engineering (American Society of Civil Engineers)* 64 (January 1994): 38–41.

Duffy, D. "To Still the Waters: Levees, Flumes, Riprap, and the Rivers." *Conservationist* 46 (March-April 1992): 40–47.

Duncan, J. M., and W. H. Houston. "Estimating Failure Probabilities for California Levees [Discussion of 109 (February 1983): 260–268]." *Journal of Geotechnical Engineering* 110 (July 1984): 993–996.

Dyhouse, Gary R. "Effects of Federal Levees and Reservoirs on 1993 Flood Stages in St. Louis." *Transportation Research Record* 1483 (July 1995): 11–17.

Faber, Scott E. "Letting Down the Levees." *National Wetlands Newsletter* 15 (November-December 1993): 5–7.

Goldman, D. "Estimating Expected Annual Damage for Levee Retrofits." *Journal of Water Resources Planning and Management* 123 (March-April 1997): 89–94.

Lee, H.-L., and L. W. Mays. "Hydraulic Uncertainties in Flood Levee Capacity." *Journal of Hydraulic Engineering* 112 (October 1986): 928–934.

Mansur, C. I., and R. I. Kaufman. "Control of Underseepage, Mississippi River Levees, St. Louis District." *American Society of Civil Engineers Proceedings* 82 (January 1956): 1–21.

Olsen, J. R., et al. "Input-Output Economic Evaluation of System of Levees." *Journal of Water Resources Planning and Management* 124 (September-October 1998): 237–245.

Peterson, Dave. "Levee Breach Inundation Study: Sacramento County, California." *Proceedings of the National Conference on Hydraulic Engineering, Part 1, San Francisco, CA,* 1993, pp. 833–835.

Randall, C. "Water Table Data Helps Process Flood Control Levees." *Public Works* 127 (March 1996): 56–57.

Skonberg, E. R., and C. W. Berry. "Directionally Drilled Crossing Constructed under River Levee." *Pipeline and Gas Journal* 223 (June 1996): 26–28.

Wang, F. C. "Effects of Levee Extension on Marsh Flooding." *Journal of Water Resources Planning and Management* 113 (March 1987): 161–176.

Channels

Abt, S. R., et al. "Analysis of ARS Low-Drop Grade-Control Structure." *Journal of Hydraulic Engineering* 118 (October 1992): 1424–1434.

Afshar, A., et al. "Optimizing River Diversion under Hydraulic and Hydrologic Uncertainties." *Journal of Water Resources Planning and Management* 120 (January-February 1994): 36–47.

Aldama, Alvaro A. "Least-Square Parameter Estimation for Muskingum Flood Routing." *Journal of Hydraulic Engineering* 116 (April 1990): 580–586.

Bartholomew, M. J., and H. H. Mills. "Old Courses of the New River: Its Late Cenozoic Migration and Bedrock Control Inferred from High-Level Stream Gravels, Southwestern Virginia." *Geological Society of America Bulletin* 103 (January 1991): 73–81.

Carroll, R., et al. "Riverbank Renewal." *Civil Engineering (American Society of Civil Engineers)* 61 (October 1991): 39–41.

Chung, Wei-Hao, Alvaro A. Aldama, and James A. Smith. "On the Effects of Downstream Boundary Conditions on Diffusive Flood Routing." *Advances in Water Resources* 16 (1993): 259–275.

"Citizens Want Ponds, Not Widened Channels [Sims Bayou, Houston]." *Engineering News-Record* 227 (November 11, 1991): 23–24.

"Corps Channeling Plan Faces Varied Opposition [Los Angeles River]." *Engineering News-Record* 227 (November 18, 1991): 14+.

Crum, James, and Michael Mulvihill. "Expert System for the Planning and Design of Flood Control Channels." *Proceedings of the Eighteenth Annual Conference and Symposium on Water Resources Planning and Management and Urban Water Resources, New Orleans, LA,* 1991, pp. 429–433.

Darby, S. E., and C. R. Thorne. "Predicting Stage-Discharge Curves in Channels with Bulk Vegetation." *Journal of Hydraulic Engineering* 122 (October 1996): 583–586.

Fread, D. L., and K. S. Hou. "Applicability of Two Simplified Flood Routing Methods: Level Pool and Muskingum Cunge." *Proceedings of the National Conference on Hydraulic Engineering, San Francisco, CA,* 1993, pp. 1564–1568.

French, R. H. "Design of Flood Protection for Transportation Alignments on Alluvial Fans." *Journal of Irrigation and Drainage Engineering* 118 (March-April 1992): 320–330.

Guzman, A. G., et al. "Simulating Effect of Channel Changes on Stream Infiltration." *Journal of Hydraulic Engineering* 115 (December 1989): 1631–1645.

Harding, M. A. "Diversion Channel Helps Arizona Canal Control Flooding." *Aberdeen's Concrete Construction* 40 (May 1995): 462–464+.

Hicks, Faye E. "Hydraulic Flood Routing with Minimal Channel Data: Peace River, Canada." *Canadian Journal of Civil Engineering* 23 (April 1996): 524–535.

"Hidden Deflectors Confine Wandering Rivers to Their Beds." *New Scientist* 121 (March 4, 1989): 35.

Hite, John E., Scott E. Stonestreet, and Michael E. Mulvihill. "Model Study of Rio Hondo Flood Control Channel, Los Angeles, California." *Proceedings of the National Conference on Hydraulic Engineering, San Francisco, CA*, 1993, pp. 1695–1700.

Hjelmfelt, A. T., Jr. "Negative Overflows from Muskingum Flood Routing." *Journal of Hydraulic Engineering* 111 (June 1985): 1010–1014; discussion, 113 (August 1987): 1083–1085.

Huang, J., and C. C. S. Song. "Stability of Dynamic Flood Routing Schemes." *Journal of Hydraulic Engineering* 111 (December 1985): 1497–1505, discussion, 113 (August 1987): 1090–1095.

Huckleberry, G. "Contrasting Channel Response to Floods on the Gila River, Arizona." *Geology* 22 (December 1994): 1083–1086.

Jha, A. K., et al. "Modeling Unsteady Open-Channel Flows: Modification to Beam and Warming Scheme." *Journal of Hydraulic Engineering* 120 (April 1994): 461–476.

Lagasse, P. F., et al. "Erosion Risk Analysis for a Southwestern Arroyo." *Journal of Urban Planning and Management.* 111 (November 1985): 10–24.

McDonald, E. V., and A. J. Busacca. "Record of Pre-late Wisconsin Giant Floods in the Channeled Scabland Interpreted from Loess Deposits." *Geology* 16 (August 1988): 728–731.

Miller, Andrew J., Diane M. L. Mas, James A. Smith, and Wei-Hao Chung. "Boundary Conditions and Flow Patterns in a Mountain River." *Proceedings of the ASCE National Conference on Hydraulic Engineering, Buffalo, NY*, 1994, pp. 762–765.

Myers, W. R. "Velocity and Discharge in Compound Channels." *Journal of Hydraulic Engineering* 113 (June 1987): 753–766; discussion, 115 (May 1989): 688–691.

Naot, D., et al. "Hydrodynamic Behavior of Partly Vegetated Open Channels." *Journal of Hydraulic Engineering* 122 (November 1996): 625–633.

Peterson, W. C., and F. H. Verhoff. "Muskingum-like Approximations for Water Routing." *American Society of Civil Engineers Proceedings* 108 (November 1982): 1387–1393.

Pridal, D. B., and W. P. James. "Routing Procedure for Ungaged Channels." *Journal of Water Resources Planning and Management* 115 (January 1989): 108–120.

Rosenbaum, D. B. "Channel Sneaks through Problems." *Engineering News-Record* 229 (December 7, 1992): 49–50+.

Sabur, M. A. "Conservative Diffusion Wave Flood Routing Scheme for Channel Networks." *Canadian Journal of Civil Engineering* 23 (April 1996): 566–570.

Shankman, David, and Scott A. Samson. "Channelization Effects on Obion River Flooding, Western Tennessee." *Water Resources Bulletin* 27 (March-April 1991): 247–254.

Shiau, S.-E. "Scottsdale Plans $58 Million Channel Improvements." *Public Works* 126 (February 1995): 52–53.

Singh, V. P., and P. D. Scarlatos. "Analysis of Nonlinear Muskingum Flood Routing." *Journal of Hydraulic Engineering* 113 (January 1987): 61–79.

Stephenson, D., and P. Kolovopoulos. "Effects of Momentum Transfer in Compound Channels." *Journal of Hydraulic Engineering* 116 (December 1990): 1512–1522.

Stonestreet, Scott E., Michael E. Mulvihill, and John E. Hite Jr. "Revised Hydraulic Design of the Rio Hondo Flood Control Channel." *Proceedings of the ASCE National Conference on Hydraulic Engineering, Buffalo, NY,* 1994, pp. 401–405.

Sturm, T. W., and A. Sadiq. "Water Surface Profiles in Compound Channel with Multiple Critical Depths." *Journal of Hydraulic Engineering* 122 (December 1996): 703–709.

Temple, D. M. "Velocity Distribution Coefficients for Grass-Lined Channels." *Journal of Hydraulic Engineering* 112 (March 1986): 193–205; discussion, 113 (September 1987): 1221–1226.

Ting, Y.-K. "River Flood Routing by Nonlinear Muskingum Method." *Journal of Hydraulic Engineering* 111 (December 1985): 1447–1460.

Trieste, D. J. "Evaluation of Supercritical/Subcritical Flows in High-Gradient Channel." *Journal of Hydraulic Engineering* 118 (August 1992): 1107–1118, discussion, 120 (February 1994): 270–273.

Wasimi, S. A. "Estimation of Channel Depth during Floods by Canonical Correlation Analysis." *Journal of Hydraulic Engineering* 119 (January 1993): 81–94.

Wetmore, T. E. "Flooding Controlled by Bridge Relocation." *Public Works* 121 (June 1990): 86–87.

White, D. L. "Morganza Floodway to Steal 600,000 cfs [cubic feet per second] of Mississippi's Thunder." *Civil Engineering* 22 (April 1952): 272–277.

Williams, P. "Inviting Trouble Downstream." *Civil Engineering (American Society of Civil Engineers)* 69 (February 1998): 50–53.

Spillways

Afshar, A., and M. A. Marino. "Optimizing Spillway Capacity with Uncertainty in Flood Estimation." *Journal of Water Resources Planning and Management* 116 (January-February 1990): 71–84.

Blaisdell, F. W., and C. L. Anderson. "Pipe Plunge Pool Energy Dissipator." *Journal of Hydraulic Engineering* 117 (March 1991): 303–323; correction, 122 (January 1996): 55; discussion, 118 (October 1992): 1448–1453.

Chamani, M. R., and N. Rajaratnam. "Jet Flow on Stepped Spillways." *Journal of Hydraulic Engineering* 120 (February 1994): 254–259; discussion, 121 (May 1995): 441–448.

Chanson, H. "Self-Aerated Flows on Chutes and Spillways." *Journal of Hydraulic Engineering* 119 (February 1993): 220–243; discussion, 120 (June 1994): 778–782.

Christodoulou, G. C. "Energy Dissipation on Stepped Spillways." *Journal of Hydraulic Engineering* 119 (May 1993): 644–650.

Falvey, H. T., and P. Treille. "Hydraulics and Design of Fusegates." *Journal of Hydraulic Engineering* 121 (July 1995): 512–518.

Hager, W. H., and R. Sinniger. "Flood Storage in Reservoirs." *Journal of Irrigation and Drainage Engineering* 11 (March 1985): 76–85.

Khan, A. A., and P. M. Staffler. "Vertlcally Averaged and Moment Equations Model for Flow Over Curved Beds." *Journal of Hydraulic Engineering* 122 (January 1996): 3–9.

Lee, W., and J. A. Hoopes. "Prediction of Cavitation Damage for Spillways." *Journal of Hydraulic Engineering* 122 (September 1996): 481–488.

Mettel, C., et al. "Money-Saving Model." *Civil Engineering (American Society of Civil Engineers)* 64 (January 1994): 54–56.

Rice, C. E., and K. C. Kadavy. "Model Study of a Roller Compacted Concrete Stepped Spillway." *Journal of Hydraulic Engineering* 122 (June 1996): 292–297.

Sehgal, C. K. "Design Guidelines for Spillway Gates." *Journal of Hydraulic Engineering* 122 (March 1996): 155–165.

Tullis, J. P., et al. "Design of Labyrinth Spillways." *Journal of Hydraulic Engineering* 121 (March 1995): 247–255.

Woodbury, M. S., et al. "Minimizing the Probable Maximum Flood." *Civil Engineering (American Society of Civil Engineers)* 64 (June 1994): 64–65.

Dams

Alam, M. M., and M. A. Bhuiyan. "Collocation Finite-Element Simulation of Dam-Break Flows." *Journal of Hydraulic Engineering* 121 (February 1995): 118–128.

Attey, John Wilson, and Drew Randall Liebert. "Clean Water,

Dirty Dams: Oxygen Depletion and the Clean Water Act [of 1982, Legislative and Regulatory Policies That Would Prevent Environmental Degradation Caused by Dams and Hydroelectric Power Plants]." *Ecology Law Quarterly* 11 (1984): 703–729.

Auhl, O. "Economy in Materials Handling Features Bluestone Dam Construction: Power and Flood-Control Structure in West Virginia." *Civil Engineering* 18 (June 1978): 352–357.

Blackwelder, Brent. "In Lieu of Dams [Various Nonstructural Solutions to Flood Problems]." *Water Spectrum (Corps of Engineers)* 9 (Fall 1997): 40–46.

Bloomberg, R. "Dam Is Designed to Trap Sediment [Runoff from Mt. St. Helens Volcanic Eruption]." *Engineering News-Record* 220 (January 7, 1988): 30–31.

"Conference of the Association of State Dam Safety Officials, Albuquerque, NM." *Civil Engineering (American Society of Civil Engineers)* 59 (December 1989): 13–14.

"Delaware Dams Helped: Governor Asks Another." *Engineering News* 155 (September 8, 1955): 25.

Ellingson, D. "Foundation Problems Are Blamed for Reservoir Embankment Failure." *Engineering News-Record* 222 (January 12, 1989): 10–11.

Ellingwood, B., et al. "Assessing Cost of Dam Failure." *Journal of Water Resources Planning and Management* 119 (January-February 1993): 64–82.

Enzel, Yehouda, Lisa L. Ely, Juan Martinez-Goytre, and Vivian R. Gwinn. "Paleofloods and a Dam-Failure Flood on the Virgin River, Utah and Arizona." *Journal of Hydrology* 153 (January 1994): 291–315.

French, R. H. "Cisterns for Water Conservation and Flood Control." *Journal of Water Resources Planning and Management* 114 (September 1988): 565–577.

Horty, J. I. "Union Village Dam, Vermont: First Step in Program to Control Flood Waters of Connecticut River." *Explosives Engineer* 26 (September 1948): 135–139.

Jayyousl, Enan F., David S. Bowles, and Ronald W. Jeppson. "Natural and Dam Break Flood Routing in Mountain Rivers." *Proceedings of the ASCE National Conference on Hydraulic Engineering, Buffalo, NY,* 1994, pp. 371–375.

Johnson, D. B., and R. H. McCuen. "Slit Dam Design for Debris Flow Mitigation." *Journal of Hydraulic Engineering* 115 (September 1989): 1293–1296.

Kochel, R. C., et al. "Role of Tree Dams in the Construction of

Pseudo-terraces and Variable Geomorphic Response to Floods in Little River Valley, Virginia." *Geology* 15 (August 1987): 718–721.

Kollmorgen, W. M. "Deliver Us from Big Dams." *Land Economics* 30 (November 1954): 333–346.

Kriz, Margaret. "Dueling Over Dams: The Operating Licenses of 234 Hydroelectric Facilities across the Nation Will Expire at the End of 1993; Environmental Activists Want Federal Regulators to Use the Relicensing Process to Make the Facilities More Environment-Friendly: The Hydroelectric Industry Doesn't Like the Idea One Bit." *National Journal* 25 (December 11, 1993): 2935–2937.

Krohe, James, Jr. "Dams, Floods, Rainmaking, and Droughts [Illinois]." *Illinois Issues* 8 (August 1982): 23–29.

Lagassa, G. "What Price Dam Safety?" *Independent Energy* 19 (May-June 1989): 44–46+.

Lynch, Christopher J. "Wynoochee Lake and Dam Flood Storage Reevaluation Study." *Proceedings of the Twentieth Anniversary Conference on Water Management in the '90s, Seattle, WA,* 1993, pp. 372–375.

Mason, P. J., and K. Arumugam. "Free Jet Scour below Dams and Flap Buckets." *Journal of Hydraulic Engineering* 111 (February 1985): 220–2335; discussion, 113 (September 1987): 1192–1205.

McEnroe, B. M. "Preliminary Sizing of Detention Reservoirs to Reduce Peak Discharges." *Journal of Hydraulic Engineering* 118 (November 1992): 1540–1549; discussion, 120 (March 1994): 417–425.

Morris, R. "It Was a Dam Disaster [Colorado River Flood of 1983]." *National Wildlife* 23 (October-November 1985): 42–47.

Patrick, Joseph. "The Battle of the Dams: Those Who Think Some of Our Rivers Are a Damned Shame Argue for the Structure to Come Down." *Smithsonian* 19 (November 1988): 48–61.

Pattison, Kermit. "Why Did the Dam Burst? [St. Francis Dam North of Los Angeles]." *Invention and Technology* 14 (Summer 1998): 22–31.

Prakash, A. "Design-Basis Flood for Rehabilitation of Existing Dams." *Journal of Hydraulic Engineering* 118 (February 1992): 291–305.

Reisner, Marc. "America's Newest Old Energy Source: Hydro Power: Whatever Flows and Drops an Appreciable Distance, Someone, Somewhere Is Contemplating a Dam." *Amicus Journal* 6 (Spring 1985): 42–52.

Schafer, Kristopher T. "Creatively Cost Sharing a Large Flood

Control Dam." *Water Resources Infrastructure: Needs, Economics, and Financing, Forth Worth, TX,* 1990, pp. 62–65.

Siegrist, R. "Defense against Deluge: Whitney Point Dam Provides Protection to New York State Area Devastated in 1935 Flood Disaster." *Explosives Engineer* 20 (February 1942): 42–52.

Soast, A. "Tall Earthfill Dam Key to Flood Plan [Seven Oaks Dam, Santa Ana River Basin, California]." *Engineering News-Record* 233 (November 7, 1994): 26–28.

Soltys, Peter W. "Formulating an Effective Dam-Break Emergency Action Plan." *Journal of Professional Issues in Engineering Education and Practice* 117 (April 1991): 115–122.

Thompson, K. D., et al. "Evaluation and Presentation of Dam Failure and Flood Risks." *Journal of Water Resources Planning and Management* 123 (July-August 1997): 216–227.

U.S. Congress, House Committee on Interior and Insular Affairs. *Grand Canyon Projection Act of 1990: Hearings, April 26 and May 22, 1990, before the Subcommittee on Water Power and Offshore Energy Resources and the Subcommittee on National Parks and Public Lands, on H.R. 4498 to Amend the Colorado River Storage Project Act, to Direct the Secretary of the Interior to Establish and Implement Emergency Interim Operational Criteria at Glen Canyon Dam, and for Other Purposes.* 101st Cong., 2d sess. Washington: GPO, 1991, 710 pp.

U.S. Congress, Senate Select Committee on Indian Affairs. *Northern Cheyenne Indian Reserved Water Rights Settlement Act of 1991: Hearings, November 15, 1991, on S. 1607, to Provide Claims of the Northern Cheyenne Tribe.* 102d Cong. 1st sess. Washington: GPO, 1992, 170 pp.

Wallace, M. "Grout-Filled Bags Save Lives [Slope of Dam Face is Changed to Eliminate Dangerous Undertow]." *Concrete Construction* 31 (August 1986): 721–723.

Wang, J. S. "Dam-Break Study for Large Floodplain Area: A Case Study." *Proceedings for the Symposium on Engineering Hydrology, San Francisco, CA,* 1993, pp. 581–586.

"Windrows Survive the Flood." *BioCycle* 35 (June 1994): 40.

Wu, Chao, et al. "Model of Dam-Break Floods for Channels of Arbitrary Cross Section." *Journal of Hydraulic Engineers* 119 (August 1993): 911–923.

Wurbs, Ralph A. "Dam-Breach Flood Wave Models." *Journal of Hydraulic Engineering* 113 (January 1987): 29–45; discussion, 114 (May 1988): 565–569.

Reservoirs

Lovell, Troy Lynn, J. Russell Killen, and Bill S. Eichert. "Reservoir Regulation and Real-Time Models for Trinity River Flood Prevention and Control." *Proceedings of the Symposium on Engineering Hydrology, San Francisco, CA,* 1993, pp. 778–783.

"Reservoir Plan Challenged for Kansas Flood Control." *Engineering News* 151 (August 20, 1953): 53–55.

Williams, Philip B. "Assessing the True Value of Flood Control Reservoirs: The Experience of Folsom Dam in the February 1986 Flood." *Proceedings of the National Conference on Hydraulic Engineering, San Francisco, CA,* 1993, pp. 1969–1974.

Detention Basins

Akan, A. O. "Storm Runoff Detention for Pollutant Removal." *Journal of Environmental Engineering* 118 (May-June 1992): 380–389; discussion, 119 (November-December 1993): 1255–1258.

Akan, A. O., and E. N. Antoun. "Runoff Detention for Flood Volume or Erosion Control." *Journal of Irrigation and Drainage Engineering* 120 (January-February 1994): 168–178.

Antoun, Edward N., and A. Osman Akan. "Detention Basin Design to Control Flood Volumes." *Proceedings of the National Conference on Hydraulic Engineering, Nashville, TN,* 1991, pp. 1067–1071.

"Basin Stores Wet Weather Sewage Overflows." *Water/Engineering and Management* 140 (March 1993): 21.

Guo, J. C. Y., and B. Urbonas. "Maximized Detention Volume Determined by Runoff Capture Ratio." *Journal of Water Resources Planning and Management* 122 (January-February 1996): 33–39.

Hefner, J. W., et al. "Dallas' Flood Caverns." *Civil Engineering (American Society of Civil Engineers)* 61 (March 1991): 79–81.

Henderson, Frank E. "10th Street Detention Basin and Recreation Facilities [Phoenix, AZ]." *Proceedings of the Twenty-fourth Annual Water Resources Planning and Management Conference, Houston, TX,* 1997, pp. 217–222.

Klemens, T. L. "Precast, Slope Protection Proves Key to Speed." *Highway and Heavy Construction* 134 (February 1991): 44–45.

Lee, G. F., and A. Jones-Lee. "Stormwater Runoff Management: Are Real Water Quality Problems Being Addressed by Current Structural Best Management Practices?" *Public Works* 126 (January 1995): 54–56.

Loganathan, G. V. "Sizing Storm-Water Detention Basins for Pollutant Removal." *Journal of Environmental Engineering* 120 (November-December 1994): 1380–1399.

Maldonato, T. J. "Petroleum Hydrocarbons in Detention-Basin Sediments." *Journal of Environmental Engineering* 120 (May-June 1994): 683–690.

Molzahn, Robert E. "Estimating Maintenance Cost of Existing Stormwater Retention Ponds." *Proceedings of the Twentieth Anniversary Conference on Water Management in the '90s, Seattle, WA,* 1993, pp. 368–371.

"Oakland Braces for Storm Overflow." *Civil Engineering (American Society of Civil Engineers)* 62 (November 1992): 23.

Ponce, V. M., et al. "Large Basin Deterministic Hydrology: A Case Study." *Journal of Hydraulic Engineering* 111 (September 1985): 1227–1245; discussion, 113 (November 1987): 1461–1471.

Shafer, Kevin L., and David E. Westfall. "Utilizing Wetlands for Stormwater Retention." *Proceedings of the International Conference on Hydropower, Denver, CO,* 1991, 1130–1137.

Stanley, D. W. "Pollution Removal by a Stormwater Dry Detention Pond." *Water Environment Research* 68 (September-October 1996): 1076–1083.

Dikes

Christenson, J. A. "A Workable Compromise on Flood Control." *Civil Engineering (American Society of Civil Engineers)* 64 (September 1994): 6.

"Dikes Delay Bridge Repairs [Washed out by Midwest Flood]." *Engineering News-Record* 231 (November 29, 1993): 21.

"Dikes Open to Quake Threat." *Engineering News Record* 214 (March 14, 1985): 15–16.

Fritzinger, S. A., and D. S. Smith. "Rising from the River." *Civil Engineering (American Society of Civil Engineers)* 65 (December 1996): 48–50.

Leshchinsky, D., et al. "Geosynthetic Tubes for Confining Pressurized Slurry: Some Design Aspects." *Journal of Geotechnical Engineering* 122 (August 1996): 682–690.

"Recycled Conveyor Belt Protects Ash-Pond Dikes." *Power* 139 (June 1995): 107–108.

"Soft Dikes an Answer to Stone-Dike Collisions." *Civil Engineering (American Society of Civil Engineers)* 64 (September 1994): 20–21.

Tompkins, Mark E. "South Carolina's Diked Tidal Wetlands: The Persisting Dilemmas." *Coastal Management* 15 (1987): 135–155.

Floodgates

Berry, B. "Clarifier Changes Minimize I&I [Inflow and Infiltration] Effects." *Water Environment and Technology* 6 (August 1994): 22+.

"Corps-Modified Levees Just Ducky For Waterfowl [Winter Flooding of Farmland to Create Temporary Wetlands]." *Civil Engineering (American Society of Civil Engineers)* 64 (April 1994): 22+.

Halstead, Kenneth C., and Surya Bhamidipaty. "West Columbus, OH, LPP Gate Closure Analysis: A Study of the Requirements for Multiple Closures." *Proceedings of the ASCE National Conference on Hydraulic Engineering, Buffalo, NY, 1994*, pp. 472–476.

Jimenez, O. F., and M. H. Chaidhry. "Water-Level Control in Hydropower Plants." *Journal of Energy Engineering* 118 (December 1992): 180–193; discussion, 120 (August 1994): 98–101.

"Morganza: A $20 Million Flood Gate." *Engineering News* 148 (June 12, 1952): 34–36+.

Ohtsu, I., and Y. Yasuda. "Characteristics of Supercritical Flow below Service Gates." *Journal of Hydraulic Engineering* 120 (March 1994): 332–346.

Reina, P. "Giant Floating Steel Gates Guard against Sea Surges." *Engineering News-Record* 230 (April 19, 1993): 24–25+.

Rodellar, J., et al. "Control Method for On-Demand Operation of Open-Channel Flow." *Journal of Irrigation and Drainage Engineering* 119 (March-April 1993): 225–241.

Smith, R. J., and C. Chasten. "Corrosion Protection for Meter Gates." *ASTM Standardization News* 23 (May 1993): 52–54.

———. "Evaluation for Aging Steel Structures—Miter Gates." *ASTM Standardization News* 21 (March 1993): 50–53.

Soast, A. "Record Size Lock and Dam Project Gets a Soggy Launch as Rains Swell the Lower Ohio River for Months." *Engineering News-Record* 232 (May 30, 1994): 24–26.

Swamee, P. K., et al. "Analysis of Rectangular Side Service Gates." *Journal of Irrigation and Drainage Engineering* 119 (November-December 1993): 1026–1035.

Flood Walls

"Flood Wall Protects Jobs in Rural Community." *Water/Engineering and Management* 145 (November 1998): 12.

"Forming of Floodwall Meets Requirements." *Concrete International* 16 (September 1994): 80–81.

Reina, P. "Welsh Waterfront Barrier Generates a Barrage of Controversy." *Engineering News-Record* 240 (January 12, 1998): 38–39.

Slakter, A., and A. Soast. "Floodwall Is Tight Fit [Huntington, WV]." *Engineering News-Record* (June 16, 1988): 16.

Taylor, R. E., and D. F. Meadows. "Cellular Sheet-Pile Floodwall." *Civil Engineering (American Society of Civil Engineers)* 61 (January 1995): 58–60.

Lakes—Water Level

Cheng, X., and M. P. Anderson. "Numerical Simulation of Ground-Water Interaction with Lakes Allowing for Fluctuating Lake Levels." *Ground Water* 31 (November-December 1993): 929–933.

Cornman, R. E. "Bring Great Salt Lake Floods under Control." *Public Works* 118 (September 1987): 111–113.

Gibb, R. "Battling a Rising Great Salt Lake." *Engineering News Record* 217 (November 13, 1986): 25+.

"The Great Lakes Rise While the Corps Stands By." *Engineering News-Record* 216 (April 10, 1986): 13–14.

Janssen, Robert H. A., and Frederick A. Locher. "Simulation of Rapid Reservoir Drawdown for Flood Control, Cowlitz Falls Project." *Proceedings of the National Conference on Hydraulic Engineering, San Francisco, CA,* 1993, pp. 1842–1847.

Lee, Deborah H., and Anne H. Clites. "Great Lakes Water Level Extremes and Risk Assessment." *Proceedings of the First International Conference on Water Resources, Part 1, San Antonio, TX,* 1995, pp. 129–133.

Naim, Robert, and Darryl Hatheway. "Benefits of Hazard Mitigation Planning to Reduce Shoreline Impacts Due to Great Lakes Water Level Management Fluctuations and Severe Storms." *Proceedings of the ASCE National Conference on Hydraulic Engineering, Buffalo, NY,* 1994, pp. 182–186.

Reeve, D. E. "Coastal Flood Risk Assessment." *Journal of Waterway, Port, Coastal, and Ocean Engineering* 124 (September-October 1998): 219–228.

Schindler, H. "Salt Lake Fury Breaks Dike." *Engineering News-Record* 216 (June 19, 1986): 27.

Vance, R. E., et al. "7000-Year Record of Lake-Level Change on the Northern Great Plains: A High-Resolution Proxy of Past Climate." *Geology* 20 (October 1992): 879–882.

Sea Walls

Kirkgoz, M. S. "Breaking Wave Impact on Vertical and Sloping Coastal Structures." *Ocean Engineering* 22 (January 1995): 35–48.

Sinclair, J. "Rising Sea Levels Could Affect 300 Million." *New Scientist* 125 (January 28, 1990): 27.

Sundaresan, J. "Protection of Tropical Barrier Beaches: A Potential Remedial Measure." *Environmental Geology* 22 (November 1993): 272–275.

"Tahoe Walls Anchored Quickly and Cleanly." *Civil Engineering (American Society of Civil Engineers)* 64 (January 1994): 90.

Wang, K.-H., and X. Ren. "An Effective Wave-Trapping System." *Ocean Engineering* 21 (February 1994): 155–178.

Protection

Akan, A. O. "Storm Runoff Detention for Pollutant Removal." *Journal of Environmental Engineering* 118 (May-June 1992): 380–389.

Bakall, Ergun, Jeff Moncrief, Jon Walters, and Howard Chang. "Emergency Protection, San Luis Rey River Aqueducts." *Proceedings of the National Conference on Hydraulic Engineering, Part 1, San Francisco, CA,* 1993, pp. 962–967.

Braga, B. P. F., and P. S. F. Barbosa. "Hydropower and Flood Control Trade-Offs in a Multireservoir System." *Energy Sources* 14 (1992): 43–49.

Cozzens, H. F. "Steel Rails for Bank Protection on Salinas River, California. *Civil Engineering* 113 (March 1946): 113–115.

Hatfield, D. "Research Under Way for Flood-Resistant Treatment Plants." *Water Environment and Technology* 6 (April 1994): 20+.

Laura, R. A., and J. D. Wang. "Two-Dimensional Flood Routing on Steep Slopes." *Journal of Hydraulic Engineering* 110 (August 1984): 1121–1135.

Marcus, W. A. "Lag-Time Routing Suspended Sediment Concentrations during Unsteady Flow." *Geological Society of America Bulletin* 101 (May 1989): 644–651.

Nash, A. M. "How Flexible Wire Mattress and Riprap Was Placed along Section of Redwood Highway, California, to Stop Bank Erosion." *Roads and Streets* 87 (December 1944): 85–88.

O'Keefe, W. "Is Add-On Flood Protection Worthwhile for Old Plants? [Questions and Answers]." *Power* (April 1991): 175–177.

Smith, G. S. "Town Helps Itself to Flood Prevention: Princeton, W.Va." *Public Works* 93 (October 1962): 130–131.

Wiley, William N. *Elevated Housing: Flood Protection through Raising Existing Structures.* Research Report no. 186. Frankfort, KY: Kentucky Legislative Research Commission, 1981, 62 pp.

Transportation

Adams, Lea, Richard Palmer, and George Turkiyyah. "Expert System for Evaluating Scour Potential and Stream Stability at Bridges." *Proceedings of the Twenty-second Annual Conference on Integrated Water Resources Planning for the Twenty-first Century, Cambridge, MA,* 1995, pp. 786–789.

"After the Deluge, Highway Work Begins." *Engineering News-Record* 231 (August 23, 1993): 16.

Fischer, Edward E. "Contraction Scour at a Bridge over Wolf Creek, Iowa." *Proceedings of the First International Conference on Water Resources, Part 1, San Antonio, TX,* 1995, pp. 430–434.

Kaatz, K. J., and W. P. James. "Analysis of Alternatives for Computing Backwater at Bridges." *Journal of Hydraulic Engineering* 123 (September 1997): 784–792.

Laurie, R. A., and W. F. Dotson. "Bridge Evaluations after Catastrophes." *Concrete International* 20 (March 1998): 59–61.

Rosta, P. "Spare Tires Stand against Flood." *Engineering News-Record* 240 (April 20, 1998): 22–23.

Shen, H. W. "Risk Evaluation on Low Water-Crossing Structures." *Journal of Transportation Engineering* 117 (May-June 1991): 362–368.

Southard, Rodney E. *Simulation of the Effect of Traffic Barricades on Backwater along U.S. Highway 54 at Jefferson City, Missouri: 1993 Flood on the Missouri River.* Rolla, MO: Missouri Department of Transportation; and Denver CO: U.S. Geological Survey, 1997, 13 pp.

Umbrell, E. R., et al. "Clear-Water Contraction Scour under Bridges in Pressure Flow." *Journal of Hydraulic Engineering* 124 (February 1998): 236–240.

Mathematical Models

Akanbi, A. A., and N. D. Katopodes. "Model for Flood Propagation on Initially Dry Land." *Journal of Hydraulic Engineering* 114 (July 1988): 689–706; discussion, 116 (February 1990): 292–294.

Aldama, A. A. "Least-Square Parameter Estimation for Muskingum Flood Routing." *Journal of Hydraulic Engineering* 116 (April 1990): 580–586.

Arnell, N. W. "Expected Annual Damages and Uncertainties in Flood Frequency Estimation." *Journal of Water Resources Planning and Management* 115 (January 1989): 94–107; discussion, 116 (November-December 1990): 847–850.

Basco, D. R. "Limitations of de Saint Venant Equations in Dam-Break Analysis." *Journal of Hydraulic Engineering* 115 (July 1989): 950–965.

Bhaskar, N. R., and C. A. O'Connor. "Comparison of Method of Residuals and Cluster Analyses for Flood Regionalization." *Journal of Water Resources Planning and Management* 45 (November 1989): 793–808.

Cappelaere, B. "Accurate Diffusive Wave Routing." *Journal of Hydraulic Engineering* 123 (March 1999): 174–181.

Chowdhury, J. U., and J. R. Stedinger. "Confidence Interval for Design Floods with Estimated Skew Coefficient." *Journal of Hydraulic Engineering* 118 (July 1991): 811–831; discussion, 118 (July 1992): 1074–1076.

"Computer Paints Environmental Portrait." *Public Works* 119 (June 1988): 80–81.

Costanza, R., et al. "Modeling Coastal Landscape Dynamics [Atchafalaya River, LA]." *BioScience* 40 (February 1990): 91–107.

Crippen, J. R. "Envelope Curves for Extreme Flood Events." *American Society of Civil Engineers Proceedings* 108 (October 1982): 1208–1212.

Davis, Stuart A. *Guidelines to Estimating Existing and Future Residential Content Valves.* Ft. Belvoir, VA: U.S. Army Corps of Engineers, Water Resources Support Center, Institute for Water Resources, 1993, 98 pp. Microfiche.

Dawdy, David R., and Vijay K. Gupta. "Comment on Multiscaling and Skew Separation in Regional Floods." *Water Resources Research* 33 (January 1997): 271–275.

Debo, T. N. "Urban Flood Damage Estimating Curves." *American Society of Civil Engineers Proceedings* 108 (October 1982): 1059–1069.

Fahmy, H. E. S., and H. J. Morel-Seytoux. "Hybrid Noninertia and Statistical Model Versus Hydrodynamic Routing." *Journal of Hydraulic Engineering* 120 (June 1994): 706–721.

Garcia-Navarro, P., and V. Zorraquino. "Numerical Modeling of Flood Propagation through System of Reservoirs." *Journal of Hydraulic Engineering* 119 (March 1993): 380–389.

Gill, M. A. "Numerical Solution of Muskingum Equations." *Journal of Hydraulic Engineering* 118 (May 1992): 804–809; discussion, 119 (September 1993): 1073–1078.

———. "Response of Muskingum Equation to Step Input." *Journal of Irrigation and Drainage Engineering* 115 (August 1989): 736–738; discussion, 117 (July-August 1991): 605–607;

119 (March-April 1973): 410–415; 120 (May-June 1994): 695–701.

Goel, N. K., et al. "Multivariate Modeling of Flood Flows." *Journal of Hydraulic Engineering* 124 (February 1998): 146–155.

Han, G., and Deguan Wang. "Numerical Modeling of Anhul Debris Flow." *Journal of Hydraulic Engineering* 122 (May 1996): 262–265.

Hjalmarson, H. W., and J. V. Phillips. "Potential Effects of Translating Waves on Estimation of Peak Flows." *Journal of Hydraulic Engineering* 124 (November 1998): 1178–1179.

———. "Potential Effects of Translating Waves on Estimation of Peak Flows." *Journal of Hydraulic Engineering* 123 (June 1997): 571–575.

Jha, A. K., et al. "First-and-Second-Order Flux Difference Splitting Schemes for Dam-Break Problem." *Journal of Hydraulic Engineering* 121 (December 1995): 877–884.

Jin, M., and D. L. Fread. "Dynamic Flood Routing with Explicit and Implicit Numerical Solution Schemes." *Journal of Hydraulic Engineering* 123 (March 1997): 166–173.

Katopodes, N. D., and D. R. Schamber. "Applicability of Dam-Break Flood Wave Models." *Journal of Hydraulic Engineering* 109 (May 1983): 702–721.

Koussis, A. D. "Unified Theory for Flood and Pollution Routing." *Journal of Hydraulic Engineering* 109 (December 1983): 1652–1664; discussion; 112 (October 1986): 981–985.

Krzysztofowicz, R. "Probabilistic Hydrometeorological Forecasts: Toward a New Era in Operational Forecasts." *Bulletin of the American Meteorological Society* 79 (February 1998): 243–251.

Lambert, J. H., and D. Li. "Evaluating Risk of Extreme Events for Univariate-Loss Functions." *Journal of Water Resources and Planning Management* 120 (May-June 1994): 382–399.

Lee, C. F. "Watershed Modeling and Flood Routing for Safety Assessment of an Existing Dam." *Journal of Water Resources Planning and Management* 122 (September-October 1996): 334–341.

Lee, H.-L., and L. W. Mays. "Hydraulic Uncertainties in Flood Levee Capacity." *Journal of Hydraulic Engineering* 112 (October 1986): 928–934.

Lee, J., et al. "Modelling the Effect of Data Error on Feature Extraction from Digital Elevation Models." *Photogrammetric Engineering and Remote Sensing* 38 (October 1992): 1461–1467.

Lichty, R. W., and M. R. Karlinger. "Spatial Trends in Pearson

Type III Statistical Parameters." *Journal of Hydraulic Engineering* 121 (September 1995): 672–678.

Madsen, H., and D. Rosbjerg. "The Partial Duration Series Method in Regional Index-Flood Modeling." *Water Resources Research* 33 (April 1997): 737–746.

McCuen, R. H., and T. V. Hromadka. "Flood Skew in Hydrologic Design on Ungaged Watersheds." *Journal of Irrigation and Drainage Engineering* 114 (May 1988): 301–310; discussion, 115 (October 1989): 914–915.

McCuen, R. H., et al. "Regionalized Partial-Duration Balanced-Hydrograph Model." *Journal of Irrigation and Drainage Engineering* 119 (November-December 1993): 1036–1051.

McGraw, David, and Susanne Strater. "Money-Saving Model." *Civil Engineering (American Society of Civil Engineers)* 64 (January 1994): 54–56.

Miller, S., and M. H. Chaudhry. "Dam-Break Flows in Curved Channel." *Journal of Hydraulic Engineering* 115 (November 1989): 1465–1478.

Myers, R. C., and J. F. Lyness. "Discharge Ratios in Smooth and Rough Compound Channels." *Journal of Hydraulic Engineering* 123 (March 1997): 182–188.

Nguyen, Q. K., and K. Kawano. "Simultaneous Solution for Flood Routing in Channel Networks." *Journal of Hydraulic Engineering* 121 (October 1995): 744–750.

O'Donnell, T., et al. "Improved Fitting for Three-Parameter Muskingum Procedure." *Journal of Hydraulic Engineering* 114 (May 1988): 516–528; discussion, 116 (August 1990): 1056–1058.

Perkins, S. P., and A. D. Koussis. "Stream-Aquifer Interaction Model with Diffusive Wave Routing." *Journal of Hydraulic Engineering* 122 (April 1996): 210–218.

Perumal, M. "Unification of Muskingum Difference Schemes." *Journal of Hydraulic Engineering* 115 (April 1989): 536–543; correction, 115 (December 1989): 1721.

Robinson, J. S., and M. Sivapalan. "Temporal Scales and Hydrological Regimes: Implications for Flood Frequency Sealing." *Water Resources Research* 33 (December 1997): 2981–2999.

Shome, M. L., and P. M. Steffler. "Lateral Flow Exchange in Transient Compound Channel Flow." *Journal of Hydraulic Engineering* 124 (January 1998): 77–80.

Singh, V. P., and P. D. Scarlatos. "Analysis of Gradual Earth-Dam Failure." *Journal of Hydraulic Engineering* 114 (January 1988): 21–42.

Sinha, J., et al. "Comparison of Spectral and Finite-Difference Methods for Flood Routing." *Journal of Hydraulic Engineering* 121 (February 1995): 108–117.

Sturm, T. W., and A. Sadiq. "Water Surface Profiles in Compound Channel with Multiple Critical Depths." *Journal of Hydraulic Engineering* 122 (December 1996): 703–707.

Tung, Y-K. "River Flood Routing by Nonlinear Muskingum Method." *Journal of Hydraulic Engineering* 111 (December 1985): 1447–1460; discussion, 113 (August 1987): 1086–1090.

Tung, Y. K., and L. W. Mays. "Reducing Hydrologic Parameter Uncertainty." *American Society of Civil Engineers Proceedings* 107 (March 1981): 245–262.

Uddin, M. S., et al. "Estimation of the Surface Velocity of Debris Flow with Computer-Based Spatial Filtering." *Applied Optics* 37 (September 10, 1998): 234–239.

Vreugdenhil, C. B., and J. H. A. Wijbenga. "Computation of Flow Patterns in Rivers." *American Society of Civil Engineers Proceedings* 108 (November 1982): 1296–1310.

Wagner, M. J. "GIS Shines in Florida." *GIS World* 11 (July 1998): 60–63.

Walder, J. S., and J. E. O'Connor. "Methods for Predicting Peak Discharge of Floods Caused by Failure of Natural and Constructed Earthen Dams." *Water Resources Research* 33 (October 1997): 2337–2348.

Wang, K.-H., et al. "Hydrodynamic Flow Modeling at Confluence of Two Streams." *Journal of Engineering Mechanics* 122 (October 1996): 994–1002.

Whitley, R., and T. V. Hromadka. "Approximate Confidence Intervals for Design Floods for a Single Size Site Using a Neural Network." *Water Resources Research* 35 (January 1999): 203–209.

Wohl, E. E. "Uncertainty in Flood Estimates Associated with Roughness Coefficient." *Journal of Hydraulic Engineering* 124 (February 1998): 219–223.

Wurbs, R. A. "Dam-Breach Flood Wave Models." *Journal of Hydraulic Engineering* 113 (January 1987): 29–45.

Yoon, J., and G. Padmanabhan. "Parameter Estimation of Linear and Nonlinear Muskingum Models." *Journal of Water Resources Planning and Management* 119 (September-October 1993): 600–610.

Zhao, B., and L. W. Mays. "Uncertainty and Risk Analyses for FEMA Alluvial-Fan Method." *Journal of Hydraulic Engineering* 122 (June 1996): 325–332.

Computer Simulation

Boyle, S. J., et al. "Developing Geographic Information Systems for Land Use Impact Assessment in Flooding Conditions." *Journal of Water Resources Planning and Management* 124 (March-April 1998): 89–98.

Brimicombe, A. J. "Flood Risk Assessment Using Spatial Decision Support Systems." *Simulation* 59 (December 1992): 379–380.

Buzzi, A., et al. "Numerical Simulations of the 1994 Piedmont Flood: Role of Orography and Moist Processes." *Monthly Weather Review* 126 (September 1998): 2369–2383.

Cohn, T. A., et al. "An Algorithm for Computing Moments-Based Flood Quantile Estimates when Historical Flood Information Is Available." *Water Resources Research* 33 (September 1997): 2089–2096.

"Computer Program Planned for 1983 Season to Predict Flood Levels and Building Damages." *Bulletin of the American Meteorological Society* 64 (February 1983): 169–170.

Fabry, K. "Fighting Flood Waters [Watertown, SD]." *Water Environment and Technology* 10 (April 1998): 40–41.

Feldman, A. D. "Systems Analysis Applications at the Hydrologic Engineering Center." *Journal of Water Resources Planning and Management* 118 (May-June 1992): 249–261.

Gross, L. J., and M. J. Small. "River and Floodplain Process Simulation for Subsurface Characterization." *Water Resources Research* 34 (September 1998): 2365–2376.

Hjalmarson, H. W., and B. E. Thomas. "New Look at Flood-Frequency Relations for Arid Lands." *Journal of Hydraulic Engineering* 118 (June 1992): 868–886.

Hoegberg, S. "New Computer Program Aids Flood Prediction/Response Process." *Public Works* 127 (December 1996): 32–33.

Komura, S. "Method for Computing Bed Profiles during Floods." *Journal of Hydraulic Engineering* 112 (September 1986): 833–846.

Lipschultz, M. S., and D. E. Glaser. "Rainy Season Flooding Being Tracked by GIS." *Water/Engineering and Management* 139 (June 1992): 22–25.

Marche, C., et al. "Simulation of Dam Failures in Multidike Reservoirs Arranged in Cascade." *Journal of Hydraulic Engineering* 123 (November 1997): 950–961.

Nair, U. S., et al. "Numerical Simulation of the 9–10 June 1972 Black Hills Storm Using CSU RAMS." *Monthly Weather Review* 125 (August 1997): 1753–1766.

O'Brien, J. S., et al. "Two-Dimensional Water Flood and Mudflow Simulation." *Journal of Hydraulic Engineering* 119 (February 1993): 244–261; discussion, 120 (June 1994): 771–774.

Ogawa, H., and J. W. Male. "Simulating the Flood Mitigation Role of Wetlands." *Journal of Water Resources Planning and Management* 112 (January 1986): 114–128.

Rutledge, J. "Computers Help Solve Structural Problems of Dams." *American City and County* 107 (November 1992): 42–43.

Spencer, P. L., and D. J. Stensrud. "Simulating Flash Flood Events: Importance of the Subgrid Representation of Convection." *Monthly Weather Review* 126 (November 1998): 2884–2912.

Tucci, C. E. M., et al. "Hydrodynamic Analysis of Floods in Urban System." *Journal of Water Resources Planning and Management* 115 (July 1989): 523–540.

Uddin, M. S., et al. "Estimation of the Surface Velocity of Debris Flow with Computer-Based Spatial Filtering." *Applied Optics* 37 (September 10, 1998): 234–239.

Wagner, M. J. "GIS Shines in Florida." *GIS World* 11 (July 1998): 60–63.

Zhang, D.-L., and J. M. Fritsch. "Numerical Evolution of the Meso-6 Scale Structure and Evolution of the 1977 Johnstown Flood: Internal Gravity Waves and the Squall Line." *Journal of the Atmospheric Sciences* 45 (April 1, 1989): 1252–1268.

———. "Numerical Simulation of the Meso-5 Scale Structure and Evolution of the 1977 Johnstown Flood." *Journal of the Atmospheric Sciences* 43 (September 15, 1986): 1913–1943; 44 (September 15, 1987): 2593–2612.

Forecasting

Awwad, H. M., and J. B. Valdes. "Adaptive Parameter Estimation for Multisite Hydrologic Forecasting." *Journal of Hydraulic Engineering* 118 (September 1992): 1201–1221.

Bae, D.-H., et al. "Operational Forecasting with Real-Time Databases." *Journal of Hydraulic Engineering* 121 (January 1995): 49–60.

Baker, Lori, "'Attention! This Neighborhood Is under Mandatory Evacuation: You Must Leave Immediately.'" *Family Circle* 110, no. 15 (November 1, 1997): 56–65.

Beard, L. R. "Practical Determination of Hypothetical Floods." *Journal of Water Resources Planning and Management* 116 (May-June 1990): 389–401.

Bishop, R., and W. E. Watt. "Development from Expert System for Selection of Flood Forecasting Methods." *Canadian Water Resources Journal* 14 (1989): 5–17.

Colon, Raul, James R. Wallace, Robert W. Olson, and Kristina L. Massey. "Flood Forecasting: An Alternate Response for PMF at Saluda Dam." *Proceedings of the Fifty-first American Power Conference, Chicago, IL,* 1989, pp. 999–1002.

"Conference on Weather Analysis and Forecasting, 13th, Including Symposium on Flash Floods, Vienna, VA, August 2–6, 1993 [Revised Program]." *Bulletin of the American Meteorological Society* 74 (May 1993): 959–967.

D'Aleo, J., and W. Junker. "Summary of the 13th Conference on Weather Analysis and Forecasting and Fifth Conference on Aviation Weather Systems [Tyson's Corner, VA, August 10, 1993]." *Bulletin of the American Meteorological Society* 75 (February 1994): 245–257.

Diaz, Gustavo E., Jose D. Salas, and William R. Hansen. "Relation between Largest Known Flood Discharge and Elevation in Montana." *Proceedings of the ASCE National Conference on Hydraulic Engineering, Buffalo, NY,* 1994, pp. 870–874.

Dotson, Harry W., and John C. Peters. "Hydrologic Aspects of Flood Warning—Preparedness Program." *Proceedings of the National Conference on Hydraulic Engineering, San Diego, CA,* 1990, pp. 1239–1244.

Fan, Shou-shan. "Problems of Stream Flood Simulation and Prediction." *Proceedings of the ASCE National Conference on Hydraulic Engineering, Buffalo, NY,* 1994, pp. 1110–1114.

"Flood Forecasting: Susquehanna River Basin." *Public Works* 90 (September 1959): 113–115.

Hoegberg, S. "New Computer Program Aids Flood Prediction/Response Process." *Public Works* 127 (December 1996): 32–33.

Ingram, John J., Edwin Welles, and Dean T. Braatz. "Advanced Hydrologic Forecasting Products for Flood and Drought Mitigation." *Proceedings of the 1996 Conference on Natural Disaster Reduction, Washington, DC,* 1996, pp. 227–228.

James, W. P., et al. "Radar-Assisted Real-Time Flood Forecasting." *Journal of Water Resources Planning and Management* 119 (January-February 1993): 32–44.

Jarrett, Robert D. "Historic-Flood Evaluation and Research Needs in Mountainous Areas." *Proceedings of the ASCE National Conference on Hydraulic Engineering, Buffalo, NY,* 1994, pp. 875–879.

Kouwen, N., E. D. Soulis, A. Pietroniro, and R. A. Harrington. "Application of Remote Sensing to Flood Forecasting." *Proceedings of the ASCE Seventeenth Annual National Conference on Optimizing the Resources for Water Management, Fort Worth, TX,* 1990, pp. 208–212.

Kunkel, K. E., et al. "A Regional Response to Climate Information Needs during the 1993 Flood." *Bulletin of the American Meteorological Society* 76 (December 1995): 2415–2421.

Madsen, H., and D. Rosbjerg. "The Partial Duration Series Method in Regional Index-Flood Modeling." *Water Resources Research* 33 (April 1997): 737–746.

Melching, Charles S. "Reliability Assessment Method for Flood Forecasts." *Proceedings of the National Conference on Hydraulic Engineering, Nashville, TN,* 1991, pp. 984–989.

Miller, N. L., and J. Kim. "Numerical Prediction of Precipitation and River Flow over the Russian River Watershed during the January 1995 California Storm." *Bulletin of the American Meteorological Society* 77 (January 1996): 101–105.

Mimikou, M. A., and E. A. Baltas. "Flood Forecasting Based on Radar Rainfall Measurements." *Journal of Water Resources Planning and Management* 122 (May-June 1996): 151–156.

Mukherjee, D., and N. Mansour. "Estimation of Flood Forecasting Errors and Flow-Duration Joint Probabilities of Exceedance." *Journal of Hydraulic Engineering* 122 (March 1996): 130–140.

Nelson, M. E. "Appropriate Technology for Flood Warnings." *Civil Engineering (American Association of Civil Engineers)* 62 (June 1992): 64–66.

Pessos, M. L., et al. "Use of Weather Radar for Flood Forecasting in the Sieve River Basin: A Sensitivity Analysis." *Journal of Applied Meteorology* 32 (March 1993): 462–475.

Shalaby, A. I. "Sensitivity to Probable Maximum Flood." *Journal of Irrigation and Drainage Engineering* 121 (September-October 1995): 327–337.

Stover, Charles M., David W. Widener, and Edmund C. Burkett. "Real Time Forecasting at a Major Flood Control Project." *Proceedings of the Eighteenth Annual Conference and Symposium on Water Resources Planning and Management and Urban Water Resources, New Orleans, LA,* 1991, pp. 16–21.

Susquehanna River Basin Commission. *Recommendations for an Improved and Expanded Flood Forecasting System for the Susquehanna River Basin.* Mechanicsburg, PA: Susquehanna River Basin Commission, 1973, 15 leaves.

Tao, Tao, and Nicholas Kouwen. "Remote Sensing and Fully Distributed Modeling for Flood Forecasting." *Journal of Water Resources Planning and Management* 115 (November 1989): 809–823.

Unver, O., et al. "Real-Time Flood Management Model for Highland Lake System." *Journal of Water Resources Planning and Management* 113 (September 1987): 620–638.

U.S. Congress. House Committee on Science and Technology. Subcommittee on Investigations and Oversight. *Forecasting and Technology for Water Management: Hearings, October 13–14, 1983.* 98th Cong., 1st sess. Washington, DC: GPO, 1984, 492 pp.

Vogel, R. M., et al. "The Regional Persistence and Variability of Annual Streamflow in the United States." *Water Resources Research* 34 (December 1998): 3445–3459.

Wall, D. J., et al. "Flood Peak Estimates from Limited At-Site Historic Data." *Journal of Hydraulic Engineering* 113 (September 1987): 1159–1174.

Woodbury, Mark S., Douglas T. Eberlein, and Nicholas Pansic. "Minimizing the Probable Maximum Flood." *Civil Engineering (American Society of Civil Engineers)* 64 (June 1994): 64–65.

Woodward, Carl W. "Real-Time Flood Forecasting in Harris County, Texas, with HEC-1." *Proceedings of the First International Conference on Water Resources, Part 2, San Antonio, TX,* 1995, pp. 986–990.

Zevin, S. F. "Steps toward an Integrated Approach to Hydrometeorological Forecasting Services." *Bulletin of the American Meteorological Society* 75 (July 1994): 1267–1276.

Frequency

Adamowski, K., and W. Feluch. "Nonparametric Flood-Frequency Analysis with Historical Information." *Journal of Hydraulic Engineering* 116 (August 1990): 1035–1047.

Arnell, Nigel W. "Expected Annual Damages and Uncertainties in Flood Frequency Estimation." *Journal of Water Resources Planning and Management* 115 (January 1989): 94–107.

Ashkar, Fahim, and Taha B. M. J. Ouarda. "Assessment of Flood Magnitude Estimator Uncertainty: Tolerance Limits for the Gamma and Generalized Gamma Distributions." *Proceedings of the International Conference on Hydropower, Part 3, San Francisco, CA,* 1995, pp. 2456–2465.

Balocki, James B., and Stephen J. Burges. "Relationships Between n-Day Flood Volumes for Infrequent Large Floods." *Journal of Water Resources Planning and Management* 120 (November-December 1994): 794–817.

Beard, Leo R. "Estimating Flood Frequency and Average Annual Damage." *Journal of Water Resources Planning and Management* 123 (March-April 1997): 84–88.

Beard, Leo R., W. H. Espey, Phil Combs, and Ben M. Littlepage. "Probability and Impact of an Observed Rare Sequence of Floods." *Proceedings of the National Conference on Hydraulic Engineering, San Francisco, CA,* 1993, pp. 2345–2349.

Bodhaine, G. L. "Flood Frequency Relationships in the Pacific Northwest." *American Society of Civil Engineers Proceedings* 86 (November 1960): 1–10.

Bogardi, Istvan, Ronald Reiter, and Peter Nachtnebel. "Fuzzy Rule-Based Estimation of Flood Probabilities under Climatic Fluctuations." *Proceedings of the Seventh Conference on Risk-Based Decision Making in Water Resources, Santa Barbara, CA,* 1995, pp. 61–79.

Boughton, W. C., et al. "Flood Frequency Estimates in Southeastern Arizona." *Journal of Irrigation and Drainage Engineering* 113 (November 1987): 469–478.

Bradley, A. A. "Regional Frequency Analysis Methods for Evaluating Changes in Hydrologic Extremes." *Water Resources Research* 34 (April 1998): 741–750.

Burn, Donald H. "Cluster Analysis as Applied to Regional Flood Frequency." *Journal of Water Resources Planning and Management* 115 (September 1989): 567–582.

———. "Delineation of Groups for Regional Flood Frequency Analysis." *Journal of Hydrology* 104 (December 30, 1988): 345–361.

Clement, Ralph W. *Floods in Kansas and Techniques for Estimating Their Magnitude and Frequency on Unregulated Streams.* Lawrence, KS: Department of the Interior, U.S. Geological Survey, Denver, CO, and Kansas Department of Transportation, 1987, 50 pp.

Escalante-Sandoval, C. A., and J. A. Raynal-Villasensor. "A Trivariate Extreme Value Distribution Applied to Flood Frequency Analysis." *Journal of Research of the National Institute of Standards and Technology* 99 (July-August 1994): 369–375.

Fang, Xin Yu, and Babak Naghavi. "Selection of Flood Frequency Analysis Procedure for Evaluating Flood-Estimation Models." *Transportation Research Record* 1483 (July 1995): 56–63.

Garros-Berthel, H. "Station-Year Approach: Tool for Estimation of Design Floods." *Journal of Water Resources Planning and Management* 120 (March-April 1994): 135–160.

Giese, G. L., and M. A. Franklin. *Magnitude and Frequency in the Suwannee River Water Management District, Florida.* Series: Water Resources Investigations Report 96-4176. Tallahassee, FL: Suwannee River Water Management District; and Washington, DC: U.S. Geological Survey, 1996, 14 pp.

Gingras, Denis, and Kaz Adamowski. "Performance of L-Moments and Nonparametric Flood Frequency Analysis." *Canadian Journal of Civil Engineering* 21 (October 1994): 856–862.

Hirsch, Robert M., and Jerry R. Stedinger. "Plotting Positions for Historical Floods and Their Precision." *Water Resources Research* 23 (April 1987): 715–727.

Hjalmarson, Hjmalmar W., and Blakemore E. Thomas. "New Look at Regional Flood-Frequency Relations for Arid Lands." *Journal of Hydraulic Engineering* 118 (June 1992): 868–886.

Hromadka, T. V., and R. J. Whitley. "Checking Flood Frequency Curves Using Rainfall Data." *Journal of Hydraulic Engineering* 115 (April 1989): 544–548.

Jacques, J. E., and D. L. Lorenz. *Techniques for Estimating the Magnitude and Frequency of Floods in Minnesota.* Denver, CO: U.S. Geological Survey, 1988, 48 pp.

Jennings, M. E. "Plans for National Flood Frequency by Microcomputer." *Proceedings of the National Conference on Hydraulic Engineering, New Orleans, LA,* 1989, pp. 386–391.

Kirby, W. H., and M. E. Moss. "Summary of Flood-Frequency Analysis in the United States." *Journal of Hydrology* 96 (December 15, 1987): 5–14.

Kurothe, R. S., et al. "Derived Flood Frequency Distribution for Negatively Correlated Rainfall Intensity and Duration." *Water Resources Research* 33 (September 1977): 2103–2107.

Lichty, R. W., and M. R. Karlinger. "Climate Factor for Small-Basin Flood Frequency." *Water Resources Bulletin* 26 (August 1990): 577–586.

Loaicisa, Hugo A. "Frequency of Flood Extremes." *Proceedings of the National Conference on Hydraulic Engineering, Colorado Springs, CO,* 1988, pp. 806–812.

Magilligan, Francis J., and Brian E. Graber. "Hydroclimatological and Geomorphic Controls on Timing and Spatial Variability of Floods in New England, USA." *Journal of Hydrology* 178 (April 15, 1996): 159–180.

Marco, J. B., and J. B. Valdes. "Partial Area Coverage Distribution for Flood Frequency Analysis in Arid Regions." *Water Resources Research* 34 (September 1998): 2309–2317.

Melcher, Nick B., and Patsy G. Martinez. "Frequency Analyses for Recent Regional Floods in the United States." *Proceedings of the Conference on Natural Disaster Reduction, Washington, DC,* 1996, pp. 59–61.

Moon, Young, Upmaner Lall, and Ken Bosworth. "Comparison of Tail Probability Estimators for Flood Frequency Analysis." *Journal of Hydrology* 151 (November 1993): 343–363.

Neely, Braxtel L., Jr. *Magnitude and Frequency of Floods in Arkansas.* Denver, CO: U.S. Geological Survey, 1987, 51 pp.

Newton, D. W. "Realistic Assessment of Maximum Flood Potentials." *Journal of Hydraulic Engineering* 110 (August 1984): 1166–1178.

Olin, D. A. *Flood Depth Frequency Relations for Streams in Alabama.* Denver, CO: U.S. Geological Survey, 1986, 46 pp.

Perry G. R., and K. L. Shafer. "Frequency-Related Temporally and Spatially Varied Rainfall." *Journal of Hydraulic Engineering* 116 (October 1990): 1215–1231.

Raines, Timothy H., and Juan B. Valdes. "Assessment of Derived Flood Frequency Distributions." *National Conference on Water Resources Planning and Management—Water Forum, Baltimore, MD,* 1992, pp. 268–273.

———. "Estimation of Flood Frequencies for Unengaged Catchments." *Journal of Hydraulic Engineering* 119 (October 1993): 1138–1154.

Robinson, J. S., and M. Sivapalan. "An Investigation into the Physical Causes of Scaling and Heterogeneity of Regional Flood Frequency [Appalachian Region]." *Water Resources Research* 33 (May 1997): 1045–1059.

Sauer, Vernon B. "New Studies of Urban Flood Frequency in the Southeastern United States." *Transportation Research Record* 1073 (1986): 10–15.

Schickedanz, Norman L., James E. Lindell, Ben C. Trammell Jr., and John M. Boknect. "Rocky Mountain Project: Probable Maximum Floods." *Proceedings of the International Conference on Horsepower, Denver, CO,* 1991, pp. 1108–1117.

Shalaby, A. I. "Sensitivity to Probable Maximum Flood." *Journal of Irrigation and Drainage Engineering* 121 (September-October 1995): 327–337.

Shen, H. W., et al. "Physically Based Flood Features and Frequencies." *Journal of Hydraulic Engineers* 116 (April 1990): 494–514; discussion, 118 (April 1992): 637–638.

Swain, Robert E. "Colorado River Probable Maximum Floods." *Proceedings of the International Conference on Hydropower, Denver, CO,* 1991, pp. 1445–1454.

Tasker, Gary D., Scott A. Hodge, and C. Shane Barks. "Region of Influence Regression for Estimating the 50-Year Flood at Ungaged Sites." *Water Resources Bulletin* 32 (February 1996): 163–170.

Thomas, Wilbert O., Jr., Minoru Kuriki, and Todashi Suatougi. "Evaluating Frequency Distributions for Flood Hazard Analysis." *Proceedings of the First International Conference on Water Resources, Part 1, San Antonio, TX,* 1995, pp. 124–128.

Vogel, Richard M., Wilbert O. Thomas Jr., and Thomas McMahon. "Flood-Flow Frequency Model Selection in Southwestern United States." *Journal of Water Resources Planning and Management* 119 (May-June 1993): 353–366.

Walsh, James J. "Case History: 100-Year Flood Event in San Francisco." *Proceedings of the National Conference on Hydraulic Engineering, Part 1, San Francisco, CA,* 1993, pp. 347–352.

Wolff, C. Gary, and Stephen J. Burges. "Analysis of the Influence of River Channel Properties on Flood Frequency." *Journal of Hydrology* 153 (January 1994): 317–337.

Zrinji, Zolt, and Donald H. Burn. "Flood Frequency Analysis for Ungaged Sites Using a Region of Influence Approach." *Journal of Hydrology* 153 (January 1994): 1–21.

———. "Regional Flood Frequency with Hierarchial Region of Influence." *Journal of Water Resources Planning and Management* 122 (July-August 1996): 245–252.

Warning

Bartfeld, Ira, and Verrie F. Pearce. "City of Roseville, California, Alert System: Real Times Microcomputer Based Flood Warning System." *Proceedings of the Third Water Resources Operations Management Workshops, Fort Collins, CO,* 1988, pp. 656, 665.

Booy, C., and L. M. Lye. "New Look at Flood Risk Determination." *Water Resources Bulletin* 25 (1989): 933–943.

Brown, W. "Flood Warning as Sea Defenses Weaken." *New Scientist* 127 (September 1, 1990): 20.

Curtis, David C., and Donald E. Colton. "Flood Warning Using Wide-Area Computer Network." *Proceedings of the Third Water Resources Operations Management Workshop, Fort Collins, CO,* 1988, pp. 666–671.

Duan, Li, Yacov Y. Haimes, Eugene Stakhiv, and David Moser. "Optimal Flood Warning Threshold: A Case Study of Connellsville, Pennsylvania." *Proceedings of the Fifth Conference on Risk-Based Decision Making in Water Resources, Santa Barbara, CA,* 1992, pp. 260–283.

"Flood-Warning System for San Antonio." *Water Engineering and Management* 137 (April 1990): 13.

"Flood [Warning] System Installed in Northern New Jersey." *Civil Engineering (American Society of Civil Engineers)* 57 (November 1987): 20–21.

"Flood Warning System Purchased by San Antonio." *American City and County* 105 (March 1990): 31–32.

Fontaine, Thomas A., and Kenneth W. Potter. "Estimating Exceedance Probabilities of Extreme Floods." *Proceedings of the Symposium on Engineering Hydrology, San Francisco, CA,* 1993, pp. 635–640.

Georgakakos, K. P. "On the Design of National, Real-Time Warning Systems with Capability for Site-Specific, Flash-Flood Forecasts." *Bulletin of the American Meteorological Society* 67 (October 1986): 1233–1239.

Goulter, I. C. "Flood Warnings and Flood Responses for the Red River of the North." *Water Resources Bulletin* 20 (August 1984): 599–610.

Graham, Wayne J., and Curtis A. Brown. "Flood Warning Systems As a Means for Reducing Urban Flood Losses." *Proceedings of the National Water Conference Specialty Conference, Newark, DE,* 1989, pp. 281–285.

Gruntfest, Eve. "Report on 18 Warning Systems in America." *Proceedings of the Third Water Resources Operation Management Workshop, Fort Collins, CO,* 1988, pp. 750–758.

Hampton, Terry L. "Probable Maximum Flood Determination Using EPRI [Electric Power Research Institute] Research Results." *Proceedings of the International Conference on Hydropower, Part 2, San Francisco, CA,* 1995, pp. 1715–1723.

"How Forecasters Kept Flood Warnings to Themselves." *New Scientist* 121 (March 25, 1989): 18.

Johnson, Lynn E. "Flood Warning System Product Usage Patterns." *Proceedings of the Twenty-second Annual Conference on Integrated Water Resources Planning for the Twenty-first Century, Cambridge, MA,* 1995, pp. 779–781.

———. "Flood Warning Systems." *Proceedings of the Third Water Resources Operation Management Workshop, Fort Collins, CO,* 1988, pp. 648–655.

Kachic, Albert S. "Planning and Implementing a Wide Area Flood Warning System: The IFLOWS Experience." *Proceedings of the Third Water Resources Operations Management Workshop, Fort Collins, CO,* 1988, pp. 672–682.

Krzystofowicz, R., et al. "Reliability of Flood Warning Systems." *Journal of Water Resources Planning and Management* 120 (November-December 1994): 906–926.

Linsley, Ray K. "Flood Estimates: How Good Are They?" *Water Resources Research* 22 (August 1986): 159–164.

Miller, John. *Floods: People at Risk, Strategies for Prevention.* New York: United Nations, 1997, 93 pp.

Nelson, Mark E. "Appropriate Technology for Flood Warnings." *Civil Engineering (American Society of Civil Engineers)* 62 (June 1992): 64–66.

Taylor, Dolores B. "Economic Benefits of a Flood Warning System: The Ventura County, California, Experience." *Proceedings of the Seventeenth Annual National Conference on Optimizing the Resources for Water Management, Fort Worth, TX,* 1990, pp. 353–359.

U.S. National Advisory Committee on Oceans and Atmosphere. *The Agnes Floods: A Post-audit of the Effectiveness of the Storm and Flood Warning System of the National Oceanic and Atmospheric Administration.* Washington, DC: GPO, 1972, 35 pp.

Wall, David J., David F. Kibler, Donald W. Newton, and Janet Herrin. "Flood Peak Estimates from Limited At-Site Historical Data." *Journal of Hydraulic Engineering* 113 (September 1987): 1159–1176.

Woodbury, M. S., et al. "Minimizing the Probable Maximum Flood." *Civil Engineering (American Society of Civil Engineers)* 64 (June 1994): 64–65.

Plans and Projects

Argent, Gala. "Keeping California above Water: Flood Control." *Western Water* (January-February 1989): 4–11.

Brown, E. A. "Missouri River Flood Problems." *Midwest Engineer* 4 (March 1952): 7–9+.

Callahan, J. P. "Single Purpose Flood Control Pays Off in Ohio." *Public Utilities* 42 (July 15–29, 1949): 63–76, 159–166.

Cassidy, W. F. "California Water Plan: Flood Control Problems." *American Water Works Association Journal* 49 (February 1957): 126–131.

Chatry, F. M. "Flood Distribution Problems below Old River."

American Society of Civil Engineers Proceedings 86 (August 1960): 1–15.

Cookson, G. M. "Plan for Closure of Old River." *American Society of Civil Engineers Proceedings* 86 (September 1960): 83–102.

Evelyn, Joseph B., and Michael E. Mulvihill. "Santa Ana River Project Overview." *Proceedings of the National Conference on Hydraulic Engineering, New Orleans, LA,* 1989, pp. 820–826.

Flood Plain Information, Antietam and Heister Creek, Berks County, Pennsylvania. Prepared for the Berks County Planning Commission, Springfield, VA, Corps of Engineers, U.S. Army, Philadelphia District. 1974, 24 pp.

Ford, D. T., and J. R. Killen. "PC-Based Decision-Support Systems for Trinity River, Texas." *Journal of Water Resources Planning and Management* 121 (September-October 1995): 375–381.

Freeman, D. B. "Pick-Sloan Flood Control Plan Develops Resources of Missouri River Basin." *Civil Engineering* 17 (November 1947): 652–657.

Gilcrest, B. R., et al. "Flood Control Plan for the Ohio River Basin." *American Society of Civil Engineers Proceedings* 83 (April 1957): 1–16.

Graham, R. "Hydrologic Study of Large Basin in Eastern Wyoming." *Journal of Water Resources Planning and Management* 114 (January 1988): 52–65.

Hall, C. L. "Corps of Engineers Plans Ohio Flood Control." *Civil Engineer* 15 (June 1945): 249–252.

Hardin, J. R. "Evolution of the Mississippi Valley Flood Control Plan." *American Society of Civil Engineers Proceedings* 83 (May 1957): 1–18.

Johnson, W. E. "Missouri River Basin Plan in Operation." *American Society of Civil Engineers Proceedings* 81 (September 1955): 1–19.

Leonard, G. K., and D. H. Mattern. "Planning the Watauga Project: Flood Control and Power Project of Tennessee Valley Authority." *Civil Engineering* 18 (March 1948): 142–146+.

Lewis, W. E. "Tunnel Construction by Peripheral Sawing at the Fort Randall Reservoir, Pickstown, S.D." *U.S. Bureau of Mines Circular* 7610 (1951): 1–21.

Mansur, C. I., and R. I. Kaufman. "Dewatering Excavation: Low Sill Structure: Old river, LA." *American Society of Civil Engineers Proceedings* 84 (February 1958): 1–32.

Ohlemutz, Rudolf E. "Mission Creek Flood Control Project." *Proceedings of the Twenty-second Annual Conference on Integrated Water Resources Planning for the Twenty-first Century, Cambridge, MA,* 1995, pp. 812–815.

Pick, L. A. "Missouri River Development Program." *American Water Works Association Journal* 38 (July 1946): 859–867.

Richman, M. "Communities Upgrading Management Programs to Prevent Flood Damage." *Water Environment and Technology* 9 (July 1997): 28–29.

Schriver, Weldon K. "Abilene, Texas, Flood Control Study: Case History." *Proceedings of the Seventeenth Annual National Conference on Optimizing the Resources for Water Management, Fort Worth, TX,* 1990, pp. 519–524.

Shen, H. W., et al. "Kissimmee River Restoration Study." *Journal of Water Resources and Planning Management* 120 (May-June 1994): 230–249.

Troch, Peter A., Jamie A. Smith, and Eric F. Wood. "Hydrologic Controls of Large Floods in a Small Basin: Central Appalachian Case Study." *Journal of Hydrology* 156 (April 1994): 285–309.

U.S. Army. Corps of Engineers. *Floods and Flood Control on the Mississippi, 1973.* Washington, DC: 1973.

Management

Bedient, Philip B., and Peter G. Rowe, eds. "Urban Watershed Management: Flooding and Water Quality." [Proceedings of a Symposium held at Rice University, May 25–26, 1978]. *Rice University Studies* 65 (Winter 1979): 1–205.

Begel, Nancy E., and Gary M. Pettit. "Dallas Floodway Past and Present Successes in Flood Protection Benefits." *Proceedings of the Seventeenth Annual National Conference on Optimizing Resources for Water Management, Forth Worth, TX,* 1990, pp. 381–386.

Burkett, Edmund B., and Cheryl L. Struble. "Alberto Flood of 1994 Water Management and Flood Forecasting Aspects." *Proceedings of the Twenty-second Annual Conference on Integrated Water Resources Planning for the Twenty-first Century, Cambridge, MA,* 1995, pp. 767–770.

California Department of Water Resources. *California Flood Management: An Evaluation of Flood Damage Prevention Programs.* Bulletin 199. Sacramento, CA: 1980, 277 pp.

Changnon, S. A., Jr. "Research Agenda for Floods to Solve Policy Failure." *Journal of Water Resources Planning and Management* 111 (January 1985): 54–64.

Cheng, M. S. "User-Friendly GIS Aids in Flood Management." *Water Environment and Technology* 6 (April 1994): 34.

Contract Program Supplements to Flood Control Maintenance." *Public Works* 118 (December 1987): 40–41.

Corcoran, C., et al. "County Develops a Comprehensive Stormwater Management Plan." *Public Works* 124 (November 1993): 48–50.

Danilevesky, A. "Development of the Rio de La Plata System." *Journal of Water Resources Planning and Management* 113 (November 1987): 761–778.

Dawdy, David R. "Sorry State of Flood/Hydrology in the Arid Southwest." *Proceedings of the International Symposium on Hydraulics/Hydrology of Arid Lands and the National Conference on Hydraulic Engineering, San Diego, CA,* 1990, pp. 743–748.

Dzurik, Andrew A. "Floodplain Management Trends." [Role of the United States federal government in flood control]. *Water Spectrum (Corps of Engineers)* 12 (Summer 1980): 35–42.

"Flood Management." *Compressed Air* 100 (April-May 1995) 20–28.

Galuzzi, M. R., and J. M. Pflaum. "Integrating Drainage, Water Quality, Wetlands, and Habitat in a Planned Community Development." *Journal of Urban Planning and Development* 122 (September 1996): 101–108.

Grimm, M. "Floodplain Management." *Civil Engineering (American Society of Civil Engineers)* 68 (March 1998): 62–64.

Hawley, M. E., and R. H. McCuen. "Elements for a Comprehensive Stormwater Management Program." *Journal of Water Resources Planning and Management* 113 (November 1987): 793–809.

Heaney, James P. "Sustainable Stormwater Management." *Proceedings of the Twenty-second Annual Conference on Integrated Water Resources Planning for the Twenty-first Century, Cambridge, MA,* 1995, pp. 165–168.

Hegemier, Tom. "Alternative Flood Management Approaches." *Proceedings of the First International Conference on Water Resources, Part 2, San Antonio, TX,* 1995, pp. 1824–1828.

Herring, B. E., and W. B. Stevenson. "The Alabama Floodplain Management Information System." *Surveying and Mapping* 46 (December 1986): 279–286.

Holway, James M., and Raymond J. Burby. "Reducing Flood Losses: Local Planning and Land Use Controls." *American Planning Association Journal* 59 (Spring 1993): 205–216.

Horn, D. R. "Prioritizing Flood Control Planning Needs." *Journal of Water Resources Planning and Management* 113 (March 1987): 283–292.

"Indianapolis Faces Flooding Problem." *Water/Engineering and Management* 136 (May 1989): 18–19.

Jones, D. E., Jr., and J. E. Jones. "Floodway Delineation and Management." *Journal of Water Resources Planning and Management* 113 (March 1987): 228–242; discussion, 114 (March 1988): 246–247.

Lamb, B. L., and N. P. Lovrich. "Strategic Use of Technical Information in Urban Instream Flow Plans." *Journal of Water Resources Planning and Management* 113 (January 1987): 42–52.

Lee, H.-L., et al. "Performance Evaluation of Lake Shelbyville by Stochastic Dynamic Programming." *Journal of Water Resources Planning and Management* 118 (March-April 1992): 185–204; discussion, 119 (July-August 1993): 502–503.

Lewis, G. L. "Jury Verdict: Frequency versus Risk-Based Culvert Design." *Journal of Water Resources Planning and Management* 118 (March-April 1992) 166–184; discussion, 120 (November-December 1994): 994–999; 121 (September-October 1995): 400.

Lichty, R. W., and M. R. Karlinger. "Spatial Trends in Pearson Type III Statistical Parameters." *Journal of Hydraulic Engineering* 121 (September 1995): 672–678.

"Low-Leak Sluice Gates Control Flooding at Wastewater Plant." *Water/Engineering and Management* 134 (September 1987): 26.

Lydon, Donna. "HEC's [Hydraulic Engineering Center] Project Benefit Accomplishment Program." *Proceedings of the Symposium on Engineering Hydrology, San Francisco, CA,* 1993, pp. 1200–1205.

McCallum, Brian E. "Flood Monitoring Network in Southeastern Louisiana." *Proceedings of the ASCE National Conference on Hydraulic Engineering, Buffalo, NY,* 1994, pp. 346–350.

McCuen, R. H., and G. E. Moglen. "Multicriterion Stormwater Management Methods." *Journal of Water Resources Planning and Management* 114 (July 1988): 414–431.

Merli, Kevin, and Michael Goetz. "Case Studies of Multi-objective Management in New England." *Proceedings of the Twenty-second Annual Conference on Integrated Water Resources Planning for the Twenty-first Century, Cambridge, MA,* 1995, pp. 747–750.

Miller, H., and E. Silberhorn. "Managing Water Resources in the New Orleans Area." *Journal of the Water Pollution Control Federation* 56 (September 1984): 995–1002.

Momatiuk, Y., and J. Easteatt. "Liquid Land [Regulation of Atchafalaya River, LA]." *Audubon* 97 (September-October 1995): 48–57+.

Newson, M. D., and D. Sear. "The Role of Geomorphology in Monitoring and Managing River Sediment Systems." *Water and Environmental Management Journal* 12 (February 1998): 18–24.

Nichols, A. B. "Kissimmee Restoration Project Breaks New Ground." *Water Environment and Technology* 4 (July 1992): 18.

Noppeney, R., and C. Kranenburg. "Dilution Discharge Measurement during Flood Wave." *Journal of Hydraulic Engineering* 115 (November 1989): 1582–1586.

Oliver, Clifford E., and Harry B. Thomas. "Joint Effort of ASCE [American Society of Civil Engineers] and FEMA [Federal Emergency Management Agency] to Develop Flood Hazard Mitigation Standards." *Proceedings of the Conference on Natural Disaster Reduction, Washington, DC,* 1996, pp. 337–338.

Ormsbee, L. E., et al. "Design of Stormwater Detention Basins for Multiple Design Frequencies." *Journal of Hydraulic Engineering* 113 (May 1987): 601–614.

Pate, Mary Lynne. *Introduction to Urban Stormwater Management in Georgia.* Circular 9. Prepared for the Federal Emergency Management Agency as part of Cooperative Agreement EMA-K-0079. Atlanta, GA: Department of Natural Resources; Environmental Protection Agency; and Geologic Surgery, 1983, 20 pp.

Platt, R. H. "Sharing the Challenge: Floodplain Management into the Twenty-first Century." *Environment* 37 (January-February 1995): 25–28.

Plazak, D. J. "Flood Control Benefits Revisited." *Journal of Water Resources Planning and Management* 112 (April 1986): 265–276; discussion, 113 (July 1987): 594–597.

Rahn, Perry H. "Flood-Plain Management Program in Rapid City, South Dakota." *Geological Society of America Bulletin* 95 (July 1984): 838–843.

Russell, S. O., and Ken-Beck Lee. "Estimating the Probabilities of Combined Events." *Canadian Journal of Civil Engineering* 21 (December 1994): 1088–1091.

Sokolove, R. D. "Subrogation: Enforcing Flood Plain Management." *Journal of Professional Issues in Engineering* 109 (July 1983): 195–207.

Stiftel, Bruce, and Raymond J. Burby. "State and Local Programs for Flood Hazard Management in the Southeast." *Carolina Planning* 9 (Summer 1983): 29–31.

Tasker, Gary D., and Raymond M. Slade. "Interactive Regional Regression Approach to Estimating Flood Quantiles." *Pro-*

ceedings of the Twenty-first Annual Conference on Water Policy and Management: Solving the Problems, Denver, CO, 1994, pp. 782–785.

Tettemer, J. M. "Stormwater Plan Avoids Flood Control Projects." *Water Environment and Technology* 6 (April 1994): 17.

Unver, O., et al. "Real-Time Flood Management Model for Highland Lake System." *Journal of Water Resources Planning and Management* 113 (September 1987): 620–638; discussion, 119 (January 1987): 125–127.

U.S. Congress, House Committee on Interior and Insular Affairs. *Colorado River Management: Oversight Hearings, September 7–8, 1983.* 98th Cong., 1st sess. Washington, DC: GPO, 1983, 798 pp.

Vaughan, Memphis, Jr. "Water Management Aspects of Southeastern Flood of 1994." *Proceedings of the First International Conference on Water Resources, Part 1, San Antonio, TX,* 1995, pp. 760–764.

Wang, Z., et al. "Seismic Monitoring of Water Floods? A Petrophysical Study." *Geophysics* 56 (October 1991): 1614–1623.

Weaver, W. J. "Stormwater Management in an Urbanized Area." *Public Works* 119 (October 1988): 60–62.

Westhaver, David S., and Alison H. Boyce. "Alaska Flood Recovery Project: Management of a Disaster Recovery by a General Contractor." *Proceedings of the Conference on Natural Disaster Reduction.* Washington, DC, 1996, pp. 111–112.

Whipple, W., Jr. "Flood Management for Small Urban Streams." *American Society of Civil Engineers Proceedings* 103 (November 1977): 315–324; discussion, 104 (November 1978): 104.

Williams, P. B. "Flood Control vs. Flood Management." *Civil Engineering (American Society of Civil Engineers)* 64 (May 1994): 51–54.

Wood, D. W., et al. "Development of a Flood Management Plan." *Journal of Water Resources Planning and Management* 111 (October 1985): 417–433.

Flood Damage

Albertson, M. L. "Big Thompson Flood Damage Was Severe, But Some Could Have Been Prevented." *Civil Engineering* 48 (February 1978): 74–77.

Appelbaum, Stuart J. "Determination of Urban Flood Damage." *Journal of Water Resources Planning and Management* 111 (July 1985): 269–283.

Barr, D. W., and K. L. Heuer. "Quiet Response on the Mississippi." *Civil Engineering (American Society of Civil Engineers)* 59 (September 1989): 50–52.

Batzel, R. "Overflow Control Protects Mississippi River." *Water Environment and Technology* 6 (June 1994): 29–30+.

Berry, M. A., et al. "Suggested Guidelines for Remediation of Damage from Sewage Overflow into Buildings." *Journal of Environmental Health* 57 (October 1994): 9–15.

Davis, Stuart A. *Business Depth-Damage Analysis Procedures.* Ft. Belvoir, VA: U.S. Army Corps of Engineers, Engineer Institute for Water Resources, 1985, 100 pp. Microfiche.

"Deluge of Damage." *Public Works* 123 (November 1992): 67.

"Drowned-and-Out Town Is On the Move, Really [English, IN, Relocating to Higher Ground]." *Engineering News-Record* 225 (October 25, 1990): 17–18.

Evensen, J. S. "A Water District's Recovery from Storm Damage." *Public Works* 118 (October 1987): 71–74.

"Florida Assesses Damage." *Engineering News-Record* 221 (September 22, 1988) 13–14.

Frazier, B. "GIS and SCADA Converge to Minimize Flood Damage." *Public Works* 126 (April 1995): 40–42+.

Freund, A. "Fast-Track Electrical Rebuilding after Flood Disaster [Ramada O'Hare Hotel, Chicago, IL]." *Electrical Construction and Maintenance* 87 (August 1988): 74–79.

Johnson, W. K. "Significance of Location in Computing Flood Damage." *Journal of Water Resources Planning and Management* 111 (January 1985): 65–81.

Karlsson, P.-O., and Y. Y. Haimes. "Risk Assessment of Extreme Events: Application." *Journal of Water Resources Planning and Management* 115 (May 1989): 299–320.

Koen, A. D. "Southeast Texas Pipelines Recovering from Flood." *Oil and Gas Journal* 92 (November 7, 1994): 34–35.

Lawrie, R. A., and W. F. Dotson. "Bridge Evaluation after Catastrophe." *Concrete International* 20 (March 1998): 59–61.

Lee, L. T., and T. L. Essex. "Urban Headwater Flooding Damage Potential." *Journal of Hydraulic Engineering* 109 (April 1983): 519–535.

Lewis, Gary L. "Management of Regional Flood Damage to Railroads." *Proceedings of the Twenty-second Annual Conference on Integrated Water Resources Planning for the Twenty-first Century, Cambridge, MA,* 1995, pp. 808–811.

Lloyd, Glenn D., Jr. "Analysis of Negative Effects of Major Floods on Man." *Proceedings of the First International Conference on*

Water Resources, Part 1, San Antonio, TX, 1995, pp. 864–868.

"Los Angeles Aqueduct Damaged by Flooding." *Engineering News-Record* 223 (August 14, 1989): 14.

McBean, Edward, Michael Fortin, and Jack Gorrie. "Critical Analysis of Residential Flood Damage Estimation Curves." *Canadian Journal of Civil Engineering* 13 (February 1986): 86–94.

McBean, Edward, et al. "Adjustment Factors for Flood Damage Curves." *Journal of Water Resources Planning and Management* 114 (November 1988): 635–646; discussion, 116 (November-December 1990): 843–846.

———. "Flood Depth-Damage Curves by Interview Survey." *Journal of Water Resources Planning and Management* 114 (November 1988): 613–634.

McManamy, R. "Chicago Shifts to Finger Pointing." *Engineering News-Record* 228 (May 4, 1992): 10–11.

———. "Receding Floodwater Bares Massive Restoration Needs." *Engineering News-Record* 231 (August 16, 1993): 9.

Monk, W. Curtis. "July 1993 Flood Damage to US-71 Bridge Over Brushy Creek, Carroll County, Iowa: Case Study." *Transportation Research Record* 1483 (July 1995): 38–46.

Ouellette, P., et al. "Application of Extreme Value Theory to Flood Damage." *Journal of Water Resources Planning and Management* 11 (October 1985): 467–477.

Rosenbaum, D. B. "Protecting Bridges from Floods." *Engineering News-Record* 230 (February 22, 1993): 38.

Thrash, M. M. "When the Allegheny Dropped Its Ice: People's Natural Gas Handling of a Mid-Winter Flood Emergency." *Gas Age* 123 (April 16, 1959): 36–37.

U.S. Congress, House Committee on Public Works, Subcommittee on Flood Control and Internal Development. *South Dakota Flood Disaster: Hearing, June 27, 1972.* 92d Cong. 2d sess. Washington, DC: GPO, 1972, 103 pp.

U.S. Congress, House Committee on Public Works and Transportation, Subcommittee on Water Resources. *Flood Damage along the Monongahela and Cheat Rivers in Pennsylvania and West Virginia as the Result of Severe Flooding in November 1985.* Hearing before the Subcommittee on Water Resources of the Committee on Public Works and Transportation, House of Representatives, February 7, 1986, at Point Marion, PA. 99th Cong. 2d sess. Washington, DC: GPO, 1986, 215 pp.

Williams, P. "Inviting Trouble Downstream." *Civil Engineering (American Society of Civil Engineers)* 69 (February 1998): 50–53.

Wurbs, Ralph A. "Optimal Sizing of Flood Damage Reduction Measures Based on Economic Efficiency." *International Journal of Water Resources Development* 12 (March 1996): 5–16.

Yeh, C.-H. "Floods Prove Need for Project." *Engineering News-Record* 241 (October 26, 1998): 99; discussion, 242 (January 18, 1999): 5–6.

Yoe, Charles. "Ice-Related Flood Damage Estimation." *Journal of Water Resources Planning and Management* 110 (April 1984): 141–152.

Economic Aspects

"$1.3-Billion Flood Job in Jersey Creeps Ahead [Passaic River]." *Engineering News-Record* 229 (July 13, 1992): 10–11.

Abt, S. R., R. J. Wittler, and A. Taylor. "Predicting Human Instability in Flood Flows." *Proceedings of the National Conference on Hydraulic Engineering, New Orleans, LA*, 1989, pp. 70–76.

Betzler, R. L., and A. F. Calley. "Cost Reporting Procedures Help Speed Recovery from Flood Disaster." *Public Works* 105 (April 1974): 58–61.

"Big Damage Happened in a Flash." *Engineering News-Record* 239 (August 11, 1997): 22–23.

Bollens, Scott A. "Public Policy and Land Conversion: Lessening Urban Growth Pressure in River Corridors." *Growth and Change* 21 (Winter 1990): 40–58.

Brennan, M. "Storm Hits Colorado State University Hard." *Chemical and Engineering News* 75 (August 4, 1997): 12.

Christian, G. L. "How TWA Beat Disaster at Overhaul Base: Maintained 85.1 Percent of Schedules during Flood." *Aviation Week* 55 (December 31, 1951): 35–36+.

Collins, Patrick S. "Financing the Future of Storm Water." *Civil Engineering (American Society of Civil Engineers)* 63 (March 1996): 64–66.

Das, Sujit, and Lee Russell. "Nontraditional Methodology for Flood Stage-Damage Calculations." *Water Resources Bulletin* 24 (December 1988): 1263–1272.

Donnelly, William A. "Hedonic Price Analysis of the Effect of a Floodplain on Property Values." *Water Resources Bulletin* 25 (June 1989): 581–586.

Evensen, J. A. "A Water District's Recovery from Storm Damage." *Public Works* 118 (October 1987): 71–74.

Eliatamby, Deepal, and Michael E. Meadows. "Impact of Urbanization on Main Stream Flooding." *Proceedings of the Sympo-*

sium on Watershed Planning and Analysis in Action, Durango, CO,* 1990, pp. 48–57.

Farr, Cheryl. "Land Development and the Environment: Decision Making for Flood-Prone Areas." *Public Management* 64 (February 1982): 5–13.

Foster, E. E. "Evaluation of Flood Losses and Benefits of Control." *American Society of Civil Engineers Proceedings* 67 (May 1941): 805–828.

Gunnison, D., et al. "Relationship of Materials in Flooded Soils and Sediments to the Water Quality of Reservoirs: Oxygen Consumption Rates." *Water Research* 17 (1983): 1609–16–17.

Harrison, R. W. "New Mississippi Problem." *Land Economics* 27 (November 1952): 297–305.

Huffman, Roy G., and Darryl Davis. "Is the National Economic Development Plan the Best Plan?" *Proceedings of the Twenty-second Annual Conference on Integrated Water Resources Planning for the Twenty-first Century, Cambridge, MA,* 1995, pp. 790–793.

Ichniowski, T., and A. Roe. "Wave of Relief Funds Hits Flood-Damaged Plains States." *Engineering News-Record* 238 (June 23, 1997): 9–10.

Johnson, N. L., Jr. "Economics of Permanent Flood-Plain Evacuation." *American Society of Civil Engineers Proceedings* 102 (September 1976): 273–283.

Kunkel, K. E., et al. "Climatic Aspects of the 1993 Upper Mississippi River Basin Flood." *Bulletin of the American Meteorological Society* 75 (May 1994): 811–822.

Laska, Shirley Bradway. "Involving Homeowners in Flood Mitigation." *Journal of the American Planning Association* 52 (Autumn 1986): 452–466.

Lawrie, R. J. "Flooded Motors: What to Do." *Electrical Construction and Maintenance* 92 (September 1993): 33.

Pascocello, A. J., Jr. "Saving Property: Salvage Operations, Part I." *Fire Engineering* 149 (September 1996): 70–72.

Patterson, F. M. "TVA's All over the Place: Economically Undesirable." *Public Utilities* 35 (February 1, 1945): 155–160.

Plazak, David J. "Flood Control Benefits Revisited." *Journal of Water Resources Planning and Management* 112 (April 1986): 265–276.

Rhodes, Jennifer, and Roy Trent. "Economics of Floods, Scour, and Bridge Failures." *Proceedings of the National Conference on Hydraulic Engineering, Part 1, San Francisco, CA,* 1993, pp. 928–933.

Shabman, Leonard. "Measuring the Benefits of Flood Risk Reduction." *Proceedings of the Sixth Conference on Risk-Based Decision Making in Water Resources, Santa Barbara, CA,* 1994, pp. 122–135.

Stadinger, J. R. "Expected Probability and Annual Damage Estimators." *Journal of Water Resources Planning and Management* 123 (March-April 1997): 125–135; discussion, 124 (November-December 1998): 365–366.

Steffen, Constance C. "The Great Salt Lake: Major Economic Impacts of High Lake Levels." *Utah Economic and Business Review* 43 (September-October 1983): 1–7.

Thunberg, Eric. "Determinants of Landowner's Willingness to Pay for Flood Hazard Reduction." *Water Resources Bulletin* 27 (July-August 1991): 657–665.

Wittler, R. J., A. Taylor, and D. J. Love. "Human Stability in a High Flood Hazard Area." *Water Resources Bulletin* 25 (August 1989): 881–890.

Wurbs, R. A. "Economic Feasibility of Flood Control Improvements." *Journal of Water Resources Planning and Management* 109 (January 1983): 29–47.

Flood Insurance

"Afterstorm Cleanup Needs Care and Common Sense." *Water/Engineering and Management* 131 (November 1984): 23–25.

Attanasi, E. D., and M. R. Karlinger. "Worth of Geophysical Data in Natural Disaster–Insurance Rate Setting." *Journal of Applied Meteorology* 21 (April 1982): 453–460.

"Can You Insure for Floods?" *Steel* 137 (October 31, 1955): 42.

"Companies Ease Policy Terms in Flood Areas." *National Underwriter Life Insurance Edition* 55 (July 20, 1951): 5.

Coulton, Kevin G. "Coastal Flood Insurance Study Procedure for Puget Sound." *Proceedings of the National Conference on Hydraulic Engineering, Colorado Springs, CO,* 1988, pp. 294–299.

Davison, Todd A. "National Flood Insurance Program and Coastal Hazards." *Proceedings of the Eighth Symposium on Coastal and Ocean Management, Part 2, New Orleans, LA,* 1993, pp. 1377–1391.

Draper, Stephen E. "Governmental Immunity from Liability in Flood Control Operations." *Proceedings of the Eighteenth Annual Conference and Symposium on Water Resources Planning and Management and Urban Water Resources, New Orleans, LA,* 1991, pp. 511–516.

"Federal Flood Bill Passes by Senate." *Eastern Underwriter* 57 (May 18, 1956): 22+.

"Flood Insurance: Can It Work?" *Business Week* (June 14, 1952): 134–136.

Foster, H. A. "Flood Insurance." *American Society of Civil Engineers Proceedings* 80 (August 1954): 1–35.

Hunter, J. Robert. "Flood Insurance: A Growth Story [United States]." *Water Spectrum (Corps of Engineers)* 9 (Spring 1977): 37–43.

"Kansas City Grain Loss in 1951 Due to Flood, Not Explosion: Federal Court Rules for Insurers." *Eastern Underwriter* 54 (November 6, 1953): 1.

Langbein, W. B. "Flood Insurance." *Land Economics* 29 (November 1953): 323–330.

Lulott, A. E., and Kenneth P. Wilkinson. "Participation in the National Flood Insurance Program: A Study of Community Activeness [Pennsylvania]." *Rural Sociology* 44 (Spring 1979): 137–152.

Maloney, Frank E., and Dennis C. Dambly. "The National Flood Insurance Program: A Model Ordinance for Implementation of Its Land Management Criteria." *Natural Resources Journal* 16 (July 1976): 665–736.

McManamy, R. "Great Lakes Settles Claim Over Flood and Keeps Growing [Great Lakes Dredge & Dock Co.]" *Engineering News-Record* 236 (June 3, 1996): 20.

Millemann, Beth. "The National Flood Insurance Program." *Oceanus* 36 (Spring 1993): 6–8.

Millemann, Beth, and Elise Jones. "Improving the National Flood Insurance Program." *National Wetlands Newsletter* 12 (May-June 1990) 2–4.

O'Connell, John J. "National Flood Insurance: Arizona's Experience." *Arizona Business* 26 (April 1979): 19–24.

Platt, Rutherford H. "The National Flood Insurance Program: Some Midstream Perspectives." *Journal of the American Institute of Planners* 42 (July 1976): 303–313.

Power, Fred B., and E. Warren Shows. "A Status Report on the National Flood Insurance Program, Mid-1978." *Journal of Risk and Insurance* 46 (June 1979): 61–76.

Pritchett, S. Travis, and Harvey W. Rubin. "A Case Study of Flood Losses: Implications for Flood Insurance Product Development [Types and Amounts of Losses Which Were Incurred by Businesses in Richmond, VA, during the Agnes Food of June 1972]." *Journal of Risk and Insurance* 42 (March 1975): 105–116.

Rogers, Spencer M., Jr. "Flood Insurance Construction Standards: Can They Work on the Coast?" *Proceedings of the Seventh Symposium on Coastal and Ocean Management Part 2, Long Beach, CA,* 1991, pp. 1064–1078.

Rossmiller, R. "Planning Can Lower Flood Insurance Costs." *American City and County* 110 (March 1995): 15–16.

Seifert, R. E. "Insurance Men Now Doing Effective Relief Work in Kansas-Missouri Flood Area." *Weekly Underwriter* 165 (July 28, 1951): 188–189.

Shaw, Peter H. "Use of Remote Sensing and G.I.S. in the Economic Analyses of Flood Damage Reduction." *Proceedings of the Seventeenth Annual National Conference on Optimizing the Resources for Water Management, Forth Worth, TX,* 1990, pp. 213–218.

Stossel, J. "Ocean View, Thanks to You [National Flood Insurance Program]." *Reader's Digest* 148 (January 1996): 181–182.

Tsai, Frank Y., and Joseph H. Coughlin. "Coastal Barrier Resources Act and the National Flood Insurance Program Six Years After." *Proceedings of the Sixth Symposium on Coastal and Ocean Management, Charleston, SC,* 1989, pp. 3430–3440.

"Underwriters Salvage Co. Reduced Greatly Kansas City Flood Losses." *Eastern Underwriter* 52 (August 31, 1951): 25.

U.S. Congress, House Committee on Banking, Finance, and Urban Affairs, Subcommittee on Consumer Credit and Insurance. *The Status of the National Flood Insurance Program: Hearing, June 24, 1993.* 103d Cong., 1st sess. Washington: GPO, 1994, 210 pp.

U.S. Congress, House Committee on Banking, Finance, and Urban Affairs, Subcommittee on Housing and Community Development. *Federal Flood Insurance, 1983: Hearing, September 15, 1983.* 98th Cong., 1st sess. Washington, DC: GPO, 1983, 83 pp.

———. *Oversight of the Federal Flood Insurance Programs: Hearings, September 7–8, 1977.* 95th Cong., 1st sess. Washington, DC: GPO, 1977, 506 pp.

U.S. Congress, House Committee on Banking, Finance, and Urban Affairs, Subcommittee on Policy Research and Insurance. *Coastal Erosion and Erosion Management: Hearing, July 13, 1990.* 101st Cong., 2d sess. Washington, DC: GPO, 1990, 626 pp.

———. *Flood Disaster Protection Act of 1973: Hearing, March 8, 1990.* 101st Cong., 2d sess. Washington, DC: GPO, 1990, 272 pp.

———. *Insurance Concepts and Funding Mechanisms: Hearing July 11, 1990.* 101st Cong., 2d sess. Washington, DC: GPO, 1990, 196 pp.

———. *National Flood Insurance Program: Hearing, May 3–31, 1989.* 101st Cong., 1st sess. Washington, DC: GPO, 1989, 801 pp.

U.S. Congress, Senate Committee on Governmental Affairs, Subcommittee on Governmental Efficiency and the District of Columbia. *National Flood Insurance Program: Hearings, April 11–November 19, 1977.* 95th Cong., 1st sess. Washington, DC: GPO, 1978, 598 pp.

Flood Plain

General

Bradley, A. Allen, and Kenneth W. Potter. "Estimating Floodplain Limits for Complicated Hydrologic and Hydraulic Conditions." *Proceedings of the Symposium on Engineering Hydrology, San Francisco, CA,* 1993, pp. 575–580.

Bradley, A. Allen, Paula J. Cooper, Kenneth W. Potter, and Thomas Price. "Floodplain Mapping Using Continuous Hydrologic and Hydraulic Simulation Models." *Journal of Hydraulic Engineering* 122 (April 1996): 63–68.

Cheang, C. Y., and P. B. Bedient. "PIBS Model for Surcharged Pipe Flow." *Journal of Hydraulic Engineering* 112 (March 1986): 181–192.

Christen, K. "Recent Floods Compel Harder Look at Floodplain Control Efforts." *Water Environment and Technology* 10 (July 1998): 28–29.

Cigler, Beverly A., et al. "Rural Community Responses to a National Mandate: An Assessment of Floodplain Land-Use Management." *Publius* 17 (Fall 1987): 113–130.

Crayford, Forrest J., Jr., Gregory W. Lowe, and Arland W. Whitlock. "Benefits from Floodplain Management Activities in Relation to Operating South Holston Dam." *Proceedings of the ASCE Seventeenth Annual National Conference on Optimizing the Resources for Water Management, Fort Worth, TX,* 1990, pp. 681–685.

Cunniff, Shannon E., and Gerald E. Galloway Jr. "Sharing the Challenge of Effective Floodplain Management." *Proceedings of the Twenty-second Annual Conference on Integrated Water Resources Planning for the Twenty-first Century, Cambridge, MA,* 1995, pp. 743–746.

Dagerty, D. J., et al. "Near-Bank Impacts of River Stage Control." *Journal of Hydraulic Engineering* 121 (February 1995): 196–207.

Ford, D. T., and A. Oto. "Floodplain Management Plan Enumeration." *Journal of Water Resources Planning and Management* 115 (July 1989): 472–485.

Ford, D. T., and J. R. Killen. "PC-Based Decision-Support System for Trinity River, Texas." *Journal of Water Resources Planning and Management* 121 (September-October 1995): 375–381.

Froehlich, D. C. "Peak Outflow from Breached Embankment Dam." *Journal of Water Resources Planning and Management* 121 (January-February 1995): 90–97; discussion, 122 (July-August 1996): 314–319.

Galloway, G. E. "New Directions in Floodplain Management." *Water Resources Bulletin* 31 (June 1995): 351–357.

Graf, J. B., et al. "Relation of Sediment Load and Flood Plain Formation to Climatic Variability, Paria River Drainage Basin, Utah and Arizona." *Geological Society of America Bulletin* 103 (November 1991): 1405–1415.

Grimm, M. "Floodplain Management." *Civil Engineering (American Society of Civil Engineers)* 68 (March 1998): 62–64.

Gross, L. J., and M. J. Small. "River and Floodplain Process Simulation for Subsurface Characterization." *Water Resources Research* 34 (September 1978): 2365–2376.

Hannan, T. C., and I. C. Goulter. "Model for Crop Allocation in Rural Floodplains." *Journal of Water Resources Planning and Management* 114 (January 1988): 1–19.

Hunt, B. "Perturbation Solution for Dam-Break Floods." *Journal of Hydraulic Engineering* 110 (August 1984): 1058–1071.

James, L. D., and B. Hall. "Risk Information for Floodplain Management." *Journal of Water Resources Planning and Management* 112 (October 1986): 485–499; discussion, 114 (January 1988): 120–123.

Kennelly, John R. "Nonstructural Flood Mitigation Projects in New England." *Proceedings of the Twenty-second Annual Conference on Integrated Water Resources Planning for the Twenty-first Century, Cambridge, MA,* 1995, pp. 751–754.

Knight, D. W., and J. D. Demetriou. "Flood Plain and Main Channel Flow Interaction [Discussion of 109 (August 1983): 1073–1092]." *Journal of Hydraulic Engineering* 111 (May 1985): 881–891; discussion, 112 (November 1986): 1097–1101.

Kouchakzadeh, S., and R. D. Townsend. "Maximum Scour Depth at Bridge Abutments Terminating in the Floodplain Zone." *Canadian Journal of Civil Engineering* 24 (December 1997): 996–1006.

Krishnappan, B. G., and Y. L. Lau. "Turbulence Modeling of

Flood Plain Flows." *Journal of Hydraulic Engineering* 112 (April 1986): 251–266.

Kusler, J., and L. Larson. "Beyond the Ark: A New Approach to U.S. Floodplain Management." *Environment* 36 (June 1993): 6–11+.

Lloyd, Glenn D., Jr. "Engineer-Economic Approach to Better Floodplain Usage." *Proceedings of the Twenty-second Annual Conference on Integrated Water Resources Planning for the Twenty-first Century, Cambridge, MA,* 1995, pp. 755–758.

Pasche, E., and G. Rouve. "Overbank Flow with Vegetatively Roughened Flood Plains." *Journal of Hydraulic Engineering* 111 (September 1985): 1262–1278; discussion, 113 (May 1987): 692–696.

Penning-Rowsell, E. C., et al. "Comparative Aspects of Computerized Floodplain Data Management." *Journal of Water Resources Planning and Management* 113 (November 1987): 725–744.

Ports, M. A., and C. Riling. "Tug Fork Flood Plain Modifications and Wetlands Mitigation." *Proceedings of the Twenty-first Annual Conference on Water Policy and Management: Solving the Problems, Denver, CO,* 1994, pp. 766–769.

Rahn, P. H. "Flood-Plain Management Program in Rapid City, South Dakota." *Geological Society of America Bulletin* 95 (July 1984): 838–843.

Rosenberg, Cecelia. "Floodplain Management for Alluvial Fan Areas." *Proceedings of the International Symposium on Hydraulics/Hydrology of Arid Lands and 1990 National Conference on Hydraulic Engineering, San Diego, CA,* July 30–August 2, 1990, pp. 20–24.

Schamber, D. R., and N. D. Katopodes. "One Dimensional Models for Partially Breached Dams." *Journal of Hydraulic Engineering* 110 (August 1984): 1086–1102.

Skipwith, Walter, Laura Morland, Michael Denton, and Mike Askew. "Advances in Flood Plain Management Techniques." *Sixth Conference on Computing in Civil Engineering, New York.* 1989, pp. 346–352.

Skipwith, Walter, et al. "Closing the Floodgates [Floodplain Management Techniques]." *Civil Engineering (American Society of Civil Engineers)* 60 (July 1990): 54–55.

Soltys, P. W. "Floodplain Management." *Public Works* 125 (October 1994): 51–53+.

Sparks, R. E. "Need for Ecosystem Management of Large Rivers and Their Floodplains." *BioScience* 45 (March 1995): 168–182.

Stevens, E. W. "Multilevel Model for Gage and Paleoflood Data." *Journal of Water Resources Planning and Management* 120 (July-August 1994): 444–457.

Swenson, S. "Squalicum Creek Floodplain Management Plan." *Public Works* 123 (June 1992): 68–69.

Thomas, W. O., Jr. "A Uniform Technique for Flood Frequency Analysis." *Journal of Water Resources Planning and Management* 111 (July 1985): 321–337.

Tingsanchali, T., and S. K. Manandhar. "Analytical Diffusion Model for Flood Routing." *Journal of Hydraulic Engineering* 111 (March 1985): 435–454.

U.S. Congress, Senate Committee on Environment and Public Works. *Floodplain Management and Flood Control: Hearings, May 26 and July 20, 1994.* 103d Cong., 2d sess. Washington: GPO, 1994, 205 pp.

Vogel, R. M., and J. R. Stedinger. "Flood-Plain Delineation in Ice Jam Prone Regions." *Journal of Water Resources Planning and Management* 110 (April 1984): 206–219; discussion, 112 (October 1986): 565–567.

Waugh, Peter D., Leo Eisel, and Mark R. Bonner. "Flood Control and Floodplain Planning for the Havasupai Indian Reservation." *Proceedings of the Twenty-second Annual Conference on Integrated Water Resources Planning for the Twenty-first Century, Cambridge, MA*, 1995, pp. 763–766.

Wilkerson, Worth. "Getting Away from Floods: Unusual Plan to Purchase Homes and Relocate Families Offers Only Hope for Those Most Vulnerable in Three Towns in Virginia and Tennessee." *Tennessee Valley Perspective* 8 (Fall 1977): 4–9.

Wood, A., R. Palmer, and C. Petroff. "Comparison and Assessment of Zero-Rise Floodplain Ordinances." *Journal of Water Resources Planning and Management* 123 (July-August 1997): 239–245.

Yeh, C.-H. "Floods Prove Need for Project." *Engineering News-Record* 241 (October 26, 1998): 99; discussion, 242 (January 18, 1999): 5–6.

Alluvial Fans

Faltas, Muna E. "Evaluating Flood Hazards on Alluvial Fans." *Proceedings of the National Conference on Hydraulic Engineering, Colorado Springs, CO*, 1988, pp. 161–166.

Flippin, S. J., and R. H. French. "Comparison of Results from Alluvial Fan Design Methodology with Historical Data." *Journal of Irrigation and Drainage Engineering* 120 (January-

February 1994): 195–210; discussion, 121 (March-April 1995): 228–231.

French, R. H. "Preferred Directions of Flow on Alluvial Fans." *Journal of Hydraulic Engineering* 118 (July 1992): 1002–1013; discussion, 119 (November 1993): 1313–1323.

French, R. H., et al. "Alluvial Fan: Proposed New Process-Oriented Definitions for Arid Southwest." *Journal of Water Resources Planning and Management* 119 (September-October 1993): 588–598; discussion, 122 (May-June 1996): 229–231.

Grindeland, Thomas R., J. S. O'Brien, and Ruh-Ming Li. "Flood Hazard Delineation on Alluvial Fans." *Proceedings of the International Symposium on Hydraulics/Hydrology of Arid Lands and the National Conference on Hydraulic Engineering, San Diego, CA,* 1990, pp. 268–273.

Kouchakzadeh, S., and R. D. Townsend. "Maximum Scour Depth at Bridge Abutments Terminating in the Floodplain Zone." *Canadian Journal of Civil Engineering* 24 (December 1997): 996–1006.

Mertes, L. A. K. "Documentation and Significance of the Perirheic Zone on Inundated Floodplains." *Water Resources Research* 33 (July 1997): 1749–1762.

Rupprecht, C. F. "Disaster: Relief Work of the American Red Cross." *Spectator (Life ed.)* 153 (November 1945): 56–63+.

Schell, James D., Douglas W. Bender, and Frank J. Peairs. "Flood Control Improvements on Alluvial Fans." *Proceedings of the International Symposium on Hydraulics/Hydrology of Arid Lands and 1990 National Conference on Hydraulic Engineering, San Diego, CA,* 1990, pp. 165–170.

Seindel, G. E. "Tiered Training Approach to Swift-Water Rescue." *Fire Engineering* 147 (March 1994): 104+.

Mitigation Benefits

DeVera, Maximo R. "Flooding Problems Mitigation in Metropolitan Phoenix." *Proceedings of the Twenty-fourth Annual Water Resources Planning and Management Conference, Houston, TX,* 1997: 309–314 pp.

Isiminger, George F., and John S. Yeend. "Benefits of Flood Hazard Mitigation at Ports." *Conference on Port Engineering and Development for the Twenty-first Century, Part 1, Tampa, FL,* 1995: pp. 161–165.

Laska, Shirley Bradway. "Involving Homeowners in Flood Mitigation." *Journal of the American Planning Association* 52 (Autumn 1986): 42–66.

"Maps Mitigate Cincinnati Flood Damage." *Public Works* 129 (March 1998): 50.

Stallings, Eugene A. "Benefits and Costs Associated with Flood Mitigation in the United States." *Proceedings of the 1996 Conference on National Disaster Reduction, Washington, DC,* 1996, pp. 153–154.

Federal Government

Clinton, William J. "Remarks, Announcing Federal Flood Relief for Georgia, Alabama, and Florida in Albany, Georgia, July 13, 1994." *Weekly Compilation of Presidential Documents* 30 (July 18, 1994): 1474–1476.

"Corps Moves Quickly on Emergency Repairs." *Engineering News-Record* 224 (April 5, 1990): 25.

"Corps Studies Calif. Flooding." *Engineering News-Record* 217 (December 4, 1986): 13–14.

"Flood Control Project Ended by Controversy." *Engineering News-Record* 223 (July 5, 1989): 13.

Ichniowski, T., and A. Rose. "Wave of Relief Funds Hit Flood-Damaged Plain States." *Engineering News-Record* 238 (June 23, 1997): 9–10.

Koski, J. A. "U.S. Army Corps of Engineers: New Orleans District." *Aberdeen's Concrete Construction* 39 (January 1994): 33–34+.

McManamy, R. "Corps [of Engineers] Finds Itself in Middle of a Heated Policy Debate." *Engineering News-Record* 231 (July 26, 1993): 14–15.

Morland Laura, Rajindra Juyal, Terry Hampton, and Jerrold W. Gotzmer. "Using Tropical Storm Alberto to Evaluate FERC [Federal Energy Regulatory Commission] Guidelines on Probable Maximum Flood Development." *Proceedings of the International Conference on Horsepower, Part 2, Atlanta, GA,* 1997, pp. 824–833.

New Jersey General Assembly, Independent and Regional Authorities Committee. *Public Hearing: A Record of Testimony on Assembly Bills 2047, 2048, and 2750 (Flood Control Bills): Wayne, New Jersey, May 26, 1987, Trenton NJ,* 1987, 98 pp.

Philippi, N. "Plugging the Gaps in Flood-Control Policy." *Issues in Science and Technology* 11 (Winter 1994–1995): 71–78.

"Planning Bucks Opposition (Passaic River Basin Flood Tunnel)." *Engineering News-Record* 232 (March 21, 1994): 12.

Purves, Amy J., Peter L. Croswell, and Timothy W. Foresman.

"Regional Flood Control District GIS Applications." *Second National Specialty Conference on Civil Engineering Applications of Remote Sensing and Geographic Information Systems, Washington, DC, May 14–16, 1991*. 1991, pp. 328–335.

Riley, A. L. "Overcoming Federal Water Policies: The Wildcat–San Pablo Creek Case." *Environment* 31 (December 1989): 12–20+.

Sanders, Johnny G. "Yazoo River Basin: A New Direction for the Corps." *ASCE National Convention, Orlando, FL*, 1991, pp. 59–66.

Setzer, S. W., and P. Kemerzis. "Two States Accuse the Corps of Environmental Degradation." *Engineering News-Record* 222 (March 30, 1989): 10–11.

Simons, Daryl B., and Robert K. Simons. "Reducing the Potential for Flood Litigation." *Proceedings of the National Conference on Hydraulic Engineering, New Orleans, LA*, 1989, pp. 58–63.

Wolman, A. "Problems in Developing a National Flood-Protection Policy." *American Society of Civil Engineers Proceedings* 63 (March 1937): 429–439.

Environmental Impact—Human Reaction

Adler, T. "Healing Waters [Deliberate Flooding of Grand Canyon to Restore Damage Done by Dam: Cover Story]." *Science News* 150 (September 21, 1996): 188–189.

Ainsworth, S. "Houston Area Floods: Shutdowns Vex Tight Chemical Markets." *Chemical and Engineering News* 72 (October 31, 1994): 3–4.

Aldridge, B. N. "Effects of Vegetation on Floods at Four Arizona States." *Proceedings of the National Conference on Hydraulic Engineering, New Orleans, LA*, 1989, pp. 392–397.

Atwater, B. F. "Periodic Floods from Glacial Lake Missoula into the Sanpoie Arm of Glacial Lake Columbia, Northeastern Washington." *Geology* 12 (August 1984): 464–467.

Bailey, J. "Emergency Work at Earthquake Site Prevented Flood Disaster." *Civil Engineering* 29 (October 1959): 751–752.

Baker, B. "Water, Everywhere—and Not a Drop to Drink." *Journal of Environmental Health* 56 (November 1993): 25–27.

Barber, L. B., and J. H. Writer. "Impact of the 1993 Flood on the Distribution of Organic Contaminants in Bad Sediments of the Upper Mississippi River." *Environmental Science and Technology* 32 (July 15, 1998): 2077–2083.

Bonan, G. B., and L. M. Stillwell-Soller. "Soil Water and the Persistence of Floods and Droughts in the Mississippi River Basin." *Water Resources Research* 34 (October 1998): 2693–2701.

Bradley, A. A., and J. A. Smith. "The Hydrometeorological Environment of Extreme Rainstorms in the Southeastern Plains of the United States." *Journal of Applied Meteorology* 33 (December 1994): 1418–1431.

Brannan, R. W. "Drainage Problems in an Area Changing from Rural to Urban: Lucas County, Ohio." *Public Works* 93 (October 1962): 130–131.

Carter, R. H., Jr. "Control of Arroyo Floods at Albuquerque, N.M." *American Society of Civil Engineers Proceedings* 81 (September 1955): 1–8.

Collier, C. A., and J. R. Williams Jr. "Optimum Floor Elevation in Storm Tide Flood Zones." *Journal of Waterway, Port, Coastal, and Ocean Engineering* 109 (February 1983): 41–53.

Collier, M. P., et al. "Experimental Flooding in Grand Canyon." *Scientific American* 276 (January 1997): 82–89.

Collins, J. "Environmental Health Effects of the Red River Flood of 1997." *Journal of Environmental Health* 60 (September 1997): 17–22.

"Conservation Group Urges Flood-Control Reform." *Civil Engineering (American Society of Civil Engineers)* 64 (September 1994): 18.

"Control of Aquatic Vegetation Aids Flood Control Efforts." *Public Works* 122 (June 1991): 60–61.

Creisler, J. "Three-Phase Sanitation Program in the Klamath Flood Disaster." *Public Health Reports* 72 (September 1957): 801–808.

Darby, S. E., and C. R. Thorne. "Predicting Stage-Discharge Curves in Channels with Bank Vegetation." *Journal of Hydraulic Engineering* 122 (October 1996): 83–86.

Eden, E. W., Jr. "Floods of the Florida Everglades." *American Society of Civil Engineers Proceedings* 85 (June 1959): 43–59; discussion, 85 (December 1959): 121–123; 86 (January 1960): 95–97.

Ely, Lisa L., and Victor R. Baker. "Large Floods and Climate Change in the Southwestern United States." *Proceedings of the International Symposium on Hydraulic/Hydrology of Arid lands and the National Conference on Hydraulic Engineering, San Diego, CA,* 1990, pp. 361–366.

Fischenich, J. Craig, E. A. Dardeau, and Kenneth D. Parrish. "Use of Flood Control Features for Environmental Mitigation." *Proceedings of the Twentieth Anniversary Conference on Water Management in the '90s, Seattle, WA,* 1993, pp. 101–104.

"Flooded Substations Need Re-engineering." *Electrical World* 208 (April 1994): 68+.

Gomez, B., et al. "Sediment Characteristics of an Extreme Flood: 1993 Upper Mississippi River Valley." *Geology* 23 (November 1995): 963–966.

Greising, David, and Julia Flynn. "My Kind of Town Chicago Is: The City's Freak Flood Points Up the Need to Fix Aging Infrastructures." *Business Week* (April 27, 1992): 42.

Hall, R. D. "Flood Recovery in the Wyoming Buried Valley to Displace Many Billion Gallons." *Coal Age* 41 (September 1936): 355–360.

Herndon, L. W. "Drainage in the Mississippi River Valley." *American Society of Civil Engineers Proceedings* 83 (September 1957): 1–11; discussion, 84 (September 1958): 11–15; reply, 15–16.

Huber, Thomas P., and Eve C. Gruntfest. "Flood and Avalanche Hazard in Colorado: Political Implications of the New Federalism." *Environmental Management* 7 (November 1983): 505–510.

Jacques, J. E., and D. L. Lorenz. *Techniques for Estimating the Magnitude and Frequency of Floods in Minnesota.* Denver, CO: U.S. Geological Survey, 1988, 48 pp.

Jarrett, Robert D. "Flood Elevation Limits in the Rocky Mountains." *Proceedings of the Symposium on Engineering Hydrology, San Francisco, CA,* 1993, pp. 180–185.

Klimas, Charles V. "Anticipating Critical Impacts on Floodplain Ecosystems Resulting from Water Level Regulation." *Bulletin of the Permanent International Association of Navigation Congresses* 57 (1987): 29–33.

LeBlanc, R. D. "Terror in Village Creek [J. Lemons and C. Jackson Trapped in Flash Flood, Texas]." *Reader's Digest* 136 (February 1990): 134–139.

Li, Y., et al. "Sand Boils Induced by the 1993 Mississippi River Flood: Could They One Day Be Misinterpreted as Earthquake-Induced Liquefaction?" *Geology* 24 (February 1996): 171–174.

Magilligan, F. J., et al. "Geomorphic and Sedimentological Controls on the Effectiveness of an Extreme Flood." *Journal of Geology* 106 (January 1998): 87–95.

McCutchen, H. E., Raymond Herrmann, and David L. Stevens. *Ecological Effects of the Lawn Lake Flood of 1982, Rocky Mountain National Park.* Washington, DC: U.S. Department of the Interior, National Park Service, 1993, 214 pp.

McMullen, L. D. "Surviving the Flood: Teamwork Pays Off in

Des Moines." *Journal of the American Water Works Association* 86 (January 1994): 68–72.

Michelmore, P. "The Night the Creeks Ran Wild [Ohio]." *Reader's Digest* 138 (January 1991): 69–74.

Mick, G. E. "Boulder Creek: An Environmental Status Report." *American Society of Civil Engineers Proceedings* 100 (March 1974): 1–6.

Miller, A. J. "Fluvial Response to Debris Associated with Mass Wasting during Extreme Floods." *Geology* 18 (July 1990): 599–602.

Molloy, John J. *Flood Discharge Records Relating to Pennsylvania Streams.* Harrisburg, PA: Pennsylvania Department of Forests and Waters, Division of Hydrography, 1960, 62 pp.

Mussetter, R. A., P. F. Lagasse, and M. D. Harvey. "Procedures for Evaluating the Effects of Sedimentation on Flood Hazards in Urbanized Areas in Southwestern U.S." *Proceedings of the Twenty-first Annual Conference on Water Policy and Management: Solving the Problems, Denver, CO,* 1994, pp. 425–428.

Naghavi, B., and Yu, F. X. "Selection of Parameter-Estimation Method for LP3 Distribution." *Journal of Irrigation and Drainage Engineering* 122 (February 1996): 24–30.

O'Connor, Jim E. *Hydrology, Hydraulics, and Geomorphology of the Bonneville Flood.* Series: Special Papers (Geological Society of America) No. 274. Boulder, CO: Geological Society of America: 1993, 83 pp.

O'Connor, Jim E., and V. R. Baker. "Magnitudes and Implications of Pest Discharges from Glacial Lake Missoula." *Geological Society of America Bulletin* 104 (March 1992): 267–279.

O'Connor, Jim E., et al. "Paleohydrology of Pool-and-Rifle Pattern Development: Boulder Creek, Utah." *Geological Society of America Bulletin* 97 (April 1986): 410–420.

Pearce, M., et al. "Long-Term Monitoring of Mold Contamination in Flooded Homes." *Journal of Environmental Health* 58 (October 1995): 6–11.

Petty, J. D., et al. "Determination of Bioavailable Contaminants in the Lower Missouri River Following the Flood of 1993." *Environmental Science and Technology* 32 (April 1, 1998): 837–842.

Phillips, J. V., and H. W. Hjalmarson. "Floodflow Effects on Riparian Vegetation in Arizona." *Proceedings of the ASCE National Conference on Hydraulic Engineering, Buffalo, NY,* 1994, pp. 707–711.

Pitlick, J. "Response and Recovery of a Subalpine Stream Following a Catastrophic Flood." *Geological Society of America Bulletin* 105 (May 1993): 657–670.

Poirot, Paul L. "Flood Relief [Critical of Government Programs: United States]." *Freeman* 22 (October 1972): 591–594.

Ponce, V. M., et al. "Large Basin Deterministic Hydrology: A Case Study." *Journal of Hydraulic Engineering* 111 (September 1985): 1227–1245; discussion, 113 (November 1987): 1461–1471.

Powers, M. B. "Northeast Suffers Heavy Flooding." *Engineering News-Record* 236 (January 29, 1996): 11–12.

Powledge, G. R., et al. "Mechanics of Overflow Erosion on Embankments." *Journal of Hydraulic Engineering* 115 (August 1989): 1040–1075.

"Prompt Action Turns Back Mosquito Infestation." *Public Works* 109 (March 1978): 66.

"Raw Sewage Flowed into Homes, Schools, and Businesses [Flooding in Bartlesville, Oklahoma]." *Public Works* 118 (October 1987): 56–57.

Ray, C., et al. "Agricultural Chemicals: Effects on Wells during Floods." *American Water Works Association Journal* 90 (July 1998): 90–100+.

Reel, D. V., and L. S. Bond. "Flooding in the Desert: Taking Control." *Public Works* 119 (December 1988): 29–30+.

"Resources Development with Diesels: Control and Southern Florida's Comprehensive Water Control Project." *Diesel Power* 33 (May 1955): 38–41.

Riggle, D. "Biosolids Benefit Agricultural Land." *Biocycle* 37 (March 1996): 76–79.

Rogers, R. "Wastewater Facility Stands Up to California Floods in Napa Valley." *Water/Engineering and Management* 143 (August 1996): 25–26.

———. "Wastewater Plan Withstands Severe Floods in Napa Valley." *In Tech* 43 (June 1996): 19–20.

Roy, W. R., et al. "Off-Site Movement of Pesticide-Contaminated Fill from Agrichemical Facilities during the 1993 Flooding in Illinois." *Journal of Environmental Quality* 24 (September-October 1995): 1034–1038.

Rubin, D. M., et al. "Relation of Inversely Graded Deposits to Suspended-Sediment Grain-Size Evolution during the 1996 Flood Experiment in Grand Canyon." *Geology* 26 (February 1998): 99–102.

Schmeltzer, J. S., J. J. Miller, and D. L. Gustafson. "Flood Assessment of a Low-Level Radioactive Waste Site in Southern

Nevada." *Proceedings of the Symposium on Engineering Hydrology, San Francisco, CA,* 1993, pp. 282–287.

Schnabel, R. R., and W. L. Stout. "Denitrification Loss from Two Pennsylvania Floodplain Soils." *Journal of Environmental Quality* 23 (March-April 1994): 344–348.

Schwarz, H. E., and L. A. Dillard. "The Impact on Water Supplies [Greenhouse Effect]." *Oceanus* 32 (Summer 1989): 44–45.

Slosson, J. E., et al. "Harrison Canyon Debris Flows of 1980." *Environmental Geology and Water Sciences* 18 (July-August 1991): 27–38.

Smith, G. A. "Missoula Flood Dynamics and Magnitudes Inferred from Sedimentology of Slack-Water Deposits on the Columbia Plateau, Washington." *Geological Society of America Bulletin* 105 (January 1993): 77–100.

Smith, W. S., and D. Klingelhofer. "City Averts Economic Disaster." *Public Works* 127 (October 1996): 51–52.

"Southern Community Fights Flooding Erosion." *American City and County* 104 (August 1989): 24.

Traherne, D. "Coastline Conservation." *Civil Engineering (American Society of Civil Engineers)* 56 (November-December 1986): 37–38.

U.S. Congress, House Committee on Public Works and Transportation, Subcommittee on Water Resources. *Flooding Problems—State of Arizona: Hearings, June 1 and 2, 1979.* 96th Cong., 1st sess. Washington, DC: GPO, 1979, 380 pp.

Wheatcroft, R. A., et al. "Rapid and Widespread Dispersal of Flood Sediment on the Northern California Margin." *Geology* 25 (February 1997): 163–166.

Williams, S. H., and J. R. Zimbelman. "Desert Pavement Evolution: An Example of the Role of Sheetflood." *Journal of Geology* 102 (March 1994): 243–248.

Wootton, J. T., et al. "Effects of Disturbance on River Flood Webs." *Science* 273 (September 13, 1996): 1558–1561.

Wright, A. G. "A Last-Ditch Attempt to Save the Everglades." *Engineering News-Record* 240 (June 8, 1998): 36–37+.

Wuethrich, B. "Deliberate Flood Renews Habitats." *Science* 272 (April 19, 1996): 344–345.

Physical

Weather and Climate

Aleshire, P. "Deluge in the Desert." *Arizona Highways* 70 (March 1994): 22–33.

Ball, G. D., and M. S. Halpert. "Climate Assessment for 1997." *Bulletin of the American Meteorological Society* 79 (May 1998): S1–S50.

Bosart, L. F. "The Texas Coastal Rainstorm of September 1979: An Example of Synoptic-Mesoscale Interaction." *Monthly Weather Review* 112 (June 1984): 1108–1133.

Bradley, A. A., and J. A. Smith. "The Hydrometeorological Environment of Extreme Rainstorms in the Southern Plains of the United States." *Journal of Applied Meteorology* 33 (December 1994): 1418–1431.

Brownlee, Shannon, and Laura Tangley. "The Wrath of El Niño." *U.S. News & World Report* 123 (October 6, 1997): 16–22.

Burn, Donald H. "Stage Distribution Approach to Estimating Ice-related Flooding Probabilities." *Water Resources Bulletin* 25 (October 1989): 953–960.

Christensen, B. A., T. Y. Chiu, and John C. Dorman. "Friction Factors in Coastal Flooding." *Proceedings of the Symposium on Engineering Hydrology, San Francisco, CA,* 1993, pp. 228–233.

Churchill, D. D., et al. "The Daytona Beach Wave of 3–4 July 1992: A Shallow-Water Gravity Wave Forced by a Propagating Squall Line." *Bulletin of the American Meteorological Society* 76 (January 1995): 21–32.

Coghlan, A. "Wet, Wet, Dry . . . [Floating Doorstops Can Save Homes]." *New Scientist* 155 (August 9, 1997): 8.

Dickson, R. R. "Weather and Circulation of February 1980: California Floods." *Monthly Weather Review* 108 (May 1980): 679–684.

Duckstein, Lucien, Andras Bardassy, and Istvan Bogardi. "Linkage between the Occurrence of Daily Atmospheric Circulation Patterns and Floods: An Arizona Case Study." *Journal of Hydrology* 143 (March 15, 1993): 413–428.

Ely, L. L., et al. "A 5,000-Year Record of Extreme Floods and Climate Change in the Southwestern United States." *Science* (October 15, 1993): 410–412.

Fontaine, Thomas A. "Rainfall-Runoff Model Accuracy for an Extreme Flood." *Journal of Hydraulic Engineering* 121 (April 1995): 365–374.

Georgakakos, A. P., et al. "Impacts of Climate Variability on the Operational Forecast and Management of the Upper Des Moines River Basin." *Water Resources Research* 34 (April 1998): 799–821.

Guetter, A. K., and K. P. Georgakakos. "Are the El Niño and La Niña Predictors of the Iowa River Seasonal Flow?" *Journal of Applied Meteorology* 35 (May 1996): 690–705.

Gutowski, William J., George F. McMahon, Shing S. Schluchter, and Paul H. Kirshen. "Effects of Global Warming on Hurricane-Induced Flooding." *Journal of Water Resources Planning and Management* 120 (March-April 1994): 176–185.

———. "Projecting Climate Change to Small Basins: Potential Impact of Global Warming on Hurricane-Induced Flooding in South Florida." *Proceedings of Water Resources Planning and Management and Urban Water Resources Conference and Symposium, New Orleans, LA,* 1991, pp. 705–713.

Guttman, N. B., et al. "The 1993 Midwest Extreme Precipitation in Historical and Probabilistic Perspective." *Bulletin of the American Meteorological Society* 75 (October 1994): 1785–1792.

Kunkel, K. E., et al. "Climatic Aspects of the 1993 Upper Mississippi River Basin Flood." *Bulletin of the American Meteorological Society* 75 (May 1994): 811–822.

Lott, Neal, and Tom Ross. *1994 Weather in the Southeast: The February Ice Storm and the July Flooding.* Asheville, NC: National Climatic Data Center, Research Customer Service Group, 1994, 20 leaves. Microfiche.

Mazion, E., Jr., and B. C. Yen. "Computational Discretization Effect on Rainfall-Runoff Simulation." *Journal of Water Resources Planning and Management* 120 (September-October 1994): 715–734.

Moss, J. H., and R. C. Kochel. "Unexpected Geomorphic Effects of the Hurricane Agnes storm, Conestoga Drainage Basin, Southeastern Pennsylvania." *Journal of Geology* 86 (January 1978): 1–11.

Odom, L. M. "Atchafalaya Diversion and Its Effect on the Mississippi River." *American Society of Civil Engineers Proceedings* 76 (March 1950): 1–24; discussion, 76 (December 1950): 1–21.

Paegle, J., et al. "Dependence of Simulated Precipitation on Surface Evaporation during the 1993 United States Summer Floods." *Monthly Weather Review* 124 (March 1996): 345–361.

Pandit, A., and G. Gapalakrishman. "Estimation of Annual Storm Runoff Coefficient by Continuous Simulation." *Journal of Irrigation and Drainage Engineering* 122 (July-August 1996): 211–220.

Philander, S. G. "El Niño." *Oceanus* 35 (Summer 1992): 56–61.

Polyak, I., et al. "Multivariate Space-Time Analysis of PRE-STORM Precipitation." *Journal of Applied Meteorology* 33 (September 1994): 1079–1087.

Raymond, W. H., et al. "Evidence of an Agricultural Heat Island in the Lower Mississippi River Floodplains." *Bulletin of the American Meteorological Society.* 75 (June 1994): 1019–1025.

Schroeder, T. A. "Meteorological Analysis of an Oahu Flood." *Monthly Weather Review* 105 (April 1977): 458–468.

Seymour, R. "Wave Climate Variability in Southern California." *Journal of Waterway, Port, Coastal, and Ocean Engineering* 122 (July-August 1996): 182–186.

Shalaby, A. I. "Sensitivity to Probable Maximum Flood." *Journal of Irrigation and Drainage Engineering* 121 (September-October 1995): 327–337.

Subramanian, C., and S. Kerpedjiev. "Dissemination of Weather Information to Emergency Managers: A Decision Support Tool." *IEEE Transactions Engineering Management* 45 (May 1998): 106–114.

Wave and Tide Actions

Adams, W. M. "Conditional Expected Tsunami Inundation for Hawaii." *American Society of Civil Engineers Proceedings* 101 (November 1975): 319–329.

Chesapeake Bay Tidal Flooding Study: Main Report. Baltimore: U.S. Army Corps of Engineers, Baltimore District, 1984, 74 pp.

Dendrou, S. A., et al. "Application of Storm Surge Modeling to Coastal Flood Rate Determinations." *Marine Technology Society Journal* 19 (1985): 42–50.

El-Jabi, N., et al. "Stage Discharge Relationship in Tidal Rivers." *Journal of Waterway, Port, Coastal, and Ocean Engineering* 118 (March-April 1992): 166–174.

Green, M. O. "Wave-Height Distribution in Storm Sea: Effect of Wave Breaking." *Journal of Waterway, Port, Coastal, and Ocean Engineering* 120 (May-June 1994): 283–301.

Hall, C. L. "1938 Hurricane and Its Effect on Long Island Beach-Protection Structure." *Civil Engineering American Society of Engineers* 9 (March 1939): 169–172.

Heilberg, E. R. "A Corps Chief Looks at *Rising Tide.*" *Civil Engineering (American Society of Civil Engineers)* 69 (February 1998): 54–56.

Hertzberg, R. "Wave-Wash Control on Mississippi River Levees." *American Society of Civil Engineers Proceedings* 79 (September 1953): 1–12.

Hjalmarson, H. W., and J. V. Phillips. "Potential Effects of Translating Waves on Estimation of Peak Flows." *Journal of Hydraulic Engineering* 123 (June 1997): 571–575.

Reeve, D. E. "Coastal Flood Risk Assessment." *Journal of Waterway, Port, Coastal, and Ocean Engineering* 124 (September-October 1998): 219–228.

Smith, O. P. "Duration of Extreme Wave Conditions." *Journal of Waterway, Port, Coastal, and Ocean Engineering* 114 (January 1988): 1–17.

Tsai, Y. J., and Kevin Merli. "Overview of New England Coastal Flood Study Methodology." *Proceedings of the National Conference on Hydraulic Engineering, Colorado Springs, CO,* 1988, pp. 300–305.

Vongvisessomjai, S., and S. Rojanakamthorn. "Interaction of Tide and River Flow." *Journal of Waterway, Port, Coastal, and Ocean Engineering* 115 (January 1989): 86–104; discussion, 117 (January-February 1991): 82–84.

Westerink, J. J., et al. "Tide and Storm Surge Predictions Using Finite Element Model." *Journal of Hydraulic Engineering* 118 (October 1992): 1373–1390.

Zhang, Q., and J. N. Suhayda. "Behavior of Marine Sediment under Storm Wave-Loading." *Marine Georesources and Geotechnology* 12 (July-September 1994): 259–269.

Hurricanes

Hale, Timothy W., and Timothy C. Stamey. "Flooding in Southeastern United States from Tropical Storm Alberto, July 1994." *Proceedings of the First International Conference on Water Resources, Part 1, San Antonio, TX,* 1995, pp. 765–769.

Leavenworth, Geoffrey. "The Barrier Island Gamble: Is Galveston a Catastrophe Waiting to Happen?" *Insurance Review* 47 (September 1986): 40–50.

Mayer, E. "Agnes and the Artist." *Weatherwise* 44 (June 1991): 34–35.

Miller, Christopher, and Geraldine Bachman. "Planning for Hurricanes and Other Coastal Disturbances." *Urban Land* 43 (January 1984): 18–23.

Platt, Rutherford H. "Evolution of Coastal Hazards Policies in the United States." *Coastal Management* 22 (July-September 1994): 265–284.

U.S. Congress, House Committee on Banking, Finance, and Urban Affairs, Subcommittee on Policy Research and Insurance. *Aftermath of Hurricane Agnes: Field Hearing, June 22, 1990.* 101st Cong., 2d sess. Washington, DC: GPO, 1990, 224 pp.

Regional Floods

New England

General

"Flood Waters Force Closing of New England Mills." *Paper Trade Journal* 136 (April 3, 1953): 11–12.

Mayott, C. W. "New England Flood Control Story." *Edison Electric Institute Bulletin* 24 (February 1956): 50–52+.

McAleer, J. B., and G. E. Townsend. "Hurricane Protection Planning in New England." *American Society of Civil Engineers Proceedings* 84 (August 1958): 1–36.

McDonald, C. C. "Flood of June 16–18, 1943, in the Upper Connecticut River Basin." *Journal of the Boston Society of Civil Engineers* 30 (October 1943): 238–262.

———. "New Hampshire Flood on June 14–15, 1942." *Journal of the Boston Society of Civil Engineers* 30 (January 1943): 1–22.

Merrill, G. F. "Lessons from Floods and Hurricanes at Ware, Mass." *New England Water Works Association Journal* 54 (June 1940): 186–190.

"New England Flood Damage Production Losses." *Rubber World* 132 (September 1955): 772–773.

"No More Floods for Fitchburg: Channel Improvements on North Nashua River." *Engineering News-Record* 119 (October 7, 1937): 589–593.

Robinson, K., and K. L. Tanaka. "Magnitude of a Catastrophic Flood Event at Kasei Valley, Mass." *Geology* 18 (September 1990): 902–905.

New England Flood 1936

"Agencies Collecting and Compiling 1936 Flood Data in New England." *Boston Society of Civil Engineers Journal* 23 (April 1936): 111–114.

Barrows, H. K., M. J. Young, and H. J. Casey. "Flood Control in New England: Outlining Recommendations of Water Resources Committee and U.S. Engineer Corps, with Cost Data." *Civil Engineering* 7 (November 1937): 740–754.

Cleary, E. J. "Mopping Up after the New England Floods." *Engineering News-Record* 116 (April 16, 1936): 566–571.

Collins, R. F., and M. Schalk. "Torrential Flood Erosion in the Connecticut Valley, March 1936." *American Journal of Science 5th Series* 34 (October 1937): 293–307.

Eddy, H. P., Jr. "New England Floods of 1936." *Civil Engineering* 6 (May 1936): 301–305.

"Engineering Reports on Record Floods from New England to the Potomac." *Engineering News-Record* 116 (March 26-April 2, 1936): 441–446+, 495–498.

"Floods of March 1936: New England Rivers." *U.S. Geological Survey Water Supply Paper* 798 (1937): 1–466.

High Water Data, Floods of March 1936 and September 1938 in Massachusetts. Boston: Massachusetts Geodetic Survey, 1939, 163 pp.

Holmgren, R. S. "March, 1936, Floods in New England: Merrimack River Dams." *Boston Society of Civil Engineers Journal* 23 (October 1936): 303–308.

Nelson, H. M. "March, 1936, Floods in New England: Some Experiences in the New England Power Association Territory during the Flood of 1936." *Boston Society of Civil Engineers Journal* 23 (October 1936): 308–313.

Safford, A. T. "March 1936 Floods in New England: Merrimack River." *Boston Society of Civil Engineers Journal* 22 (October 1936): 292–300.

Stevenson, W. L. "Public Health Aspects of the Flood of March 1936." *New England Water Works Association Journal* 51 (March 1937): 80–89.

Uhl, W. F. "Flood Conditions in New England." *American Society of Civil Engineers Proceedings* 63 (March 1937): 449–483; discussion, 63 (December 1937): 1961–1966.

Weston, A. D. "Public Health Aspects of the Flood of March 1936." *New England Water Works Association Journal* 51 (March 1937): 90–102.

1938 Hurricane Flood

Dick, M. H. "New England Roads Ravaged by Floods and Hurricanes." *Railway Age* 105 (October 1, 1938): 471–477.

Harrison, W. H. "Hurricane and Flood, September 1938: Experiences of Telephone Companies." *Bell System Technical Journal* 18 (January 1939): 218–221.

Knox, J. C. "Protection of Public Water Supplies in Massachusetts during the Floods and Hurricane of 1938." *New England Water Works Association Journal* 56 (June 1939): 212–222.

Mills, C. M. "New England's Stand on Flood Control Compacts: Conflict of Federal and State's Rights." *Public Utilities* 21 (April 14, 1938): 451–462.

Paulsen, C. G., et al. "Hurricane Floods of September 1938." *U.S. Geological Survey Water Supply Paper* 867 (1940): 1–562.

Phillips, A. I., and J. G. Elder. "New England Gas Companies Maintain Service through Hurricane and Flood." *American Gas Journal* 149 (October 1938): 13–20.

Richardson, H. W., and W. G. Bowman. "Northeastern Gale and Flood." *Engineering News-Record* 121 (October 6, 1938): 424–430.

Sughrue, T. G., and C. E. Smith. "Flood and Hurricane Destruction and Rehabilitation of New England Railroads." *Boston Society of Civil Engineers Journal* 26 (April 1939): 118–146.

Wesselius, W., et al. "Experiences from the New England Hurricane." *Electrical Engineering* 58 (March 1939): 99–112.

Northeastern Flood of 1955

"$51 Million Set to Stop Northeast Floods." *Engineering News* 155 (December 8, 1955): 22.

Argraves, N. E. "Connecticut Highways and the 1955 floods." *American Society of Civil Engineers Proceedings* 84 (May 1958): 1–9.

Bogie, W. P. "How Banks Met the Seven-State Flood." *Banking* 48 (October 1955): 38–40+.

Brodersen, C. "After the Flood: Problems, Losses, and Problems." *National Petroleum News* 47 (October 1955): 38–46.

Childs, E. F. "Northeastern Floods of 1955: Flood Control Hydrology." *American Society of Civil Engineers Proceedings* 84 (June 1958): 1–24; discussion, 84 (November 1958): 91–94; 85 (January 1959): 105–110; reply, 85 (June 1959): 63–65.

"Flood-Area Newspapers Suffer Damage, Delays." *Editor and Publisher* 88 (August 17, 1955): 10–11+.

"Floodland Revisited: Naugatuck Valley Metal-Working Was Ready for It This Time." *American Machinist* 39 (November 7, 1955): 177–179.

Gilman, C. S., et al. "Northeastern Floods of 1955." *American Society of Civil Engineers Proceedings* 84 (June 1958). Papers: 1661, 37p.; 1662, 19p.; 1663, 24p.; discussion, 84 (November 1958): 89–94.

Hart, G. "Great Flood of 1955: Amateurs Aid Stricken Communities." *QST* 39 (December 1955): 11–18+.

"Industry Hit by Northeast Floods." *Chemical and Engineering News* 33 (September 5, 1955): 3661–3663.

Kopp, H. M. "Connecticut Hurricanes and Floods of 1955 as They Affected Gas Operations." *American Gas Association Proceedings* (1956): 303–308.

"Planned but Unbuilt Projects Could Have Saved $70 Million." *Engineering News* 155 (September 1, 1955): 21–25.

"Price of Diane: Black Friday for the Northeast." *Business Week* (August 27, 1955): 26–29.

"Sales Throws Lifeline to Flooded Hurricane Victims." *Sales Management* 7 (September 1, 1955): 1–4.

Sibley, A. K. "Flood Control in New England." *American Society of Civil Engineers Proceedings* 84 (January 1958): 1–31.

Smith, A. C. "Northeast Rebuilds Fast after Devastating Flood." *Construction Methods and Equipment* 37 (October 1955): 50–57.

Stocker, W. M., Jr., and R. N. Sheets. "Hell and High Water on the Naugatuck: An On-the-Spot Survey." *American Machinist* 99 (September 12, 1955): 170–178.

"Story behind the Clean-Up of Hurricane Diane Floods." *Sales Management* 75 (September 20, 1955): 103–104.

"Tributary Flash Floods Create Major Disaster." *Engineering News* 155 (August 25, 1955): 21–23.

"Utilities Repair Flood Damage: Illustrations with Text." *Electrical World* 144 (September 5, 1955): 62–65.

Williams, G. J. "Flood Damage to Gas Facilities in Connecticut." *American Gas Association Proceedings* (1955): 339–344.

East Coast

General

Carpenter, David M. *Floods in West Virginia, Pennsylvania, and Maryland.* Series: Water Resources Investigations Report, 88-4213. Towson, MD: U.S. Department of the Interior; and Denver, CO: U.S. Geological Survey, 1985, 86 pp.

Dehoff, Andrew. *The January 1996 Flood on the Lower Susquehanna River: Analysis and Recommendations of the Interior Committee on Emergencies, Jams, and Meteorological Systems.* Susquehanna River Basin Commission, no. 180, Harrisburg, PA: Susquehanna River Basin Commission, 1996, 27 pp.

Drake, A. D., and F. O. Nekin. "Review of the Olean Flood in Relation to the Mutual Aid and Civilian Protection Programs." *American Water Works Association Journal* 34 (December 1942): 1743–1754.

The Flood of July 1942 in the Upper Allegheny River and Sinnemahoning Creek Basins. Harrisburg, PA: Pennsylvania Department of Forests and Waters and U.S. Geological Survey, 1943, 35 pp.

Harrington, A. W., and H. Johnson. "New York Floods of 1935

and 1936." *American Society of Civil Engineers Proceedings* 63 (March 1937): 485–493.

"Industrial Plant Redesigned to Make Room for New Flood-Free Buildings: H. J. Heinz Pittsburgh Plant." *Architecture Forum* 90 (May 1949): 102–106.

Langbein, W. B., et al. "Major Winter and Nonwinter Floods in Selected Basins in New York and Pennsylvania." *U.S. Geological Survey Water Supply Paper* 915 (1947): 1–139.

Leathers, D. J., et al. "The Severe Flooding Event of January 1996 Across North-Central Pennsylvania." *Bulletin of the American Meteorological Society* 79 (May 1998): 785–797.

Statewide Flood in Pennsylvania, January 1996. Series: Fact Sheet, Geological Survey, U.S. FS 103-96. Reston, VA: U.S. Geological Survey, 1996, 2 pp.

Johnstown Floods

Bosart, L. F., and F. Sanders. "Johnstown Flood of July 1977: A Long-Lived Convective System." *Journal of the Atmospheric Sciences* 38 (August 1981): 1616–1642.

"Ceremony at Johnstown Opens Campaign to Curb Flood-Related Deaths." *American Meteorological Society Bulletin* 63 (August 1982): 942–943.

"City Rebuilds Fast after Violent Flood: Johnstown, Pa." *Engineering News* 203 (December 20, 1979): 60–62.

"Concrete Makes Johnstown Flood-Free: Concrete Lined Channels." *Concrete* 52 (May 1944): 8.

"The Day the Dam Broke." *Reader's Digest* 134 (May 1989): 193–196+.

Frank, W. "The Cause of the Johnstown [PA] Flood." *Civil Engineering (American Society of Civil Engineers)* 58 (May 1988): 63–66.

Guggenheim, C. "The Scene of the Crime [Life at South Fork Fishing and Hunting Club before Johnstown Flood]." *American Heritage* 43 (November 1992): 120–127.

Jackson, D. D. "When 20 Million Tons of Water Flooded Johnstown." *Smithsonian* 20 (May 1989): 50–54+.

Johnson, B. "Elise Frum Remembers a Train's Desperate Whistle 100 Years Ago—and the Great Johnstown Flood." *People Weekly* 31 (June 5, 1989): 85–88.

"Johnstown Ends Floods." *Compressed Air Magazine* 49 (April 1944): 106.

"Johnstown Flood Shuts 5 Major Mines." *Coal Age* 82 (September 1977): 36.

"Johnstown Is Inundated Again by a Record 500-Year Flood." *Engineering News* 199 (July 28, 1977): 9.

Kinney, D. G. "After the Flood." *Life* 12 (May 1989): 144–146+.

Ludlum, D. M. "The Johnstown Flood." *Weatherwise* 42 (April 1989): 88–92.

MacAllen, T. C., and R. A. Bank. "New Flood Protection Project Designed to Keep City Dry [Johnstown]. *Public Works* 126 (August 1995): 56–57.

Mangan, J. W. "Flood-Forecasting Service in Pennsylvania." *American Water Works Association Journal* 33 (February 1941): 213–218.

McCaffrey, A. H. "Flood Control for Johnstown." *Public Works* 78 (December 1977): 27–28.

"Memorial Revised: Johnstown Will Plug Its New Floodlessness." *Business Week* (December 18, 1943: 53–54.

Oxford, E. "The Johnstown Flood." *American History Illustrated* 24 (May 1989): 12–25.

Pagan, A. R. "Johnstown Flood Revisited." *Civil Engineering (American Society of Civil Engineers)* 44 (August 1974): 60–62.

Rosenthal, M. "Surviving the Johnstown, PA, Flood." *American Water Works Association Journal* 75 (August 1983): 390–393.

Ruff, C. F. "Maximum Probable Floods in Pennsylvania Streams." *American Society of Civil Engineers Proceedings* 66 (September 1940): 1239–1276; discussion, 66: 1849–1857; 67 (December 1940): 137–140; 67 (February 1941): 240–246; 67 (May 1941): 873–878.

Schuleen, E. P. "Control of Floods at Pittsburgh Planned." *Civil Engineering* 15 (October 1945): 455–458.

Steigman, H. "Environmental Health Personnel Active in Johnstown Flood Aftermath." *Journal of Environmental Health* 40 (March 1978): 274–278.

Tiffany, J. B., Jr. "Model Study Helps Prevent Johnstown Floods: Investigation at U.S. Waterways Experiment Station." *Civil Engineering* 15 (July 1945): 309–312.

East Coast Hurricane Flood 1972

Alderfer, Evan B. "Banking with Vaults Awash [Hurricane Agnes Brought Record Flooding to Many Pennsylvania Communities and Affected Everyone, Including Banks and Bankers]." *Federal Reserve Philadelphia Business Review* (August 1972): 3–7.

Appleyard, V. A., and H. V. Hetzer. "Flooding in Chester, Pa." *American Water Works Association Journal* 65 (July 1973): 480–481.

"Flood Insurance: 64 Communities May Lose Eligibility [from the Federally Subsidized Flood Insurance Programs Unless They Soon Adopt Tough Land-Use Measures to Minimize Dangers from Flooding]." *Congressional Quarterly Weekly Report* 30 (July 8, 1972): 1675–1676.

Lull, Howard W., and Kenneth G. Reinhart. *Forests and Floods in the Eastern United States.* Research Paper NE-226. Upper Darby, PA: Northeastern Forest Experiment Station, 1972, 94 pp.

U.S. Congress, Senate Committee on Labor and Public Welfare, Subcommittee on Labor. *Buffalo Creek (W.Va.) Disaster, 1972: Pt. 1, June 1972.* 92d Cong., 2d sess. Washington, DC: GPO, 1972, 225 pp.

———. *Buffalo Creek (W.Va.) Disaster, 1972: Hearings: Pts. 1–2, May 30–31, 1972, Appendices A, B, C, and D.* 92d Cong., 2d sess. Washington, DC: GPO, 1972, 2 pts. 2,717 pp.

"Where and When Flood Victims Can Be Helped: Food, Blankets, Low-Interest Loans, Temporary Housing; a Broad Array of Aid Is Being Dispensed to Victims of the Floods Triggered by Hurricane Agnes: From Officials in Charge: Details of the Help Available and Where to Go to Get It." *U.S. News & World Report* 73 (July 10, 1972): 16–19.

"Wilkes-Barre [PA]: Where Recovery Washed Out: The Storm Has Seriously Hurt the City's Effort to Build an Industrial Base." *Business Week* (July 8, 1972): 16–17.

Pennsylvania Floods of 1942

Armand, H. "Liquid Sabotage: Lukens Plant Disinfected after Flood." *Safety Engineering* 85 (January 1943): 20–22.

Bush, B. S., and M. J. Barrick. "Emergency Experiences during Flash Floods." *American Water Works Association Journal* 35 (January 1942): 81–87; 35 (January 1943): 87–92.

"Flash Floods Destroy Highway Bridges, Roads, and Railroads." *Engineering News* 128 (May 28, 1942): 884.

Hall, R. D. "Anthracite Flood Suggests Need for Better Stream Control." *Coal Age* 47 (November 1942): 66–67, 70–71.

Herber, J. L. "Repairing Damage from May 1942 Flood in Pennsylvania." *Civil Engineering* 12 (November 1942): 620–623.

Morris, R. M., and T. L. Reilly. "Operation Experiences, Tygart Reservoir." *American Society of Civil Engineers Proceedings* 67 (April 1941): 569–593; discussion, 67 (October 1941): 1465–1468; 68 (January 1942): 161–163.

"New Pennsylvania Flash Floods Wreck Allegheny River Bridges, Facilities." *Engineering News* 129 (July 23, 1942): 124.

"Pennsylvania Pushes Flood Clean-Up." *Engineering News* 128 (June 11, 1942): 954.

"Pennsylvania Sets Flood Damage Losses." *Engineering News* 129 (August 27, 1942): 273.

"Sudden Floods Disrupt Service in Anthracite Region." *Railway Age* 112 (May 30, 1942): 1097–1098.

Pennsylvania Flood of 1936

Cartwright, A. N. "Power Must Stay On: Operation of West Penn Power Company System during the Flood." *Electric Journal* 33 (May 1936): 229–236.

"Floodproof Powerhouse Built at Pittsburgh, Pa." *Railway Age* 106 (May 27, 1939): 899–903.

Garrett, C. W. *History of the Floods of March 1936 and January 1937.* Philadelphia: Pennsylvania Railroad Company, 1937, 150 pp.

Hendrickson, G. L. "Cities without Water: Pittsburgh's Waterworks Failure during the Flood." *Engineering News Record* 116 (June 25, 1936): 904–907.

Howard, N. D. "What the Floods in Pennsylvania Did to Railroads." *Railway Age* 100 (March 28, 1936): 524–533.

Kressler, C. H., and R. W. Foster. "Cities without Water: Harrisburg's Waterworks Failure during the Flood." *Engineering News-Record* 117 (July 2, 1936): 15–18.

Mitchell, T. J. "Control Surveys for Flood Projection Projects in the Pittsburgh District." *Civil Engineering* 9 (May 1939): 277–280.

Morse, E. K., and H. A. Thomas. "Floods in the Upper Ohio River and Tributaries." *American Society of Civil Engineers Proceedings* 63 (March 1937): 495–518.

Moses, H. E. "1936 Flood and Pennsylvania Public Water Supplies." *American Water Works Association Journal* 28 (December 1936): 1835–1845.

Pohl, H. H. "Ohio River Flood Control Plan." *American Water Works Association Journal* 29 (May 1937): 589–596.

"Record-Breaking Floods Put Heavy Burdens on Utilities." *Electrical World* 106 (March 28, 1936): 910–915.

Reitz, W. G. "Johnstown Comes Back after the Flood: Restoration of Transit Service." *Mass Transportation* 32 (September 1936): 280–281.

Richardson, H. W. "After the Floods in Pennsylvania and West Virginia Region: Roads, Railroads, and Municipal Conditions." *Engineering News-Record* 116 (April 23, 1936): 599–603.

———. "Johnstown Flood Rivals '89 Dam Break." *Engineering News-Record* 116 (March 26, 1936): 442–444.

Schalek, J. H. "Natural Gas Carries On during Pittsburgh's Disastrous Flood." *Gas Age* 77 (April 11, 1936): 363–366.

Tisdale, E. S. "1936 Flood and West Virginia Public Water Supplies." *American Water Works Association Journal* 28 (December 1936): 1846–1854.

Midwest Floods

General

Barney, K. R. "1951 Kansas City Flood." *American Society of Civil Engineers Proceedings* 81 (November 1955): 1–9.

Bennett, K. M. "Flood: Midwest Industry Battles Swollen Mississippi." *Iron Age* 169 (May 1, 1952): 89–81.

Bridgman, G. "Red River of the North: Spring 1989 Flooding." *QST* 73 (October 1989): 59–60.

Calkins, M. "How Kansas City Battled Its First 300-Year Killer Flood." *American City and County* 93 (February 1978): 58–59.

Carr, F. H. "Corps Tames 'Wild and Wooly' [Red] River." *Engineering News-Record* 219 (December 17, 1987): 84–85.

Carr, J. R. "Omaha Braces for Its Biggest Flood." *Engineering News* (April 17, 1952): 21–22.

Castle, L. "Fight against Flood Damage." *National Petroleum News* 43 (September 19, 1951): 72–75+.

———. "Midwest Floods Pass after Damaging Oil Installations." *National Petroleum News* 44 (April 30, 1952): 21–22.

Clinton, William J. "Statement on the Flooding in the Midwest, June 29, 1993." *Weekly Compilation of Presidential Documents* 29 (July 5, 1993): 1204.

"Construction Equipment Licks Big Muddy at Omaha." *Construction Methods and Equipment* 34 (May 1952): 50–53.

Disastrous Floods on the Trinity, Red, and Arkansas Rivers, May 1998. Series: Natural Disaster Survey Report. Silver Spring, MD: U.S. Department of Commerce, National Oceanic and Atmospheric Administration, National Weather Service, 1991.

Eash, David A. *Flood of May 19, 1990, along Perry Creek in Plymouth and Woodbury Counties, Iowa.* U.S. Geological Survey open-file report, 96–476. Denver, CO: U.S. Geological Survey, 1996, 39 pp. Microfiche.

Fabry, K. "Fighting Flood Waters [Watertown, SD]." *Water Environment and Technology* 10 (April 1998): 40–41.

"Greatest Kaw River Flood Was in Super Class." *Engineering News* 147 (July 19, 1951): 23–25.

Holmes, Robert R., and Amit Kapadia. *Floods in Northern Illinois, July 1996.* Washington, DC: U.S. Geological Survey, 1997, 4 pp.

McManamy, R. "Midwest Goes into Repair Mode." *Engineering News-Record* 231 (August 9, 1993): 8–9.

"Oil Men Battle to Supply Public Despite Heavy Flood, Fire Loss." *National Petroleum News* 43 (July 18, 1951): 24–25.

Peterson, Morris S. *Floods of June 17th and 18th, 1964, in Jefferson, St. Genevieve and St. Francois Counties, Missouri.* Rolla, MO: Prepared in Cooperation with the Missouri Geological Survey and Water Resources, 1965, 20 pp.

"Pick Raises Kaw Flood Damage Estimate to $990 Million." *Engineering News* 147 (August 2, 1951): 25–27.

Robison, R. "Taming the Red River." *Civil Engineering (American Society of Civil Engineers)* 65 (June 1995): 64–66.

Sampson, J. A. "Effects of Recent Floods on Iowa's Water Supply." *American Water Works Association Journal* 40 (February 1948): 139–143.

Serif, M. "How Gas Service Co. Met Challenge of the Nation's Worst Flood." *Gas Age* 108 (August 30, 1951): 17–19.

Smrha, R. V. "Kansas Plan for Neosho River Basin Development." *American Water Works Association Journal* 39 (July 1947): 673–679.

Southard, Rodney E. *Analyses of Backwater Flooding on Long Branch at Whiteman Air Force Base, Knob Noster, Missouri.* Rolla, MO: U.S. Department of Defense, U.S. Air Force Air Combat Command, Whiteman Air Force Base; and Denver, CO: U.S. Geological Survey, 1998, 15 pp.

"Toledo, Peoria, and Western Moved for Flood-Control Project." *Railway Age* 130 (February 26, 1951): 22–25.

U.S. Congress, House Committee on Public Works and Transportation, Subcommittee on Oversight and Review. *Flooding of the Red River of the North and Its Tributaries: Hearing, July 2, 1979.* 96th Cong., 1st sess. Washington, DC: GPO, 1979, 306 pp.

U.S. National Oceanic and Atmospheric Administration. *Kansas City Flash Flood of September 12–13, 1977: A Report to the Administrator.* Rockville, MD: National Oceanic and Atmospheric Administration, 1977, 49 pp.

Westphal, J. A., et al. "Stage-Discharge Relations on the Middle Mississippi River." *Journal of Water Resources Planning and Management* 125 (January-February, 1999): 48–53.

Ohio River Floods

"53 Miles of Railway Relocated in Ohio Flood-Control Project." *Railway Age* 101 (September 5, 1936): 345–350.

Brossmann, C. "Flood Protection in the Ohio Valley." *American Water Works Association Journal* 29 (May 1937): 597–606.

Chase, E. S. "Experiences at Louisville during the Ohio River Flood of 1937." *Boston Society of Civil Engineers Journal* 24 (July 1937): 272–288.

Crenshaw, J. C. "1937 Flood." *American Water Works Association Journal* 29 (September 1937): 1230–1236.

DeBerard, W. W. "Conditions in Flood-Beleaguered Cairo [IL]." *Engineering News-Record* 118 (February 4, 1937): 153–155+.

"Floods of Ohio and Mississippi Rivers, January-February 1937." *U.S. Geological Survey Water Supply Paper* 838 (1938): 1–746.

Geupel, L. A. "Evansville Water Works and the 1937 Flood." *American Water Works Association Journal* 29 (September 1937): 1259–1270.

Hibbs, A. S. "Water Works in the 1937 Flood." *American Water Works Association Journal* 29 (September 1937): 1237–1245.

Horn, S. J. "Flood of 1937 in the Ohio Valley." *Civil Engineering* 7 (May 1937): 326–330.

Hoskins, J. K. "Sanitation Conditions in the Flood Areas." *American Water Works Association Journal* 29 (September 1937): 1298–1307.

Morgan, A. E. "Flood Control by Reservoirs Proposed for Lower Tennessee and Ohio Valleys." *Engineering News* 119 (August 12, 1937): 263–268.

Morse, E. K., and H. A. Thomas. "Floods in the Upper Ohio River and Tributaries." *American Society of Civil Engineers Proceedings* 63 (March 1937) 495–518; discussion, 64 (April 1938): 798–801.

Munyan, E. A. "Cincinnati Safely Weathers the 1937 Record Flood: Emergency Work of the Cincinnati Gas and Electric Company." *Gas Age* 79 (April 1, 1937): 21–29.

———. "Experience in Cincinnati and the Ohio Valley during the 1937 Flood." *American Gas Association Proceedings* (1937): 821–832.

Nie, M. "The Ohio River Flood of '97." *QST* 81 (October 1997): 28–32.

Ohio-Mississippi Valley Flood Disaster of 1937: Report of Relief Operations of the American Red Cross. Washington, DC: American National Red Cross, 1938, 252 pp.

Roos, C. M. "Cairo [IL] and the Superflood of 1937." *American Water Works Association Journal* 29 (September 1937): 1230–1237.

"Service Restored Rapidly as Ohio Recedes." *Railway Age* 102 (February 6, 1937): 248–253.

Somerville, G. A. "1937 Floods in Southern Illinois." *Illinois University Engineering Experiment Station Circular* 30 (1937): 122–131.

Swenson, B. *Ohio and Mississippi Floods of January-February, 1937.* Washington, DC: U.S. Weather Bureau, 55 pp.

"System of Levees and Flood Walls Will Bar Louisville's Most Unwelcome Visitor." *Engineering News* 142 (June 9, 1949): 58–61.

Vance, L. S. "Louisville Water Company and the 1937 Flood." *American Water Works Association Journal* 29 (September 1937): 1246–1254; discussion, 29 (September 1937): 1254–1258.

Winslow, E. L., Jr., et al. "Muskingum Flood Control Work: A Symposium on the $34,500,000 Flood Control and Water-Conservation Project in Eastern Ohio." *Civil Engineering* 6 (January 1936): 1–28.

Youngquist, C. V., and W. B. Langbein. "Flood of August 1935 in the Muskingum River Basin, Ohio." *U.S. Geological Survey Water Supply Paper* 869 (1941): 1–118.

Kansas Flood of 1951

Alexander, V. "Reappraisal of Flood Control Objectives Indicated by Midwest Flood of July 1951." *Civil Engineering* 21 (November 1951): 640–643.

Carr, J. R. "Kansas Flood Cleanup: A Tale of Three Cities." *Engineering News* 147 (October 4, 1951): 30–34.

"Disaster Can Strike You: Experience of Kansas City Plant Managers." *Factory Management* 110 (June 1952): 83–91.

Hart, G. "Water in the Dust Bowl: Amateurs Supply Emergency Communications during One of the Greatest Floods in the Midwest's History." *QST* 35 (November 1951): 46–49+.

Hatcher, M. P. "Disaster Plans in Water Works Operations: Some Experiences Gained during and after the Disastrous Flood of 1951 at Kansas City." *Water and Sewage Works* 99 (April 1952): 141–146.

"How Flood Damaged Equipment Was Returned to Service Quickly: Atchison, Topeka, and Santa Fe." *Railway Age* 131 (October 22, 1951): 44–49.

"Kansas City, 1951: Contractors Work to Rehabilitate Plumbing and Heating Systems in Flood-Stricken Areas." *Domestic Engineering* 178 (September 1951): 102–104+.

Metzler, D. F., et al. "Interruption to Water Service by the Kansas

Flood of 1951." *American Water Works Association Journal* 44 (September 1952): 780–796.
"Mighty Mo Does It Again." *Public Utilities* 49 (May 8, 1952): 630–632.
Veatch, N. T. "Kansas Flood of 1951." *American Water Works Association Journal* 44 (September 1952): 765–774.

Chicago Flood of 1992

Freund, A. "Fast-Track Electrical Rebuilding after Flood Disaster [Ramada O'Hare Hotel, Chicago, IL]." *Electrical Construction and Maintenance* 87 (August 1988): 74–79.
Inouye, Randall R., and Joseph D. Jacobazzi. "Great Chicago Flood of 1992." *Civil Engineering (American Society of Civil Engineers)* 62 (November 1992): 52–55.
Lawrie, R. J. "Mobile Generators Avert Chicago Flood Disaster." *Electrical Construction and Maintenance* 91 (November 1992): 18+.
McManamy, B. "Chicago Flood Firm Sets Sail against City under Admiralty." *Engineering News-Record* 231 (September 6, 1993): 8–9.
Menkus, Belden. "Lessons Learned of the Great Chicago Flood of 1992." *Computers and Security* 11 (September 1992): 417–420.
"Rapid Delivery of MCC Helps Flooded Chicago Office Tower." *Electrical Construction and Maintenance* 9 (December 1992): 34.

Upper Mississippi River Flood of 1993

General

"America under Water [Cover Story: Special Section]." *USA Today* 123 (July 1994): 30–44.
Brownell, B. "The Great Flood of 1993." *National Geographic World* 218 (October 1993): 23–25.
Bryson, B. "Riding Out the Worst of Times [Des Moines, IA]." *National Geographic* 185 (January 1994): 82–87.
Cohen, J. "Flood Flexes Its Mussels." *Science* 265 (March 4, 1994): 1226.
Dowling Claudia Glenn. "Ain't It Grand [Grand Folk, ND]." *Life* (March 1998): 42–51.
Drew, John, and Charles De Charme. "The Record Flood of 1993." Rolla, MO: Missouri Department of Natural Resources, Division of Geology and Land Survey, 1993, 20 pp.
Dunlop, B. "Coping with Natural Catastrophes [Role of Architects]." *Architectural Record* 182 (June 1994): 38–41.

Espey, William H., Jr., Leo Beard, and John Reinfurst. "Summer of 1993 Floods Lower Missouri River." *Proceedings of the ASCE National Conference on Hydraulic Engineering, Buffalo, NY,* 1994, pp. 628–633.

"Flood, Sweat, and Tears [Cover Story: Special Section]." *Time* (July 26, 1993): 22–33.

"The Great Flood of '93." *Life* 17 (January 1994): 35–38.

Handelman, D. "After the Deluge [Effects of Flood on West Alton and Portage des Sioux, MO]." *Vogue* 183 (December 1993): 270–277+.

Hickcox, D. H. "The Great Flood of 1993." *Focus* 43 (Fall 1993): 22–25.

Mairson, A. "The Great Flood of '93." *National Geographic* 185 (January 1994): 42–81.

McManamy, R., and M. R. Anderson. "Midwest Now High and Dry." *Engineering News-Record* 223 (July 25, 1994): 9–10.

Mickelmore, P. "Fighting the Raging Mississippi [1993 Illinois Floods]." *Reader's Digest* 114 (January 1994): 80–86.

Myers, M. F., and G. F. White. "The Challenge of the Mississippi Flood [Cover Story, with Discussion and Editorial Comment by Timothy O'Riordan]." *Environment* 35 (December 1993): 6–9+.

Palm, R. "Heroics in the Heartland." *QST* 77 (December 1993): 21–26.

Parfit, M. "The Floods That Carved the West [Lake Missoula Floods]." *Smithsonian* 26 (April 1995): 48–56+.

Parratt, Charles, Nick B. Melcher, and Robert W. James Jr. "Flood Discharges in the Upper Mississippi River Basin, 1993." U.S. Geological Circular No. 1120. Washington, DC: GPO, 1993, 14 pp.

Sheehan, K., and C. Thoresen. "Des Moines, Iowa: A River Ran through It, and over It." *Waste Age* 24 (November 1993): 39–40+.

Sheets, K. R. "After the Flood." *Kiplinger's Personal Finance Magazine* 47 (October 1993): 67–71.

Sivy, M. "Three Stocks That Stand to Make a Splash When the Flood Subsides." *Money* 22 (September 1993): 58–60+.

Stallings, Eugene A. "Lessons Learned from the Great Flood of 1993." *Proceedings of the Twenty-second Annual Conference on Integrated Water Resources Planning for the Twenty-first Century, Cambridge, MA,* 1995, pp. 775–778.

———. "Some Lessons Learned during the Great Flood of 1993." *Proceedings of the First International Conference on Water Resources, Part 2, San Antonio, TX,* 1995, pp. 1794–1798.

Stephens, Dennis L., and Gary R. Dyhouse. "Great Flood of 1993: What If?" *Proceedings of the First International Conference on Water Resources, Part 2, San Antonio, TX,* 1995, pp. 956–960.

St. Louis Post-Dispatch. *High and Mighty: The Flood of '93.* Kansas City, MO: Andrews and McMeel Press, 1993, 96 pp.

Strauser, Bradford M., and James L. Keim. "Surveying and Mapping during the Great Flood of 1993." *Proceedings of the First International Conference on Water Resources, Part 2, San Antonio, TX,* 1995, pp. 961–965.

Zimmerman, R. "After the Deluge." *The Sciences* 34 (July-August 1994): 18–23.

Weather and Climate

Changnon, Stanley A., and Kenneth E. Kunkel. "Climate-Related Fluctuations in Midwestern Floods during 1921–1985." *Journal of Water Resources Planning and Management* 121 (July-August 1995): 326–334.

Dowgiallo, Michael J., ed. *Coastal Oceanic Effects of Summer 1993 Mississippi River Flooding.* Series: Special NOAA Report. Silver Spring, MD: National Oceanic and Atmospheric Administration, 1994, 77 pp.

Georgakakos, K. D., et al. "Observation and Analysis of Midwestern Rain Rates." *Journal of Applied Meteorology* 33 (December 1994): 433–444.

Guttman, N. B., et al. "The 1993 Midwest Extreme Precipitation in Historical and Probabilistic Perspective." *Bulletin of the American Meteorological Society* 75 (October 1994): 1785–1792.

Kunkel, Kenneth E. "Climatic Perspective on the 1993 Mississippi River Flood." *Proceedings of the ASCE National Conference on Hydraulic Engineering, Buffalo, NY,* 1994, pp. 600–602.

Kunkel, Kenneth E., et al. "Climatic Aspects of the 1993 Upper Mississippi River Basin Flood." *Bulletin of the American Meteorological Society* 75 (May 1994): 811–822.

———. "A Regional Response to Climate Information Needs during the 1993 Flood." *Bulletin of the American Meteorological Society* 76 (December 1995): 2415–2421.

———. "Temporal and Spatial Characteristics of Heavy-Precipitation Events in the Midwest." *Monthly Weather Review* 121 (March 1993): 858–866.

"MMS Study Helps Track Ocean Effects of Record Flooding." *Sea Technology* 34 (December 1993): 75–76.

Paegle, J., et al. "Dependence of Simulated Precipitation on Surface Evaporation during the 1993 United States Summer

Floods." *Monthly Weather Review* 124 (March 1996): 345–361.

Williams, J. "The Great Flood." *Weatherwise* 47 (February-March 1994): 18–22.

Flood Control

Budiansky, S. "Nowhere to Run, Nowhere to Hide [Controlling the Mississippi]." *U.S. News & World Report* 115 (July 26, 1993): 24–28.

Cadigan, W. J., and E. F. Niebuhr. "Flood Protection System Undergoes the Ultimate Test." *Public Works* 125 (March 1994): 57–59.

Denning, J. "When the Levee Breaks." *Civil Engineering (American Society of Civil Engineers)* 64 (January 1994): 38–41.

DiBuono, Richard J., and Gary R. Dyhouse. "1993 Flood: A Vindication of Federal Levees and Reservoirs, Or a Call for 'Back to Nature'?" *Proceedings of the Conference on Natural Disaster Reduction, Washington, DC,* 1996, pp. 163–164.

Faber, Scott E. "Letting Down the Levee." *National Wetlands Newsletter* 15 (November-December 1993): 5–7.

Ray, C., et al. "Agricultural Chemicals: Effects on Wells during Floods." *American Water Works Association Journal* 90 (July 1998): 90–100+.

Sophocleous, M., et al. "Hydrologic Impact of Great Flood of 1993 in South-Central Kansas." *Journal of Irrigation and Drainage Engineering* 122 (July-August 1996): 203–210.

"Technology Tames Midwest Floods." *Public Works* 124 (December 1993): 38–40.

Frequency

Southard, Rodney E. "Magnitude and Frequency of 1993 Flood Volumes in Upper Mississippi River Basin." *Transportation Research Record* 1483 (July 1995): 18–31.

Thomas, W. O., Jr., and D. A. Eash. "Magnitude and Frequency of Peak Discharges for Mississippi River Basin Flood of 1993." *Transportation Research Record* 1483 (July 1995): 1–10.

Recovery

Briggs, T. "Flood Damages St. Louis Treatment Facilities." *Water Environment and Technology* 5 (October 1993): 24+.

Butler, D. "Rental Power: The Pulse of Flood-Ravaged Communities." *Public Works* 125 (January 1994): 42–43.

Davis, R. A. "Treatment Plant Foils Flood." *Water Environment and Technology* 5 (October 1993): 23–24.

Hage, D. "Mississippi on the Mend: A Year after the Flood, Business Is Bustling." *U.S. News & World Report* 117 (August 22, 1994): 50–55.

Lampert, L. "After the Flood [Redecorating G. and D. Perdun's Flood-Damaged Home in Grafton, IL]." *Ladies' Home Journal* 111 (August 1994): 19–25.

Lisk, I. "Control System Helped Plant Run Unattended during 'Big Flood'." *Water/Engineering and Management* 141 (June 1994): 30–31.

McManamy, R. "Flood Recovery Begins to Gain Momentum." *Engineering News-Record* 231 (November 1, 1993): 22–24+.

Overby, P. "Beachfront Bailout." *Common Cause Magazine* 19 (Summer 1993): 12–17.

Prokopy, S. "Midwest Aggregate Operations Suffer, Help during Floods." *Rock Products* 96 (October 1993): 23–24.

Reid, J. "Overcoming the Flood: How Midwestern Utilities Managed Disaster." *American Water Works Association Journal* 85 (January 1994): 58–67.

Shorney, F. L. "Impacts and Lessons Learned from the Flood of 1993." *Public Works* 125 (June 1994): 38–40.

Silverstein, K. "Des Moines 'Rents' Power to Restore Water." *American City and Country* 109 (January 1994): 51.

"Technology 'Maps' Path for Flood Recovery." *American City and County* 109 (January 1994): 55.

"Technology Tames Midwest Floods." *Public Works* 124 (December 1993): 38–40.

"Treatment Plants Improvise during Floods." *Water/Engineering and Management* 141 (February 1994): 12–13.

Waldron, C. "Michael Espy Tackles Flood Disaster Recovery across the United States [Cover Story]." *Jet* (August 2, 1993): 4–9.

Watson, B. "A Town Makes History by Rising to New Heights [Relocation of Valmeyer, IL, after Flood]." *Smithsonian* 27 (June 1996): 110–120.

Impact of Flood

Bhowmik, Nani G. "Impacts of the 1993 Flood on the Mississippi River in Illinois." *Proceedings of the ASCE National Conference on Hydraulic Engineering, Buffalo, NY,* 1994, pp. 613–617.

Ellis, James E. "A Deluge, But Not a Total Disaster: The Flood's Effect on Farmers, Crops, and Prices May Not Be So Awful." *Business Week* (July 19, 1993): 24–35.

Hagerty, D. J., A. C. Parola, and T. E. Fenske. "Impacts of 1993

Upper Mississippi River Basin Floods on Highway Systems." *Transportation Research Record* 1483 (July 1995): 32–37.

Kamojjala, S., N. P. Gatter, A. C. Parola, and D. J. Hagerty. "Analysis of 1993 Upper Mississippi Flood Highway Infrastructure Damage." *Proceedings of the First International Conference on Water Resources, Part 2, San Antonio, TX,* 1995, pp. 1061–1065.

Southard, Rodney E. *Simulation of the Effect of Traffic Barricades on Backwater along U.S. Highway 54 at Jefferson City, Missouri: 1993 Flood on the Missouri River.* Series: Water Resources Investigations Report 97-4213. Rolla, MO: Missouri Department of Transportation; and Washington, DC: U.S. Geological Survey, 1997, 13 pp.

Turque, B. "On the Disaster Dole." *Newsweek* (August 2, 1993): 24–25.

Floodplain

Begley, S. "Lessons from the Floodplain [Midwest Flood of 1993]." *National Wildlife* 32 (April-May 1994): 38–44.

Hanback, M. "The Deluge of 1993: Litmus Test for Floodplain Forests." *American Forests* 100 (May-June 1994): 17–21+.

Kusler, J. A., and L. Larson. "Beyond the Ark: A New Approach to Floodplain Management." *Environment* 35 (June 1993): 6–11+.

Platt, R. H. "Sharing the Challenge: Floodplain Management into the Twenty-first Century." *Environment* 37 (January-February 1995): 25–28.

Environmental Problems

Allen, W. H. "The Great Flood of 1993 [Effects on Wildlife]." *BioScience* 43 (December 1993): 732–737.

Barber, L. B., and J. H. Writer. "Impact of the 1993 Flood on the Distribution of Organic Contaminants in Bed Sediments of the Upper Mississippi River." *Environmental Science and Technology* 32 (July 15, 1998): 2077–2083.

Chrzastowski, M. J., et al. *The Great Flood of 1993: Geologic Perspectives on Flooding along the Mississippi River and Its Tributaries in Illinois.* Special Report 2. Champaign, IL: Illinois State Geological Survey, 1994, 45 pp.

Currens, J. C., and C. D. R. Graham. "Flooding of Sinking Creek, Garrets Spring Karst Drainage Basin, Jessamine and Woodford Counties, Kentucky, USA." *Environmental Geology* 22 (December 1993): 337–344.

Gomez, B., et al. "Sediment Characteristics of an Extreme Flood: 1993 Upper Mississippi River Valley." *Geology* 23 (November 1995): 963–966.

Hanback, M. "Focus on Flooded Wildlife." *Outdoor Life* 192 (November 1993): 38–42.

Heimann, D. C., et al. "Agricultural Chemicals in Alluvial Aquifers in Missouri after the 1993 Flood." *Journal of Environmental Quality* 26 (March/April 1997): 361–371.

Holmes, Robert R., Jr. *Sediment Transport in the Lower Missouri and the Central Mississippi Rivers, June 26 through September 14, 1993.* U.S. Geological Survey Circular 1120-I. Washington, DC: GPO, 1996, 23 pp.

Kriz, Margaret. "The Big Spill: As the Midwest Mops Up after the Great Flood of 1993, a Host of Environmental and Land Use Questions Are Coming into View." *National Journal* 25 (September 4, 1993): 2126–2129.

Li, Y., et al. "Sand Boils Induced by the 1993 Mississippi River Flood: Could They One Day Be Misinterpreted as Earthquake-Induced Liquefaction?" *Geology* 24 (February 1996): 171–174.

Magilligan, F. J., et al. "Geomorphic and Sedimentological Controls on the Effectiveness of an Extreme Flood." *Journal of Geology* 106 (January 1998): 87–95.

Myers, M. F., and G. F. White. "The Challenge of the Mississippi Flood." *Environment* 35 (December 1993): 6–9+; discussion, 35 (December 1993): 2–5+.

Petty, J. D., et al. "Determination of Bioavailable Contaminants in the Lower Missouri River Following the Flood of 1993." *Environmental Science and Technology* 32 (April 1, 1998): 837–842.

Phillips, Steven. *The Soil Conservation Service Responds to the 1993 Midwest Floods.* Washington, DC: U.S. Department of Agriculture, Division of Economics and Social Sciences, 1994, 168 pp.

Sanders, D. A. "Damage to Wastewater Treatment Facilities from Great Flood of 1993." *Journal of Environmental Engineering* 123 (January 1997): 54–60.

Setzer, S. W. "Environmental Concerns Are Still Running Deep in Rivers' Wake." *Engineering News-Record* 231 (November 1, 1993): 231.

Sophocleous, M., et al. "Hydrologic Impact of Great Flood of 1993 in South-Central Kansas." *Journal of Irrigation and Drainage Engineering* 122 (July-August 1996): 203–210.

Wahl, R. W. "The Mississippi Flood." *Environment* 36 (June 1994): 2–3.

Williams, T. "The River Always Wins [Mississippi River after the Flood]." *Audubon* 96 (July-August 1994): 78–89+.

Government

Benenson, Bob. "Congress Must Find Flood Aid Despite Tough Budget Times: Administration Submits $2.5 Billion Emergency Supplemental amid Lawmakers' Call for More Aid, Offsetting Cuts." *Congressional Quarterly Weekly Report* 51 (July 17, 1993): 1860–1861+.

Stanfield, Rochelle L. "Conflicting Aims: FEMA's Mission Is to Help Put Things Back the Way They Were before the Flood: HUD Sees the Role as That of Making Communities Better Than They Were Before: In These Differing Views Are the Seeds of Real Conflict." *National Journal* 25 (September 4, 1993): 2130–2135.

U.S. Congress, House Committee on Appropriations. *Making Emergency Supplemental Appropriations for Relief from the Major, Widespread Flooding in the Midwest for the Fiscal Year Ending September 30, 1993 and for Other Purposes, Report (to accompany H.R. 2667).* Washington, DC: GPO, 1993, 30 pp.

U.S. Congress, House Committee on Energy and Commerce, Subcommittee on Transportation and Hazardous Materials. *Effect of Midwest Flooding on Rail Transportation: Hearing, September 23, 1993.* 103d Cong., 1st sess. Washington, DC: GPO, 1994, 217 pp.

U.S. Congress, House Committee on Public Works and Transportation, Subcommittee on Investigations and Oversight. *Federal Response to Midwest Flooding: Hearing before the Subcommittee on Investigations and Oversight of the Committee on Public Works and Transportation.* 103d Cong., 1st sess. Washington, DC: GPO, 1994, 217 pp.

U.S. Congress, Senate, *Appropriations Requests EC 1310, Communication from the President of the United States Transmitting Requests for Emergency Fiscal Year 1993 Supplemental Appropriations to Provide for Emergency Expenses Arising from the Consequences of the Flooding along the Mississippi River and Its Tributaries.* 103d Cong., 1st sess. Washington, DC: GPO, 1993, 42 pp. Microfiche.

U.S. Congress, Senate Committee on Agriculture, Nutrition, and Forestry. *Flood and Disaster Relief in the Midwest: Hearing, July 16, 1993, on the Scope and Components of Federal Disaster Relief in the Flood-Ravaged Midwest.* 103d Cong., 1st sess. Washington, DC: 1993, 78 pp.

U.S. Congress, Senate Committee on Environment and Public Works. *Federal Response to the Midwest Floods of 1993, Hearing before the Committee on Environment and Public Works.* 103d Cong., 1st sess. Washington, DC: GPO, 1994, 68 pp. Microfiche.

U.S. President. *Appropriations Request EC 1310, Communication from the President of the United States Transmitting Requests for Emergency Fiscal Year 1993 Supplemental Appropriations to Provide for Emergency Expenses Arising from the Consequences of the Flooding along the Mississippi River and Its Tributaries.* Series: Senate Document (U.S. Congress, Senate), 103-9. Washington, DC: GPO, 1993, 42 pp.

U.S. President. *Assistance to Flood-Stricken Area of the Midwest, Communication from the President of the United States Transmitting Notification Making Available Appropriations of $402.4 Million for the Department of Agriculture, Education, Labor and Transportation, and for the Legal Services.* Series: House Document (U.S. Congress, House), 103-130. Washington, DC: GPO, 1993, 3 pp. Microfiche.

U.S. President. *Emergency Supplemental Appropriations Request; Communication from the President of the United States Transmitting His Request for Emergency Supplemental Appropriations of $65,000,000 in Budget Authority for the Department of Health and Human Services to Support Public Health and Social Services Provided in Response to the Flooding along the Mississippi River and Its Tributaries, Pursuant to Public Law 103-75, Chapter 4 (107 Statute 746).* Washington, DC: GPO, 1993, 4 pp. Microfiche.

Mississippi River Floods

General

"Biggest Flood in Years [in the Mississippi River Valley]: What Kept It from Being Worse?" *U.S. News & World Report* 74 (April 23, 1973): 32+.

Carr, J. R. "Fighting the Floods at St. Louis." *Engineering News* 133 (August 21, 1947): 264–267.

"The Fate of New Orleans." *Compressed Air* 100 (April-May 1995): 30–35.

Kassner, Herbert A., and Roger P. Miller. "Flood of '73 [Lower Mississippi Valley]." *Water Spectrum* 5 (1973): 30–36.

"Memphis Prepares for Its Next Flood." *Engineering News* 133 (August 10, 1944): 166–169.

Myers, M. F., and G. F. White. "The Challenge of the Mississippi Flood." *Environment* (December 1993): 6–9+; discussion, 35 (December 1993): 2–5+.

"Plant Fights It Out with Mississippi: Clinton Floods." *Business Week* (May 5, 1951): 24–25.

Ports, Michael A. "Hydrologic Investigation of the April 1983 Flooding in New Orleans, Louisiana." *National Conference on Water Resources Planning and Management—Water Forum, Baltimore, MD,* 1992, pp. 260–267.

Read, W. E., and M. C. Robinson. "Lower Mississippi Valley Floods of 1982 and 1983." *Journal of Water Resources Planning and Management* 111 (October 1985): 434–453; discussion, 113 (November 1987): 827–829.

U.S. Department of the Army, Corps of Engineers. *Floods and Flood Control on the Mississippi River 1973.* Washington, DC: 1973, 66 pp.

Wahl, R. W. "The Mississippi Flood." *Environment* 34 (June 1994): 2–3.

Southeast

General

Bradley, B. D. "After Record Flooding, South Starts Cleanup." *Engineering News-Record* 233 (July 18, 1994): 8.

Breeding, S. D., and T. Dalrymple. "Texas Floods of 1938 and 1939." *U.S. Geological Survey Water Supply Paper* 914 (1944): 1–116.

Carpenter, David A. *Floods in West Virginia, Virginia, Pennsylvania, and Maryland, November 1985.* Denver, CO: U.S. Geological Survey, 1990, 86 pp.

Chandler, E. L. "Flood Control at Chattanooga: Local Protection Works in Conjunction with TVA Improvements." *Civil Engineering* 7 (June 1957): 405–408.

Dickson, R. R. "Weather and Circulation of August 1978: Texas Floods." *Monthly Weather Review* 106 (November 1978): 1639–1645.

Disaster Assistance: Response to West Virginia's November 1985 Flood Shows Need for Improvement: Report to Congressional Requesters. Washington, DC: General Accounting Office, 1988, 90 pp. Microfiche.

Edelen, George W., Jr., et al. "Floods of April 1979, Mississippi, Alabama, and Georgia." *Geological Survey Professional Paper* 1319 (1986): 1–220.

"Floods of August 1940 in the Southeastern States." *U.S. Geological Survey Water Supply Paper* 1066 (1949): 1–554.

"Georgia Recovers from Flood." *Engineering News-Record* 233 (July 25, 1994): 9.

"How TWA Saved Its Files." *Aviation Week* 55 (November 5, 1951): 66–68.

Kemezis, P., et al. "Record Flows Hit Southeast." *Engineering News-Record* 224 (March 29, 1990): 14+.

Lawson, L. M., and P. F. MacGregor. "International Treaty Authorizes Flood Control Structures on Lower Rio Grande." *Civil Engineering* 17 (March 1947): 117–120.

Neely, Braxtel L., Jr. *Flood of December 1987 in Central and Eastern Arkansas.* Denver, CO: U.S. Geological Survey, 1990, 16 pp.

Reid, J. "Record Floods Sweep through Georgia." *American Water Works Association Journal* 87 (May 1995): 76–80.

Ritter, D. F., and D. S. Blakeley. "Localized Catastrophic Disruption of the Gasconade River Flood Plain during the December 1982 Flood, Southeast Missouri." *Geology* 14 (June 1986): 472–476.

Rutter, E. J. "Flood-Control Operation of Tennessee Valley Authority Reservoirs." *American Society of Civil Engineers Proceedings* 76 (May 1950): 1–33; discussion, 77 (March 1951): 1–4.

Schmidt, R. A. "Flood Control without Power, Miami Conservancy District, Solved Problem by Construction of Dams Only." *Public Utilities* 40 (September 11, 1947): 333–339.

Shipley, A. "The Georgia Flood of '98." *QST* 82 (July 1998): 78–79.

U.S. Congress, Senate Committee on Labor and Public Welfare, Subcommittee on Labor. *Buffalo Creek (W.Va.) Disaster 1972.* Hearings: May 30 and 31, 1972. 92d Cong., 2d sess. Washington, DC: GPO, 1972. 2 vols. Microfiche.

Western Floods

General

"$100 Million Floods Strike Western United States." *Engineering News* 156 (January 5, 1956): 26–27.

Anderson, I. E. "Floods of the Puyallup and Chehalls River Basins." *U.S. Geological Survey Water Supply Paper* 968 (1948): 61–124.

Cerling, T. E., et al. "Cosmogenic ^{3}He and ^{21}Ne Age of the Big Lost River Flood, Snake River Plain, Idaho." *Geology* 22 (March 1994): 227–230.

Jones, Stanley H., and Chester Zenone. *Flood of October 1986 at Seward, Alaska.* Denver, CO: U.S. Geological Survey, 1988, 43 pp.

Maddox, R. A., et al. "Meteorological Characteristics of Flash Flood Events over the Western United States." *Monthly Weather Review* 108 (November 1980): 1866–1877.

Roeske, R. H., J. M. Garrett, and J. H. Eychaner. *Floods of October 1983 in Southeastern Arizona.* Denver, CO: U.S. Geological Survey, 1989, 77 pp.

Rosenbaum, D. B. "Storms Swamp Southwest." *Engineering News-Record* 230 (January 25, 1993): 13.

U.S. National Weather Service. *The Disastrous Southern California and Central Arizona Floods, Flash Floods, and Mudslides of February 1980: A Report to the Administrator.* National Disaster Survey Report NWS 81-1; National Oceanic and Atmospheric Administration NOAA-S/T 81-157. Silver Spring, MD: 1981, 5 pp.

Walsh, O. E. "Regulation of Northwest's Major Rivers Is Aim of Broad Flood Control Program." *Civil Engineering* 18 (December 1948): 748–753.

Walter, D. S. "Reclamation's Biggest Earthfill Dam: Anderson Ranch Dam in Idaho." *Engineering News* 139 (September 18, 1947): 396–402.

Big Thompson Flood of 1976

Albertson, M. L., et al. "Big Thompson Flood Damage Was Severe, But Some Could Have Been Prevented." *Civil Engineering (American Society of Civil Engineers)* 48 (February 1978): 74–77.

Balog, J. D. "Flooding in Big Thompson River, Colorado, Tributaries: Controls on Channel Erosion and Estimate of Recurrence Interval." *Geology* 6 (April 1978): 200–204.

Caracena, F., et al. "Mesoanalysis of the Big Thompson Storm." *Monthly Weather Review* 107 (January 1979): 1–17.

Costa, J. E. "Colorado Big Thompson Flood: Geologic Evidence of a Rare Hydrological Event." *Geology* 6 (October 1978): 617–620.

Gruntfest, E. C., et al. "Big Thompson Flood Exposes Need for Better Flood Reaction System to Save Lives." *Civil Engineering (American Society of Civil Engineers)* 48 (February 1978): 72–73.

Maddox, Robert A., et al. *Meteorological Aspects of the Big Thompson Flash Flood of 31 July 1976.* Washington, DC: GPO, 1977, 83 pp.

Columbia River Flood 1948

"Floods of May-June 1948 in Columbia River Basin." *U.S. Geological Survey Water Supply Paper* 1080 (1949): 1–476.

Hart, G. "Great Flood: West Coast Version." *QST* 40 (May 1956): 50–55+.

Stearns, C. "Keeping Utility Service Up in a Great Flood Emergency: Columbia River Flood." *Public Utilities* 42 (November 18, 1948): 722–727.

"What Floods Cost: Raging Columbia River." *Business Week* (June 26, 1948): 20–21.

California Floods

"California Storm Took Heavy Toll on Southern Pacific." *Railway Age* 104 (April 2, 1938): 619–623.

Cruse, R. E. "Structures to Control Torrents in Los Angeles County." *Engineering News-Record* 119 (July 8, 1937): 67–72.

Disastrous Floods from the Severe Winter Storms in California, Nevada, Washington, Oregon, and Idaho: December 1996–January 1997. Series: Natural Disaster Survey Report. Silver Spring, MD: Western Region Headquarters, National Weather Service, 1997.

Kirkbride, W. H. "Railroad Fights Floods: Southern California Deluge March 2, 1938, and Its Effect on Southern Pacific Lines." *Civil Engineer* 9 (December 1939): 711–714.

Kratch, K. "Oregon POTW's Remember the 100-Year Flood." *Water Environment and Technology* 8 (June 1996): 18–20.

McGlashan, H. D., and R. C. Briggs. "Floods of December 1937 in Northern California." *U.S. Geological Survey Water Supply Paper* 843 (1939): 1–497.

"Meeting the Challenge of Floods in Southern California: Southern Pacific Has Strengthened Lines and Rebuilt Structures." *Railway Age* 107 (August 19, 1939): 280–286.

Qualley, G. T., and M. D. Roos. "1995 Flood Events in California." *International Journal on Hydropower and Dams* 2 (July 1995): 54–57.

Rawn, A. M. "Sewerage Facilities Hard Hit by Southern California Flood." *Water Works and Sewage* 85 (April 1938): 248–256.

Rick, G. A. "Development of the Mission Bay–San Diego River Project." *American Society of Engineers Proceedings* 81 (June 1955): 1–7.

Stiles, W. W. "How a Community Met a Disaster: Yuba City Flood, Dec. 1955." *Annals of the American Academy of Political and Social Science* 309 (June 1957): 160–169.

Troxell, H. D., et al. "Floods of March 1938 in Southern California." *U.S. Geological Survey Water Supply Paper* 844 (1943): 1–399.

U.S. Congress, House Committee on Transportation and Infrastructure, Subcommittee on Water Resources and Environment. *Recent Flooding in California: Hearing before the Subcommittee on Water Resources and Environment of the Committee on Transportation and Infrastructure.* House of Representatives, 106th Cong., 1st sess. March 19, 1997. Washington, DC: GPO, 1997, 321 pp.

Selected Journal Titles

The journals listed below publish articles on many aspects of floods. Because of the destructiveness of floods and problems of recovery, floods have received a great deal of attention in a large number of journals. New journals are continually appearing. For other journals and additional information, please consult *Ulrich's International Periodicals Directory 1999,* 37th edition, New Providence, NJ, R. R. Bowker, 1998 (5 vols.).

Information on the journals listed is arranged in the following sample entry:

Journal Title
1. Editor
2. Year first published
3. Frequency of publication
4. Code
5. Special features
6. Telephone and fax numbers
7. Address of publisher

American City and County
1. Janet Ward
2. 1909
3. Monthly
4. ISSN 0149-337X
5. Advertising, book reviews, charts, illustrations, market prices, trade literature, index
6. Tel 770-955-2500; fax 770-955-0400
7. Intertec Publishing Corp.
   6151 Powers Ferry Road, NW
   Atlanta, GA 30339-2941

American Planning Association Journal

1. —
2. 1925
3. Quarterly
4. ISSN 0194-4363
5. Abstracts, advertising, book reviews, bibliographies, charts, illustrations, maps, cumulative index
6. Tel 312-431-9100; fax 312-431-9985
7. American Planning Association
   122 S. Michigan Avenue, Suite 1600
   Chicago, IL 60603-6107

American Society of Civil Engineers Proceedings

1. —
2. 1873
3. Monthly
4. ISSN 0003-1119
5. Abstracts, bibliographies, charts, illustrations, statistics, index
6. Tel 212-705-7288; fax 212-980-4681
7. American Society of Civil Engineers
   345 E. 47th Street
   New York, NY 10017-2398

American Water Works Association Journal

1. Nancy M. Zeilig
2. 1914
3. Monthly
4. ISSN 0003-150X
5. Abstracts, advertising, book reviews, bibliographies, charts, illustrations, statistics, trade literature, index, cumulative index
6. Tel 303-794-7711; fax 303-794-7310
7. American Water Works Association
   6666 W. Quincy Avenue
   Denver, CO 80235

Biocycle

1. Jerome Goldstein
2. 1960
3. Monthly
4. ISSN 0276-5055
5. Advertising, book reviews, charts, illustrations, index
6. Tel 610-967-4135

7. J. G. Press, Inc.
   419 State Avenue
   Emmaus, PA 18049

Bulletin of the American Meteorological Society
1. Richard E. Hallgren
2. 1920
3. Monthly
4. ISSN 0003-0007
5. Abstracts, advertising, book reviews, bibliographies, charts, illustrations, statistics, index
6. Tel 617-227-2425; fax 617-742-8718
7. American Meteorological Society
   45 Beacon Street
   Boston, MA 02108-3693

Business Week
1. Stephen B. Shepard
2. 1929
3. Weekly
4. ISSN 0007-7135
5. Book reviews, illustrations, statistics, index
6. Tel 212-512-2000
7. McGraw-Hill Companies
   1221 Avenue of the Americas, 39th Floor
   New York, NY 10020

Civil Engineering (New York)
1. Virginia Fairweather
2. 1930
3. Monthly
4. ISSN 0885-7024
5. Abstracts, advertising, book reviews, charts, illustrations, statistics, trade literature, index
6. Tel 212-705-7288; fax 212-980-4681
7. American Society of Civil Engineers
   345 E. 47th Street
   New York, NY 10017-2398

Coastal Management
1. Marc J. Hershman
2. 1973
3. Quarterly
4. ISSN 0892-0753

5. Abstracts, advertising, book reviews, bibliographies, charts, illustrations, statistics, index, cumulative index
6. Tel 215-785-5800; 800-821-8312; fax 215-785-5515
7. Taylor & Francis, Inc.
   1900 Frost Road, Suite 101
   Bristol, PA 19007

Electrical World
1. Robert Schwieger
2. 1874
3. Monthly
4. ISSN 0013-4457
5. Advertising, charts, illustrations, market prices, trade literature, semiannual index
6. Tel 212-512-2000
7. McGraw-Hill Companies
   1221 Avenue of the Americas
   New York, NY 10020

ENR (Engineering News-Record)
1. Howard B. Stussman
2. 1874
3. Weekly
4. ISSN 0891-9526
5. Advertising, book reviews, charts, illustrations, market prices, statistics, trade literature, semiannual index
6. Tel 212-512-2000; fax 212-512-2565
7. McGraw-Hill Companies
   Engineering News Record
   Two Penn Plaza, 9th Floor
   New York, NY 10121-0098

Environment
1. Barbara Richman
2. 1958
3. Monthly
4. ISSN 0013-9157
5. Book reviews, bibliographies, charts, illustrations, index, cumulative index
6. Tel 202-296-6267; fax 202-296-5149
7. Heldref Publications
   1319 18th Street, NW
   Washington, DC 20036-1802

Environmental Science and Technology
1. William H. Glaze
2. 1967
3. Monthly
4. ISSN 0013-936X
5. Abstracts, advertising, book reviews, bibliographies, charts, illustrations, statistics, trade literature, index
6. Tel 800-333-9511; fax 614-447-3671
7. American Chemical Society
   1155 16th Street, NW
   Washington, DC 20036

Geology
1. F. Rogers
2. 1973
3. Monthly
4. ISSN 0091-7613
5. —
6. Tel 303-447-2020; fax 303-447-1133
7. Geological Society of America
   3300 Penrose Place
   Box 9140
   Boulder, CO 80301

Journal of Applied Meteorology
1. Steven R. Hanna
2. 1962
3. Monthly
4. ISSN 0894-8763
5. Abstracts, bibliographies, charts, illustrations, statistics, index
6. Tel 617-227-2425; fax 617-742-8718
7. American Meteorological Society
   45 Beacon Street
   Boston, MA 02108-3693

Journal of Environmental Health
1. Nelson Fabian
2. 1938
3. Ten times a year
4. ISSN 0022-0892
5. Book reviews, charts, illustrations, index
6. Tel 303-756-9090; fax 303-691-9490

7. National Environmental Health Association
   720 S. Colorado Boulevard
   Tower Suite 970
   Denver, CO 80246

Journal of Environmental Quality
1. R. J. Wagenet
2. 1972
3. Quarterly
4. ISSN 0047-2425
5. Book reviews, bibliographies, charts, illustrations, statistics
6. Tel 608-273-8080; fax 608-273-2021
7. American Society of Agronomy, Inc.
   677 S. Segue Road
   Madison, WI 53711

Journal of Geology
1. Alfred T. Anderson Jr. and Robert C. Newton
2. 1893
3. Bimonthly (every two months)
4. ISSN 0022-1376
5. Advertising, book reviews, illustrations, index, cumulative index
6. Tel 773-753-3347; fax 773-753-0811
7. University of Chicago Press
   Journals Division
   Box 37005
   Chicago, IL 60637

Journal of Hydraulic Engineering
1. A. Jacob Odgaard
2. 1956
3. Monthly
4. ISSN 0733-9429
5. —
6. Tel 212-705-7288; fax 212-980-4681
7. American Society of Civil Engineers, Hydraulics Division
   345 E. 47th Street
   New York, NY 10017-2398

Journal of Irrigation and Drainage
1. A. Ramachandra Rao
2. 1956

3. Bimonthly
4. ISSN 0733-9437
5. —
6. Tel 212-705-7288; fax 212-980-4681
7. American Society of Civil Engineers,
Irrigation and Drainage Division
345 E. 47th Street
New York, NY 10017-2398

Journal of the Atmospheric Sciences
1. Robert L. Gall and G. Brant Foote
2. 1944
3. Semimonthly (twice monthly)
4. ISSN 0022-4928
5. Abstracts, bibliographies, charts, illustrations, statistics, index
6. Tel 617-227-2425; fax 617-742-8718
7. American Meteorological Society
45 Beacon Street
Boston, MA 02108-3693

Journal of Water Resources Planning and Management
1. Richard Palmer
2. —
3. Bimonthly (every two months)
4. ISSN 0733-9496
5. —
6. Tel 212-705-7288; fax 212-980-4681
7. American Society of Civil Engineers
Water Resources Planning and Management Division
345 E. 47th Street
New York, NY 10017-2398

Journal of Waterway, Port, Coastal, and Ocean Engineering
1. Nobuhisa Kobayashi
2. 1956
3. Bimonthly (every two months)
4. ISSN 0733-950X
5. —
6. Tel 212-705-7288; fax 212-980-4681
7. American Society of Civil Engineers
Waterway, Port, Coastal, and Ocean Division
345 E. 47th Street
New York, NY 10017-2398

Land Economics
1. David Bromley
2. 1925
3. Quarterly
4. ISSN 0023-7639
5. Advertising, book reviews, bibliographies, index
6. Tel 608-262-4952; fax 608-262-7560
7. University of Wisconsin Press
   Journal Division
   114 N. Murray Street
   Madison, WI 53715

Monthly Weather Review
1. T. N. Krishamurti, Peter S. Ray
2. 1872
3. Monthly
4. ISSN 0027-0644
5. Abstracts, bibliographies, charts, illustrations, statistics, index
6. Tel 617-227-2425; fax 617-742-8718
7. American Meteorological Society
   45 Beacon Street
   Boston, MA 02108-3693

National Geographic
1. William L. Allen
2. 1888
3. Monthly
4. ISSN 0027-9358
5. Advertising, illustrations, index, semiannual cumulative index
6. Tel 202-857-7000
7. National Geographic Society
   1145 17th Street, NW
   Washington, DC 20036

National Institute of Standards and Technology, Journal of Research
1. Barry Taylor
2. 1928
3. Bimonthly (every two months)
4. ISSN 1044-677X
5. Illustrations, index
6. Tel 202-512-1800; fax 202-512-2250

7. Superintendent of Documents
U.S. Government Printing Office
Box 317954
Pittsburgh, PA 15250-7954

National Journal
1. Stephen G. Smith
2. 1969
3. Weekly
4. ISSN 0360-4217
5. Advertising, book reviews, charts, illustrations, semiannual index
6. Tel 202-739-8400; fax 202-833-8069
7. National Journal, Inc.
1501 M Street, NW, Suite 300
Washington, DC 20005

National Underwriter Property and Casualty—
Risk and Benefits Management Edition
1. Sam Friedman
2. 1896
3. Weekly
4. ISSN 1042-6841
5. —
6. Tel 513-721-2140; 800-543-0874; fax 513-721-0126
7. National Underwriter Company
505 Gest Street
Cincinnati, OH 45203

New Scientist
1. Alun Anderson
2. 1956
3. Weekly
4. ISSN 0262-4079
5. Advertising, book reviews, charts, illustrations, patents, quarterly index
6. Tel 44-171-261-5000
7. IPC Magazines
Specialist Magazine Group
King's Reach Tower
Stamfort Street
London SE1 9LS
England

Oceanus
1. Vicky Cullen
2. 1952
3. Semiannual (twice a year)
4. ISSN 0029-8182
5. Advertising, book reviews, charts, illustrations, index, cumulative index
6. Tel 508-289-2719; fax 508-289-2182
7. Woods Hole Oceanographic Institution
   Research Library
   86 Water Street
   Woods Hole, MA 02543

Pipeline and Gas Journal
1. Jeff Share
2. 1859
3. Monthly
4. ISSN 0032-0188
5. Advertising, charts, illustrations
6. Tel 281-558-6930; fax 281-558-7029
7. Oildom Publishing Company of Texas, Inc.
   Box 219368
   Houston, TX 77218-9368

Public Management
1. Beth Payne
2. 1918
3. Monthly
4. ISSN 0033-3611
5. Advertising, book reviews, bibliographies
6. Tel 202-962-3619; fax 202-962-3500
7. International City-County Management Association
   777 North Capitol, NE, Suite 500
   Washington, DC 20002-4201

Public Works
1. James R. Kircher
2. 1896
3. Monthly
4. ISSN 0033-3840
5. Advertising, abstracts, book reviews, bibliographies, charts, illustrations, trade literature, index
6. Tel 201-445-5800; fax 201-445-5170

7. Public Works Journal Corporation
200 S. Broad Street
Ridgewood, NJ 07451

QST
1. Mark Wilson
2. 1915
3. Monthly
4. ISSN 0033-4812
5. Book reviews, charts, illustrations, index
6. Tel 860-594-0200; fax 860-594-0303
7. American Radio Relay League, Inc.
225 Main Street
Newington, CT 06111

Railway Age
1. Luther S. Miller
2. 1856
3. Monthly
4. ISSN 0033-8826
5. Advertising
6. Tel 212-620-7200
7. Simmons-Boardman Publishing Corporation
345 Hudson Street
New York, NY 10014-4502

Reader's Digest
1. Kenneth Y. Tomlinson
2. 1922
3. Monthly
4. ISSN 0034-0375
5. Advertising, illustrations, index
6. Tel 914-238-1000; fax 914-244-5994
7. Reader's Digest Association, Inc.
Pleasantville, NY 10570

Reason
1. Virginia I. Postrel
2. 1968
3. Monthly
4. ISSN 0048-6906
5. Advertising, book reviews, bibliographies, illustrations, index
6. Tel 815-734-1102

7. Reason Foundation
   3415 S. Sepulveda Boulevard, Suite 400
   Los Angeles, CA 90034-6060

Science
1. Floyd Bloom
2. 1880
3. Weekly
4. ISSN 0036-8075
5. Abstracts, advertising, book reviews, bibliographies, illustrations, trade literature
6. Tel 202-326-6417
7. American Association for the Advancement of Science
   1200 New York Avenue, NW
   Washington, DC 20005

Science News
1. Julie Ann Miller
2. 1921
3. Weekly
4. ISSN 0036-8423
5. Book reviews, illustrations, index
6. Tel 800-552-4412; fax 202-659-0365
7. Science Service
   1719 N Street, NW
   Washington, DC 20036

Smithsonian
1. Don Moser
2. 1970
3. Monthly
4. ISSN 0037-7333
5. Advertising, book reviews, illustrations, index
6. Tel 202-786-2900; fax 202-786-2564
7. Smithsonian Institution
   Arts and Industries Building
   900 Jefferson Drive, SW
   Washington, DC 20560

U.S. News & World Report
1. James Fallows
2. 1933
3. Weekly

4. ISSN 0041-5537
5. Advertising, charts, illustrations
6. Tel 212-830-1500
7. U.S. News & World Report, Inc.
   1290 Avenue of the Americas, Suite 600
   New York, NY 10104

Water Engineering and Management
1. Bill Swehtenberg
2. 1882
3. Monthly
4. ISSN 0273-2238
5. Abstracts, advertising, book reviews, charts, illustrations, statistics, index, cumulative index
6. Tel 847-391-1000; fax 847-390-0408
7. Scranton Gillette Communications, Inc.
   380 N. Northwest Highway
   Des Plaines, IL 60016-2282

Water Environment and Technology
1. Lisa Neal
2. 1989
3. Thirteen times a year
4. ISSN 1044-9493
5. Advertising
6. Tel 703-684-2400; fax 703-684-2492
7. Water Environment Federation
   601 Wythe Street
   Alexandria, VA 22314-1994

Weatherwise
1. Jeffrey Rosenfeld
2. 1948
3. Bimonthly (every two months)
4. ISSN 0043-1672
5. Advertising, charts, illustrations, index
6. Tel 202-296-6267; fax 202-296-5149
7. Heldref Publications
   1319 18th Street, NW
   Washington, DC 20036-1802

Western Water
1. Rita Schmidt Sudman

2. 1973
3. Bimonthly (every two months)
4. ISSN 0735-5424
5. Book reviews, illustrations, trade literature
6. Tel 916-444-6240; fax 916-448-7699
7. Water Education Foundation
   717 K Street, No. 517
   Sacramento, CA 95814-3406

U.S.G.S. Professional Papers

Professional U.S. Geological Survey papers are scientific reports of wide and lasting interest and are important to professional scientists and engineers. Listed here are also some collections of related papers on different aspects of a single scientific topic.

United States

Bailey, J. F., J. L. Patterson, and J. L. H. Paulhus. "Hurricane Agnes Rainfall and Floods, June–July 1972." 1975, P-924, 403 pp.

Carrigan, P. H. "A Flood-Frequency Relation Based on Regional Record Maxima." 1971, P-434-F, pp. F1–F22.

Chin, E. H., John Skelton, and H. P. Guy. "The Mississippi River Basin Flood: Compilation and Analyses of Meteorologic, Streamflow, and Sediment Data." 1975, P-937, 137 pp.

Dawdy, D. R., R. W. Lichty, and J. M. Bergmann. "A Rainfall-Runoff Simulation Model for Estimation of Flood Peaks for Small Drainage Basins." 1972, P-05 06-B, pp. B1–B28.

Edelen, G. W., Jr., and J. F. Miller. "Floods of March–April 1973 in Southeastern United States." 1976, P-998, 283 pp.

Hays, W. W., ed. "Facing Geologic and Hydrologic Hazards: Earth-Science Considerations." 1981, P-1240-B, pp. B1–B108.

Kilpatrick, F. A., and H. H. Barnes Jr. "Channel Geometry of Piedmont Streams as Related to Frequency of Floods." 1964, P-422-E, pp. E1–E10.

Scott, K. M., and G. C. Gravlee Sr. "Flood Surge on the Rubicon River, California: Hydrology, Hydraulics, and Boulder Transport." 1968, P-422-M, pp. M1–M40.

Shen, John. "Use of Analog Models in the Analysis of Flood Runoff." 1965, P-506-A, pp. A1–A24.

Sigafoos, R. S. "Botanical Evidence of Floods and Flood-Plain Deposition." 1964, P-485-A, pp. A1–A35.

Wolman, M. G., and L. B. Leopold. "River Flood Plains: Some Observations on Their Formation." 1957, P-282-C, pp. 87–109.

Yanosky, T. M. "Effects of Flooding upon Woody Vegetation along Parts of the Potomac Flood Plain." 1982, P-1206, 21 pp.

———. "Evidence of Floods on the Potomac River from Anatomical Abnormalities in the Wood of Flood-Plain Trees." 1983, P-1296, 42 pp.

Alabama

Edelen, G. W., Jr., K. V. Wilson, and J. R. Harkins. "Floods of April 1979, Mississippi, Alabama, and Georgia." 1986, P-1319, 212 pp.

Arizona

Burkham, D. E. "Effects of Changes in an Alluvial Channel on the Timing, Magnitude, and Transformation of Flood Waves, Southeastern Arizona." 1976, P-655-K, pp. K1–K25.

———. "Hydraulic Effects of Change in Bottom-Land Vegetation on Three Major Floods, Gila River, in Southeastern Arizona." 1976, P-655-J, pp. J1–J14.

———. "Precipitation Streamflow and Major Floods at Selected Sites in the Gila River Drainage Basin above Coolidge Dam." 1970, P-655-B, pp. B1–B33.

Chin, E. H., B. N. Aldridge, and R. J. Longfield. "Floods of February 1980 in Southern California and Central Arizona." 1991, P-1494, 126 pp.

Cooley, M. E., B. N. Aldridge, and R. C. Euler. "Effects of the Catastrophic Flood of December 1966, North Rim Area, Eastern Grand Canyon, Arizona." 1977, P-980, 43 pp.

California

Blodgett, J. C., and K. R. Poeschel. "Peak Discharge, Volume, and Frequency of the January 1982 Flood in the Santa Cruz Mountains and Vicinity." 1988, P-1434-13, pp. 229–243.

Chin, E. H., B. N. Aldridge, and R. J. Longfield. "Floods of February 1980 in Southern California and Central Arizona." 1991, P-1494, 126 pp.

Ellen, S. D., and G. F. Wieczorek, eds. "Landslides, Floods, and Marine Effects of the Storm of January 3–5, 1982, in San Francisco Bay Region, California." 1988, P-1434, 310 pp.

Frankel, Arthur, and J. E. Vidale. "A Three-Dimensional Simulation of Seismic Waves in the Santa Clara Valley, California, from an Aftershock." 1994, P-1551-A, pp. A197–A215.

Griggs, G. B. "Impact of the January 1982 Flood in Santa Cruz County." 1988, P-1434-12, pp. 205–227.

Harden, D. R. "A Comparison of Flood-Producing Storms and Their Impacts in Northwestern California." 1995, P-1454, D1-D9, 304 pp.

Helley, E. J., and V. C. La Marche Jr. "Historic Flood Information for Northern California Streams from Geological and Botanical Evidence." 1973, P-485-E, pp. E1–E16.

Stewart, J. H., and V. C. La Marche Jr. "Erosion and Deposition Produced by the Flood of December 1964 on Coffee Creek, Trinity County, California." 1967, P-422-K, pp. K1–K22.

Waananen, A. O., et al. "Flood-Prone Areas and Land-Use Planning: Selected Examples from the San Francisco Bay Region, California." 1977, P-942, 75 pp.

Young, L. E. "Flood Inundation Mapping, San Diego, California." 1964, P-486-B, pp. B163–B164.

Colorado

Shroba, R. R., et al. "Storm and Flood of July 31–August 1, 1976: Geologic and Geomorphic Effects in the Big Thompson Canyon Area, Larimer County; Damage Caused by Geologic Processes during Flood-Producing Storms." 1979, P-1115-B, pp. 87–152.

Georgia

Edelen, G. W., Jr., K. V. Wilson, and J. R. Harkins. "Floods of April 1979, Mississippi, Alabama, and Georgia." 1986, P-1319, 212 pp.

Kansas

Hauth, L. D., and W. J. Carswell Jr. "Floods in Kansas City, Missouri and Kansas, September 12–13, 1977." 1981, P-1169, 47 pp.

Schumm, S. A., and R. W. Lichty. "Channel Widening and Flood-Plain Construction along Cimarron River in Southwestern Kansas." 1963, P-352-D, pp. 71–88.

Kentucky

Runner, G. S., and E. H. Chin. "Flood of April 1977 in the Appalachian Region of Kentucky, Tennessee, Virginia, and West Virginia." 1980, P-1098, 43 pp.

Maine

Morrill, R. A., E. H. Chin, and W. S. Richardson. "Maine Coastal Storm and Flood of February 2, 1976." 1979, P-1087, 20 pp.

Mississippi

Edelen, G. W., Jr., K. V. Wilson, and J. R. Harkins. "Floods of April 1979, Mississippi, Alabama, and Georgia." 1986, P-1319, 212 pp.

Missouri

Hauth, L. D., and W. J. Carswell Jr. "Floods in Kansas City, Missouri and Kansas, September 12–13, 1977." 1981, P-1169, 47 pp.

Montana

Parrett, Charles, D. D. Carlson, G. S. Craig Jr., and E. H. Chin. "Floods of May 1978 in Southeastern Montana and Northeastern Wyoming." 1984, P-1244, 74 pp.

Nevada

Glancy, P. A., and Lynn Harmsen. "A Hydrologic Assessment of the September 14, 1974, Flood in Eldorado Canyon, Nevada." 1975, P-930, 28 pp.

Pennsylvania

Hoxit, L. R., R. A. Maddox, C. F. Chappell, and S. A. Brua. "Johnstown-Western Pennsylvania Storms and Floods of July 19–20, 1977. 1982, P-1211.

South Dakota

Schwarz, F. K., et al. "The Black Hills–Rapid City Flood of June 9–10, 1972: A Description of the Storm and Flood." 1975, P-877, 47 pp.

Tennessee

Runner, G. S., and E. H. Chin. "Flood of April 1977 in the Appalachian Region of Kentucky, Tennessee, Virginia, and West Virginia." 1980, P-1098, 43 pp.

Texas

Schroeder, E. E., B. C. Massey, and E. H. Chin. "Floods in Central Texas, August 1–4, 1978." 1987, P-1332, 39 pp.

Virginia

Runner, G. S., and E. H. Chin. "Flood of April 1977 in the Appalachian Region of Kentucky, Tennessee, Virginia, and West Virginia." 1980, P-1098, 43 pp.

West Virginia

Runner, G. S., and E. H. Chin. "Flood of April 1977 in the Appalachian Region of Kentucky, Tennessee, Virginia, and West Virginia." 1980, P-1098, 43 pp.

Wyoming

Parrett, Charles, D. D. Carlson, G. S. Craig Jr., and E. H. Chin. "Floods of May 1978 in Southeastern Montana and Northeastern Wyoming." 1984, P-1244, 74 pp.

Water Resource Investigations

Water Resource Investigations (WRI) Reports are papers of an interpretive nature made available to the public outside the formal U.S. Geological Survey publications series. Copies are reproduced on request and are also available for public inspection at depositories indicated in USGS catalogs. Early publications (1879–1970) of USGS were found under Water Supply Papers (W) but many are out of print; hence, they are not listed.

United States

Anderson, D. B., and I. L. Burmeister. *Floods of March–May 1965 in the Upper Mississippi River Basin.* 1970, W1850-A, pp. A1–A448.

Bogart, D. B. *Floods of August–October 1955, New England to North Carolina.* 1960, 854 pp.

Carter, R. W., and R. G. Godfrey. *Storage and Flood Routing.* 1960, W1543-B, pp. 81–104.

Dalrymple, Tate. *Flood Frequency Analyses.* 1960, W1543-A, pp. 1–80.

Faye, R. E., and M. E. Blalock. *Simulation of Dynamic Floodflows at Gaged Stations in the Southeastern United States.* 1984, WRI 84-4000, 114 pp.

Floods of April 1952 in the Missouri River Basin. 1955, W1260-B, pp. 49–302.

Floods of 1952 in the Basins of the Upper Mississippi River and Red River of the North. 1955, W1250-C, pp. 303–359.

Hendricks, E. L. *Summary of Floods in the United States during 1956.* 1964, W1530, 85 pp.

Majure, J. J., and P. J. Soenksen. *Using a Geographic Information System to Determine Physical Basin Characteristics for Use in Flood-Frequency Equations.* 1991, WRI 90-4162, pp. 23–29.

Matthai, H. F. *Magnitude and Frequency of Floods in the United States: Part 6-B, Missouri River Basin below Sioux City, Iowa.* 1968, W1680, 491 pp.

Parola, A. C., et al. *Streambed Stresses and Flow around Bridge Piers.* 1996, WRI 96-4142, 128 pp.

Rostvedt, J. O., et al. *Summary of Floods in the United States during 1963.* 1968, W1830-B, pp. B1–B120.

———. *Summary of Floods in the United States during 1964.* 1970, W1840-C, pp. C1–C124.

———. *Summary of Floods in the United States during 1965.* 1970, W1850-E, pp. E1–E110.

Summary of Floods in the United States during 1951. 1957, W1227-D, pp. 279–298.

Summary of Floods in the United States during 1952. 1959, W1260-F, pp. 687–713.

Summary of Floods in the United States during 1953. 1959, W1320-E, pp. 341–364.

Summary of Floods in the United States during 1954. 1959, W1370-C, pp. 201–263.

Summary of Floods in the United States during 1955. 1962, W1455-B, pp. 69–143.

Young, R. E., and R. W. Cruff. *Magnitude and Frequency of Floods in the United States: Part II, Pacific Slope Basins in California—Volume 2, Klamath and Smith River Basins and Central Valley Drainage from the East.* 1967, W1686, 308 pp.

Alabama

Atkins, J. B. *Magnitude and Frequency of Floods in Alabama.* 1996, WRI 95-4199, 234 pp.

Atkins, J. B., and T. S. Hedgecock. *Scour at Selected Bridge Sites in Alabama, 1991–94.* 1996, WRI 96-4137, 19 pp.

Floods of March–April 1951 in Alabama and Adjacent States. 1953, W1227-A, pp. 1–34.

Olin, D. A. *Flood-Depth Frequency Relations for Streams in Alabama.* 1986, WRI 85-4296, 46 pp.

Olin, D. A., and J. B. Atkins. *Estimating Flood Hydrographs and Volumes for Alabama Streams.* 1988, WRI 88-4041, 25 pp.

Pearman, J. L., T. C. Stamey, G. W. Hess, and G. H. Nelson Jr. *Floods of February and March 1990 in Alabama, Georgia, and Florida.* 1991, WRI 91-4089, 44 pp.

Alaska

Brabets, T. P. *Scour Assessment at Bridges from Flag Point to Million Dollar Bridge, Copper River Highway, Alaska.* 1994, WRI 94-4073, 57 pp.

Jones, S. H., and Chester Zenone. *Flood of October 1986 at Seward, Alaska.* 1988, WRI 87-4278, 43 pp., two oversized maps.

Lamke, R. D. *Flood Characteristics of Alaskan Streams.* 1978, WRI 78-0129.

Meyer, D. F. *Flooding in the Middle Koyukuk River Basin, Alaska, August 1994.* 1995, WRI 95-4118, 8 pp.

Arizona

Aldridge, B. N. *Floods of November 1965 to January 1966 in the Gila River Basin, Arizona and New Mexico, and Adjacent Basins in Arizona.* 1970, W1850-C, pp. C1–C176.

Carlson, D. D., and D. F. Meyer. *Flood on the Virgin River, January 1989, in Utah, Arizona, and Nevada.* 1995, WRI 94-4159, 21 pp.

Eychaner, J. H. *Estimation of Magnitude and Frequency of Floods in Pima County, Arizona, with Comparisons of Alternate Methods.* 1984, WRI 84-4142, 69 pp.

Hill, G. W., T. A. Hales, and B. N. Aldridge. *Flood Hydrology Near Flagstaff, Arizona.* 1988, WRI 87-4210, 31 pp.

Hjalmarson, H. W. *Flood of October 1983 and History of Flooding along the San Francisco River, Clifton, Arizona.* 1990, WRI 85-4225-B, 42 pp.

———. *Potential Flood Hazards and Hydraulic Characteristics of Distributary-Flow Areas in Maricopa County, Arizona.* 1994, WRI 93-4169, 56 pp.

Hjalmarson, H. W., and S. P. Kemna. *Flood Hazards of Distributary-Flow Areas in Southwestern Arizona.* 1991, WRI 91-4171, 58 pp.

Melis, Theodore S., William M. Phillips, Robert H. Webb, and Donald J. Bills. *When the Blue-Green Waters Turn Red: Historical Flooding in Havasu Creek, Arizona.* 1996, WRI 96-4059, 136 pp.

Melis, Theodore S., R. H. Webb, P. G. Griffiths, and T. J. Wise. *Magnitude and Frequency Data for Historic Debris Flows in Grand Canyon National Park and Vicinity, Arizona.* 1995, WRI 94-4214, 285 pp.

Moosburner, Otto. *Potential Flood and Debris Hazards at Katherine Landing and Telephone Cove, Lake Mead National Recreational Area, Mohave County, Arizona.* 1988, WRI 87-4081, 19 pp.

Parker, J. T. *Channel Change and Sediment Transport in Two Desert Streams in Central Arizona, 1991–92.* 1995, WRI 95-4059, 42 pp.

Roeske, R. H., J. M. Garrett, and J. H. Eychaner. *Floods of October 1983 in Southeastern Arizona,* 1989, WRI 85-4225-C, 77 pp.

Arkansas

Bedinger, M. S. *Forests and Flooding with Special Reference to the White River and Ouachita River Basins, Arkansas.* 1979, WRI 79-0068.

Gilstrap, R. C., and B. L. Neely Jr. *Floodflow Characteristics of Current River at Arkansas State Highway 328 Near Reyno, Arkansas.* 1986, WRI 86-4061, 15 pp.

Hodge, S. A., and G. D. Taska. *Magnitude and Frequency of Floods in Arkansas.* 1995, WRI 95-4224, 52 pp.

Landers, M. N. *Floodflow Frequency of Streams in the Alluvial Plain in the Lower Mississippi River in Mississippi, Arkansas, and Louisiana.* 1985, WRI 85-4150, 21 pp.

Neely, B. L., Jr. *Estimating Flood Hydrographs for Arkansas Streams,* 1989, WRI 89-4109, 19 pp.

———. *Flood Characteristics of the Buffalo River at Tyler Bend, Arkansas.* 1987 WRI 87-4180, one oversized map.

———. *Flood of December 1987 in Central and Eastern Arkansas.* 1990, WRI 89-4188, 16 pp.

———. *The Flood of December 1982 and the 100-Year and 500-Year Flood on the Buffalo River, Arkansas.* 1985, WRI 85-4192, 37 pp.

Southard, R. E. *Flood of May 19–20, 1990, in the Vicinity of Hot Springs, Arkansas.* 1992, WRI 92-4007, 48 pp.

California

Blodgett, J. C., and E. H. Chin. *Flood of January 1982 in the San Francisco Bay Area, California.* 1989, WRI 88-4236, 46 pp.

Meyer, R. W. *Potential Hazards from Floodflows within the John Muir House National Historical Site, Franklin Creek Drainage Basin, California.* 1994, WRI 93-4009, 9 pp.

Taylor, M. J., J. M. Shay, and S. N. Hamlin. *Changes in Water-Quality Conditions in Lexington Reservoir, Santa Clara County, California, Following a Large Fire in 1985 and Flood in 1986.* 1993, 92-4172, 23 pp.

Young, L. E., and E. E. Harris. *Floods of January-February 1963 in California and Nevada.* 1966, W1830-A, A1–A472.

Young, R. E., and R. W. Cruff. *Magnitude and Frequency of Floods in the United States: Part II, Pacific Slope Basins in California—Volume 2, Klamath and Smith River Basins and Central Valley Drainage from the East.* 1967, W1686, 308 pp.

Colorado

Jarrett, R. D., and J. E. Costa. *Evaluation of the Flood Hydrology in the Colorado Front Range Using Precipitation Streamflow and Paleoflood Data for the Big Thompson River Basin.* 1988, WRI 87-4117, 37 pp.

Kuhn, Gerhard, and R. C. Nickless. *Use of Frequency Analysis and the Extended Streamflow Prediction Procedure to Estimate Evacu-*

ation Dates for the Joint-Use Pool of Pueblo Reservoir, Colorado. 1994, WRI 94-4054, 46 pp.

Vaudrey, W. C. *Floods of May 1955 in Colorado and New Mexico.* 1960, W1455-A, pp. 1–68.

Delaware

Dillow, Jonathan J. *A Technique for Estimating Magnitude and Frequency of Peak Flows in Delaware.* 1996, WRI 95-4153, 27 pp., three oversized maps.

Hayes, D. C. *Scour at Bridge Sites in Delaware, Maryland, and Virginia.* 1996, WRI 96-4089, 35 pp.

———. *Site Selections and Collection of Bridge-Scour Data in Delaware, Maryland, and Virginia.* 1993, WRI 93-4017, 23 pp.

Paulachok, G. N., R. H. Simmons, and A. J. Tallman. *Storm and Flood of July 5, 1989, in Northern New Castle County, Delaware.* 1995, WRI 94-4188, 29 pp.

Florida

Franklin, M. A. *Magnitude and Frequency of Flood Volumes for Urban Watersheds in Leon County, Florida.* 1984, WRI 84-4233, 20 pp.

Franklin, M. A., and G. T. Losey. *Magnitude and Frequency of Floods from Urban Streams in Leon County, Florida.* 1984, WRI 84-4004, 37 pp.

Giese, G. L., and M. A. Franklin. *Magnitude and Frequency of Floods in the Suwannee River Water Management District, Florida.* 1996, WRI 96-4176, 14 pp.

Lopez, M. A., and R. D. Hayes. *Regional Flood Relations for Unregulated Lakes in West-Central Florida* 1984, WRI 84-4015, 60 pp.

Murphy, W. R., Jr. *Flood Profiles for Lower Brooker Creek, West Central, Florida.* 1977, WRI 77-0015.

Pearman, J. L., T. C. Stamey, G. W. Hess, and G. H. Nelson Jr. *Floods of February and March 1990 in Alabama, Georgia, and Florida.* 1991, WRI 81-4089, 44 pp.

Robertson, A. F. *Flood Profiles of the Alafia River, West-Central Florida, Computed by Step-Backwater Method.* 1977, WRI 77-0074.

Rumenik, R. P., C. A. Pascale, and D. F. Rucker. *Flood-Prone Areas of Gadson County, Florida.* 1975 (WRI 75-003).

Stone, R. B., L. V. Causey, and D. F. Tucker. *Flood-Prone Areas of the Consolidated City of Jacksonville, Duval County, Florida.* 1976, WRI 76-0054.

Georgia

Hess, G. W., and E. J. Inman. *Effects of Urban Flood-Detention Reservoirs on Peak Discharges and Flood Frequencies, and Simulation of Flood-Detention Reservoir Outflow-Hydrographs in Two Watersheds in Albany, Georgia.* 1994, WRI 94-4158, 31 pp.

———. *Effects of Urban Flood-Detention Reservoirs on Peak Discharges in Gwinnett County, Georgia.* 1994, WRI 94-4004, 35 pp.

Inman, E. J. *Comparison of the 2-, 25-, and 100-Year Recurrence Interval Floods Computed from Observed Data with the 1995 Urban Flood-Frequency Estimating Equations for Georgia.* 1997, WRI 97-4118, 14 pp.

———. *Flood-Frequency Relations for Urban Streams in Metropolitan Atlanta, Georgia.* 1983, WRI 83-4203, 38 pp.

———. *Simulation of Flood Hydrographs for Georgia Streams.* 1986, WRI 86-4004, 41 pp.

Pearman, J. L., T. C. Stamey, G. W. Hess, and G. H. Nelson Jr. *Floods of February and March 1990 in Alabama, Georgia, and Florida.* 1991, WRI 91-4089, 44 pp.

Sanders, C. L., Jr., H. E. Kubik, J. T. Hoke Jr., and W. H. Kirby. *Flood Frequency of the Savannah River in Augusta, Georgia.* 1990, WRI 90-4024, 87 pp.

Stamey, T. C., and G. W. Hess. *Techniques for Estimating Magnitude and Frequency of Floods in Rural Basins of Georgia.* 1993, WRI 93-4016, 69 pp.

Hawaii

Wong, M. F. *Estimation of Magnitude and Frequency of Floods for Streams on the Island of Oahu.* 1994, WRI 94-4052, 37 pp.

Idaho

Kjelstrom, L. C., and Charles Berenbrock. *Estimated 100-Year Peak Flows and Flow Volume in the Big Lost River and Birch Creek at the Idaho National Engineering Laboratory.* 1996, WRI 96-4163, 23 pp.

Illinois

Balding, G. O., and A. L. Ishii. *Floods of September 26–October 4, 1986, and August 14–17, 1987, in Illinois.* 1993, WRI 92-4149, 105 pp.

Curtis, G. W. *Techniques for Estimating Flood-Peak Discharges and Frequencies on Rural Streams in Illinois.* 1987, WRI 87-4207, 79 pp.

Daniels, W. S., and M. D. Hale. *Floods of October 1954 in the Chicago Area, Illinois, and Indiana.* 1958, W1370-B, pp. 107–200.

Ishii, A. L. *Floods of June 13–14, 1981, and December 2–12, 1982, in Illinois.* 1991, WRI 91-4062, 109 pp.

Indiana

Daniels, W. S., and M. D. Hale. *Floods of October 1954 in the Chicago Area, Illinois, and Indiana.* 1958, W1370-B, pp. 107–200.
Glatfelter, D. R., and G. K. Butch. *Instrumentation Methods of Flood-Data Collection and Transmission, and Evaluation of Streamflow Gaging Network in Indiana.* 1994, WRI 91-4051, 75 pp.
Glatfelter, D. R., G. K. Butch, and J. A. Stewart. *Floods of March 1982, Indiana, Michigan, and Ohio.* 1984, WRI 83-4201, 40 pp.
Miller, R. L., and J. T. Wilson. *Evaluation of Scour at Selected Bridge Sites in Indiana.* 1996, WRI 95-4259, 225 pp.

Iowa

Eash, D. A. *Flood-Plain and Channel Aggradation at Selected Bridge Sites in Iowa and Skunk River Basins, Iowa.* 1996, WRI 95-4290, 44 pp.
Floods of June 1953 in Northwestern Iowa. 1955, W1320-A, pp. 1–68.
Matthai, H. F. *Magnitude and Frequency of Floods in the United States: Part 6-B, Missouri River Basin below Sioux City, Iowa.* 1968, W1680, 491 pp.
Niehus, C. A. *Estimation of Flood Flows on the Big City Sioux River between Akron, Iowa, and North Sioux City, South Dakota.* 1996, WRI 96-4121, 20 pp.
Yost, I. D. *Floods of June 1954 in Iowa.* 1958, W1370-A, pp. 1–106.

Kansas

Clement, R. W. *Floods in Kansas and Techniques for Estimating Their Magnitude and Frequency on Unregulated Streams.* 1987, WRI 87-4008, 50 pp.
———. *Improvement of Flood-Frequency Estimates for Selected Small Watersheds in Eastern Kansas Using a Rainfall-Runoff Model.* 1983, WRI 83-4110, 26 pp.
Clement, R. W., and D. G. Johnson. *Flood of June 15, 1981, in Great Bend and Vicinity, Central Kansas.* 1982, WRI 82-4123, 12 pp.
Kansas-Missouri Floods of July 1951. 1952, W1139, 239 pp.
Perry, C. A. *A Method of Estimating Flood Volumes in Western Kansas.* 1984, WRI 84-4164, 18 pp.
Perry, C. A., and R. J. Hart. *Flood-Frequency Estimates for Five Gaged Basins in Wichita, Kansas.* 1984, WRI 84-4038, 23 pp.

Kentucky

Doyle, W. H., Jr., P. B. Curwick, and Kathleen Flynn. *A Flood Model for the Tug Fork Basin, Kentucky, Virginia, and West Virginia.* 1983, WRI 83-4014, 87 pp.

Louisiana

Floods of April–June 1953 in Louisiana and Adjacent States. 1959, W1320-C, pp. 155–320.

Landers, M. N. *Floodflow Frequency of Streams in the Alluvial Plain in the Lower Mississippi River in Mississippi, Arkansas, and Louisiana.* 1985, WRI 85-4159, 21 pp.

Lowe, A. S. *Floods in East Baton Rouge Parish and Adjacent Areas for the Period 1953–74.* 1974, WRI 74-0044.

Maine

Fontaine, R. A., and C. R. Haskell. *Floods in Maine, April–May 1979.* 1981, WRI 81-68, 70 pp.

Gadoury, R. A. *Coastal Flood of February 7, 1978, in Maine, Massachusetts, and New Hampshire.* 1979, WRI 79-0061.

Hodgkins, Glenn, and Gregory J. Stewart. *Flood of October 1996 in Southern Maine.* 1997, WRI 97-4189, 27 pp.

Maryland

Carpenter, D. H. *Floods in West Virginia, Virginia, Pennsylvania, and Maryland, November 1985.* 1990, WRI 88-4123, 86 pp.

Dillow, J. J. *Technique for Estimating Magnitude and Frequency of Peak Flows in Maryland.* 1996, WRI 95-4154, 55 pp.

Hayes, D. C. *Scour at Bridge Sites in Delaware, Maryland, and Virginia.* 1996, WRI 96-4089, 35 pp.

———. *Site Selection and Collection of Bridge-Scour Data in Delaware, Maryland, and Virginia.* 1993, WRI 93-4017, 23 pp.

Langland, M. J., and R. A. Hainly. *Changes in Bottom-Surface Elevations in Three Reservoirs on the Lower Susquehanna River, Pennsylvania and Maryland, Following the January 1996 Flood: Implications for Nutrient and Sediment Loads to Chesapeake Bay.* 1997, WRI 97-4138, 34 pp.

Massachusetts

Gadoury, R. A. *Coastal Flood of February 7, 1978, in Maine, Massachusetts, and New Hampshire.* 1979, WRI 79-0061.

Michigan

Croskey, H. M., and D. J. Holtschlag. *Estimating Generalized Flood Skew Coefficients for Michigan.* 1983, WRI 83-4194, 31 pp.

Glatfelter, D. R., G. K. Butch, and J. A. Stewart. *Floods of March 1982: Indiana, Michigan, and Ohio.* 1984, WRI 83-4201, 40 pp.

Minnesota

Ryan, G. L., and R. E. Harkness. *Flood of April 1989 in the Wahpeton-Breckenridge and Fargo-Moorhead Areas, Red River of the North Basin, North Dakota and Minnesota.* 1993, WRI 93-4155, one oversized map.

Mississippi

Colson, B. E. *Comparison of Flood Frequency Estimates from Synthetic and Observed Data on Small Drainage Areas in Mississippi.* 1986, WRI 86-4034, 23 pp.

Floyd, P. C. *Simulations of Floodflows in the Magby Creek Flood Plain Near Old Mill Road at Columbus, Mississippi.* 1993, WRI 93-4086, 39 pp.

Landers, M. N. *Floodflow-Frequency of Streams in the Alluvial Plain in the Lower Mississippi River in Mississippi, Arkansas, and Louisiana.* 1985, WRI 85-4150, 21 pp.

Landers, M. N., and K. V. Wilson Jr. *Flood Characteristics of Mississippi Streams.* 1991, WRI 91-4037, 82 pp.

Wilson, K. V., Jr. *Scour at Selected Bridge Sites in Mississippi.* 1995, WRI 94-4241, 44 pp.

Wilson, K. V., Jr. and M. N. Landers. *Annual Peak Stages and Discharges for Streamflow-Gaging Stations in Mississippi.* 1991, WRI 91-4098, 705 pp.

Missouri

Becker, L. D. *Investigation of Bridge Scour at Selected Sites on Missouri Streams.* 1994, WRI 94-4200, 40 pp.

———. *Techniques for Estimating Flood-Peak Discharges from Urban Basins in Missouri.* 1986, WRI 86-4322, 38 pp.

Becker, L. D., T. W. Alexander, and L. A. Waite. *Floods in Kansas City, Missouri, and Vicinity, August 12–13, 1982.* 1983, WRI 83-4141, 41 pp.

Becker, L. W. *Simulation of Flood Hydrographs for Small Basins in Missouri.* 1990, WRI 90-4045, 40 pp.

Kansas-Missouri Floods of July 1951. 1952, W1139, 239 pp.

Schalk, G. K., and R. B. Jacobson. *Scour, Sedimentation, and Sediment Characteristics at Six Levee-Break Sites in Missouri from the 1993 Missouri River Flood.* 1997, WRI 97-4110, 72 pp.

Southard, Rodney E. *Simulation of the Effect of Traffic Barricades on Backwater along U.S. Highway 54 at Jefferson City, Missouri: 1993 Flood on the Missouri River.* 1997, WRI 97-4213, 13 pp.

Montana

Boner, F. C., and Frank Stermitz. *Floods of June 1964 in Northwestern Montana.* 1967, W1840-B, pp. B1–B242.

Floods of May–June 1953 in Missouri River Basin in Montana. 1957, W1320-B, pp. 69–153.

Omang, R. J., *Water-Surface Profile and Flood Boundaries for the Computed 100-Year Flood, Poplar River, Fort Peck Indian Reservation, Montana.* 1990, WRI 90-4169, two oversized maps.

———. *Water-Surface Profile and Flood Boundaries for the Computed 100-Year Flood, Porcupine Creek, Fort Peck Indian Reservation and Adjacent Area, Montana.* 1993, WRI 92-4185, one oversized sheet.

———. *Water-Surface Profile and Flood Boundaries for the Computed 100-Year Flood, Rosebud Creek, Northern Cheyenne Indian Reservation, Montana.* 1995, WRI 95-4093, two oversized maps.

Omang, R. J., Charles Parrett, and J. A. Hull. *Flood Estimates for Ungaged Streams in Glacier and Yellowstone National Parks, Montana.* 1983, WRI 83-4147, 13 pp.

Parrett, Charles. *Simulation of Rain Floods on Willow Creek, Valley County, Montana.* 1986, WRI 86-4341, 89 pp.

Parrett, Charles, and D. R. Johnson. *Simulated Monthly Hydrologic Data and Estimated Flood Characteristics for Cherry Creek at a Proposed Reservoir Site Near Terry, Montana.* 1995, WRI 94-4230, 25 pp.

Parett, Charles, R. J. Omang, J. A. Hull, and J. W. Fassler. *Floods of May 1981 in West Central Montana.* 1982, WRI 82-33, 25 pp.

Nevada

Carlson, D. D., and D. F. Meyer. *Flood on the Virgin River, January 1989 in Utah, Arizona, and Nevada.* 1995, WRI 94-4159, 21 pp.

Squires, R. R., and R. L. Young. *Flood Potential of Fortymile Wash and Its Principal Southwestern Tributaries, Nevada Test Site, Southern Nevada.* 1984, WRI 83-4001, 33 pp., one oversized sheet.

Young, L. E., and E. E. Harris. *Floods of January–February 1963 in California and Nevada.* 1966, W1830-A, pp. A1–A472.

New Hampshire

Gadoury, R. A. *Coastal Flood of February 7, 1978, in Maine, Massachusetts, and New Hampshire.* 1979, WRI 79-0061.

New Jersey

Flippo, H. N., Jr., and T. M. Madden Jr. *Calibration of a Streamflow-Routing Model for the Delaware River and Its Principal Tributaries in New York, New Jersey, and Pennsylvania.* 1991, WRI 93-4160, 31 pp.

Fulton, J. L. *Application of a Distributed-Routing Rainfall Runoff Model to Flood-Frequency Estimation in Somerset County, New Jersey.* 1990, WRI 82-4210, 78 pp.

New Mexico

Aldridge, B. N. *Floods of November 1965 to January 1966 in the Gila River Basin, Arizona, and New Mexico, and Adjacent Basins in Arizona.* 1970, W1850-C, pp. C1–C176.

Thomas, R. P., and R. L. Gold. *Techniques for Estimating Flood Discharges for Unregulated Streams in New Mexico.* 1982, WRI 82-24, 47 pp.

Vaudrey, W. C. *Floods of May 1953 in Colorado and New Mexico.* 1960, W1455-A, pp. 1–68.

Waltemeyer, S. D. *Bridge Scour Analysis on Cuchillo Negro Creek at the Interstate 25 Crossing Near Truth or Consequences, New Mexico.* 1995, WRI 95-4050, 29 pp.

New York

Flippo, H. N., Jr., and T. M. Madden Jr. *Calibration of a Streamflow-Routing Model for the Delaware River and Its Principal Tributaries in New York, New Jersey, and Pennsylvania.* 1991, WRI 93-4160, 31 pp.

Flood of 1950–51 in the Catskill Mountain Region of New York. 1958, W1227-C, pp. 201–277.

Lumia, Richard. *Flood Discharge Profiles of Selected Streams in Rockland County, New York.* 1984, WRI 84-4049, 32 pp.

———. *Regionalization of Flood Discharges for Rural Unregulated Streams in New York, Excluding Long Island.* 1991, WRI 90-4197, 119 pp.

Lumia, Richard, P. M. Burke, and W. H. Johnston. *Flooding of December 29, 1984, through January 2, 1985, in Northern New York State, with Flood Profiles of the Black and Salmon Rivers.* 1987, WRI 86-4191, 53 pp.

Lumia, Richard, and W. H. Johnston. *Floods of August 7–8, 1979, in Chautauqua County, New York, with Hydraulic Analysis of Canadaway Creek in the Village of Fredonia.* 1984, WRI 83-4211, 16 pp.

Zembrzuski, T. J., and M. L. Evans. *Flood of April 4–5, 1987, in Southeastern New York State, with Flood Profiles of Schoharie Creek.* 1989, WRI 89-4084, 11 pp.

North Carolina

Mason, R. R., Jr., and J. D. Bales. *Estimating Flood Hydrographs for Urban Basins in North Carolina.* 1996, WRI 96-4085, 19 pp.

Pope, B. F. *Simulated Peak Flows and Water-Surface Profiles for Scott Creek Near Sylva, North Carolina.* 1996, WRI 96-4226, 15 pp.

Robbins, J. C., and B. F. Pope. *Estimation of Flood Frequency Characteristics of Small Urban Streams in North Carolina.* 1996, WRI 96-4084, 21 pp.

North Dakota

Emerson, D. G., and K. M. Macek-Rowland. *Flood Analysis along the Little Missouri River Within and Adjacent to Theodore Roosevelt National Park, North Dakota.* 1986, WRI 86-4090, 36 pp.

Ryan, G. L., and R. E. Harkness. *Flood of April 1989 in the Wahpeton-Breckenridge and Fargo-Moorhead Areas, Red River of the North Basin, North Dakota, and Minnesota.* 1993, WRI 93-4155, one oversized map.

Ohio

Bartlett, W. P., and J. M. Sherwood. *Flood-Profile Analysis, Big Darby Creek at State Route 762, Orient, Ohio.* 1984, WRI 84-4281, 64 pp.

Glatfelter, D. R., G. K. Butch, and J. A. Stewart. *Floods of March 1982, Indiana, Michigan, and Ohio.* 1984, WRI 83-4201, 40 pp.

Jackson, K. S., S. A. Vivian, F. J. Diam, and C. J. Crecelius. *Flood of March 1997 in Southern Ohio.* 1997, WRI 97-4149, 21 pp.

Koltun, G. F., and J. W. Roberts. *Techniques for Estimating Flood-Peak Discharges of Rural, Unregulated Streams in Ohio.* 1990, WRI 89-4126, 68 pp., one oversized map.

Kolva, J. R., and G. F. Koltun. *Flooding and Sedimentation in Wheeling Creek Basin, Belmont County, Ohio.* 1987, WRI 87-4053, 33 pp.

Roth, D. K. *Estimation of Flood Peaks from Channel Characteristics in Ohio.* 1985, WRI 85-4175, 63 pp.

Sherwood, J. M. *Estimating Peak Discharges, Flood Volumes, and Hydrograph Shapes of Small Ungaged Urban Streams in Ohio.* 1986, WRI 86-4197, 52 pp.

———. *Estimation of Flood Volumes and Simulation of Flood Hydrographs for Ungaged and Small Rural Streams in Ohio.* 1993, WRI 83-4080, 52 pp.

Shindel, H. L. *Flood of June 14–15, 1990 in Belmont, Jefferson, and Harrison Counties, Ohio, with Emphasis on Pipe and Wegee Creek Basins Near Shadyside.* 1991, WRI 91-4147, 33 pp.

Webber, E. E. *Flood of June 13–15, 1981, in the Blanchard River Basin, Northwestern Ohio.* 1982, WRI 82-4044, 35 pp.

Oklahoma

Bingham, R. H., D. L. Bergman, and W. O. Thomas Jr. *Flood of October 1973 in Enid and Vicinity, North Central Oklahoma.* 1974, WRI 74-0027.

Floods of May 1951 in Western Oklahoma and Northwestern Texas. 1954, W1227-B, pp. 135–199.

Thomas, W. O, Jr., and R. K. Corley. *Techniques for Estimating Flood Discharges for Oklahoma Streams; Techniques for Calculating Magnitude and Frequency of Floods in Oklahoma from Rural and Urban Areas under 2,500 Square Miles with Compilation of Flood Data through 1975.* 1977, WRI 77-0054.

Tortorelli, R. L. *Estimated Flood Peak Discharges on Twin, Brock, and Lightning Creeks in Southwest Oklahoma City, Oklahoma, May 8, 1993.* 1996, WRI 96-4185, 127 pp.

Tortorelli, R. L., and D. L. Bergman. *Techniques for Estimating Flood Peak Discharges for Unregulated Streams and Streams Regulated by Small Floodwater Retarding Structures in Oklahoma.* 1985, WRI 84-4358, 85 pp., two oversized sheets.

Oregon

Harris, D. D., and L. E. Hubbard. *Magnitude and Frequency of Floods in Eastern Oregon.* 1982, WRI 82-4078, 45 pp.

Hubbard, L. E. *1984 Flooding of Malheur-Harney Lake, Harney County, Southeastern Oregon.* 1989, WRI 89-4111, one oversized sheet.

———. *Urban Storm Runoff in Roseburg Area, Oregon, as Related to Urban Characteristics of the Willamette Valley.* 1992, WRI 91-4063, 28 pp.

Pennsylvania

Bailey, J. F., W. O. Thomas Jr., K. L. Wetzel, and T. R. Ross. *Estimation of Flood-Frequency Characteristics and the Effects of Urbanization for Streams in the Philadelphia, Pennsylvania, Area.* 1989, WRI 87-4194, 71 pp.

Brua, S. A. *Flow Routing in the Susquehanna River Basin: Part V, Flow-Routing Models for the West Branch Susquehanna River Basin.* 1984, WRI 82-4049, 42 pp.

Carpenter, D. H. *Floods in West Virginia, Virginia, Pennsylvania, and Maryland, November 1985.* 1990, WRI 88-4213, 86 pp.

Eisenlohr, W. S., and J. E. Stewart. *Floods of July 18, 1942, in North-Central Pennsylvania, with a Section on Descriptive Details of the Storm and Floods.* 1952, W1134-B, pp. 59–158.

Flippo, H. N., Jr. *Technique for Estimating Depths of 100-Year Floods in Pennsylvania.* 1990, WRI 86-4195, 16 pp.

Flippo, H. N., Jr., and T. M. Madden Jr. *Calibration of a Streamflow-Routing Model for the Delaware River and Its Principal Tributaries in New York, New Jersey, and Pennsylvania.* 1991, WRI 93-4160, 31 pp.

Langland, M. J., and R. A. Hainly. *Changes in Bottom-Surface Elevations in Three Reservoirs on the Lower Susquehanna River, Pennsylvania and Maryland, Following the January 1996 Flood: Implications for Nutrient and Sediment Loads to Chesapeake Bay.* 1997, WRI 97-4138, 34 pp.

Sloto, R. A. *Effects of Flood Controls Proposed for West Branch Brandywine Creek, Chester County, Pennsylvania.* 1988, WRI 86-4054, 28 pp.

Voytik, Andrew. *Statistical Analyses of Flood Frequency, Low-Flow Frequency, and Flow Direction of Streams in the Philadelphia Area, Pennsylvania.* 1986, WRI 85-4008, 34 pp.

South Carolina

Bohman, L. R. *Floodflow-Characteristics of Filbin Creek at Proposed Interstate Highway 526, North Charleston, South Carolina.* 1984, WRI 84-4323, 20 pp.

Guimaraes, W. B. *Flood of September 7–9, 1987, in Lexington and Richmond Counties in the Vicinity of St. Andrews Road and Irmo, South Carolina.* 1989, WRI 89-4077, 37 pp., two oversized maps.

Guimaraes, W. B., and L. R. Bohman. *Techniques for Estimating Magnitude and Frequency of Floods in South Carolina, 1988.* 1992, WRI 91-4157, 175 pp.

Hurley, N. M., Jr. *Flood of August 18, 1986, Newberry, South Carolina.* 1988, WRI 88-4148, 15 pp.

Lanier, T. H. *Determination of the 100-Year Flood Plain of Pen Branch, Steel Creek, and Their Selected Tributaries, Savannah River Site, South Carolina, 1996.* 1997, WRI 97-4090, 35 pp.

———. *Determination of the 100-Year Flood Plain on Fourmile Branch at the Savannah River Site, South Carolina.* 1997, WRI 96-4271, 23 pp.

———. *Determination of the 100-Year Flood Plain on Upper Three Runs and Selected Tributaries and the Savannah River at Savannah River Site, South Carolina, 1995.* 1996, WRI 96-4014, 65 pp.

Sanders, C. L. *Floodflow-Characteristics of Filbin Creek for Pre- and Post-construction Conditions, 1986, at North Charleston, South Carolina.* 1986, WRI 97-4157, 19 pp.

South Dakota

Becker, L. D. *Magnitude and Frequency of Floods from Selected Drainage Basins in South Dakota.* 1982, WRI 82-31, 95 pp.

Benson, R. D. *Analysis of Flood-Flow Frequency, Flow Duration, and Channel-Forming Flow for the James River in South Dakota.* 1988, WRI 87-4208, 136 pp.

Benson, R. D., E. B. Hoffman, and V. J. Wipf. *Analyses of Flood-Flow Frequency for Selected Gaging Stations in South Dakota.* 1985, WRI 85-4217, 202 pp.

Niehus, C. A. *Estimation of Flood Flows on the Big Sioux River between Akron, Iowa, and North Sioux City, South Dakota.* 1996, WRI 96-4121, 20 pp.

Tennessee

Bingham, R. H., and C. R. Gamble. *Floods during the Summer of 1982 in Central and East Tennessee.* 1986, WRI 84-4365, three oversized sheets.

Gamble, C. R. *Techniques for Simulating Flood Hydrographs and Estimating Flood Volumes for Ungaged Basins in East and West Tennessee.* 1989, WRI 89-4076, 40 pp.

Lewis, J. G., and C. R. Gamble. *Flood of December 25, 1987, in Millington, Tennessee, and Vicinity.* 1989, WRI 89-4019, two oversized maps.

Neely, B. L., Jr. *Flood Frequency and Storm Runoff of Urban Areas of Memphis and Shelby County, Tennessee.* 1984, WRI 84-4110, 51 pp.

Outlaw, G. S. *Flood-Frequency and Detention Storage Characteristics of Bear Branch Watershed, Murfreesboro, Tennessee.* 1996, WRI 96-4005, 24 pp.

Quiñones, Ferdinand, and C. R. Gamble. *Floods of February 1989 in Tennessee.* 1990, WRI 89-4207, 15 pp.

Robbins, C. H. *Synthesized Flood Frequency in Small Urban Streams in Tennessee.* 1984, WRI 84-4182, 24 pp.

———. *Techniques for Simulating Flood Hydrographs and Estimating Flood Volumes for Ungaged Basins in Central Tennessee.* 1986, WRI 96-4192, 32 pp.

Robbins, C. H., C. R. Gamble, and R. H. Bingham. *Flood of September 12–13, 1982, in Gibson, Carroll, and Madison Counties, West Tennessee.* 1986, WRI 85-4037, one oversized sheet.

Weaver, J. D., and C. R. Gamble. *Flood Frequency of Streams in Rural Basins of Tennessee.* 1993, WRI 92-4165, 38 pp.

Texas

Breeding, S. D., and J. H. Montgomery. *Floods of September 1952 in the Colorado and Guadalyse River Basins, Central Texas.* 1954, W1260-A, pp. 1–47.

Floods of May 1951 in Western Oklahoma and Northwestern Texas. 1954, W1227-B, pp. 135–199.

Hejl, H. R., Jr., R. M. Slade Jr., and M. E. Jennings. *Floods in Central Texas, December 1991.* 1996, WRI 95-4289, one oversized map.

Liscum, Fred, R. L. Goss, and E. M. Paul. *Effects on Water Quality Due to Flood Water Detention by Barker and Addicks Reservoir, Houston, Texas.* 1987, WRI 86-4356, 96 pp.

Mills, W. B., and E. E. Schroeder. *Floods of April 28, 1966, in the Northern Part of Dallas, Texas.* 1969, W1870-B, pp. B1–B37.

Veenhuis, J. E., and D. G. Gannett. *The Effects of Urbanization on Florida in the Austin Metropolitan Area, Texas.* 1986, WRI 86-4069, 66 pp.

Wells, F. C., T. E. Schertz, and M. W. Flugrath. *Effects of October 1981 Flood on the Quantity and Quality of Water in Selected Streams and Reservoirs in the Brazos River Basin, Texas.* 1984, WRI 84-4055, 119 pp.

Yost, I. D. *Floods of April–June 1957 in Texas and Adjacent States.* 1964, W1652-B, pp. B1–B321.

Utah

Butler, Elmer, and J. C. Mundorff. *Floods of December 1966 in Southwestern Utah.* 1970, W1870-A, pp. A1–A40.

Carlson, D. D., and D. F. Meyer. *Flood on the Virgin River, January 1989, in Utah, Arizona, and Nevada.* 1995, WRI 94-4159, 21 pp.

Virginia

Bisese, J. A. *Methods for Estimating the Magnitude and Frequency of Peak Discharges of Rural, Unregulated Streams in Virginia.* 1995, WRI 94-4148, 70 pp.

Carpenter, D. H. *Floods in West Virginia, Virginia, Pennsylvania, and Maryland, November 1985.* 1990, WRI 88-4213, 86 pp.

Doyle, W. H., Jr., P. B. Curwick, and Kathleen Flynn. *A Flood Model for the Tug Fork Basin, Kentucky, Virginia, and West Virginia.* 1983, WRI 83-4014, 87 pp.

Hayes, D. C. *Scour at Bridge Sites in Delaware, Maryland, and Virginia.* 1996, WRI 96-4089, 35 pp.

———. *Site Selection and Collection of Bridge-Scour Data in Delaware, Maryland, and Virginia.* 1993, WRI 93-4017, 23 pp.

Washington

Bartells, J. H. *Flood Elevations for the Soals River at Proposed Fish Hatchery, Clallam County, Washington: A Surface-Water Site Study.* 1978, WRI 78-0130.

Haushild, W. L. *Estimation of Floods of Various Frequencies for the Small Ephemeral Streams in Eastern Washington.* 1979, WRI 79 0081.

Hettick, O. C. *Flood Profiles along the Cedar River, King County, Washington.* 1978, WRI 78-0084.

Kresch, D. L., and Antonius Laenen. *Preliminary Estimate of Possible Flood Elevations in the Columbia River at Trojan Nuclear Power Plant Due to Failure of Debris Dam Blocking Spirit Lake, Washington.* 1984, WRI 83-4197, 11 pp.

Kresch, D. L., and T. C. Pierson. *Flood Hazard Assessment of the Hoh River at Olympic National Park Ranger Station, Washington: Debris Flow and Landslide Hazard Assessment.* 1987, WRI 86-4198, 22 pp., one oversized map.

Laenen, Antonius, and L. L. Orzol. *Flood Hazards along the Toutle and Cowlitz Rivers, Washington, from a Hypothetical Failure of Castle Lake Blockage.* 1987, WRI 87-4055, 29 pp.

Lombard, R. E. *Channel Geometry, Flood Elevations, and Flood Maps, Lower Toutle and Cowlitz Rivers, Washington, June 1980 to May 1981.* 1986, WRI 85-4080, 34 pp.

Nelson, L. M. *Flood Characteristics for the Nisqually River and Susceptibility of Sunshine Point and Longmire Facilities to Flooding in Mount Rainier National Park, Washington.* 1987, WRI 86-4179, 18 pp.

———. *Flood Elevations for the Soleduck River at Sol Duc Hot Springs, Clallam County, Washington.* 1983, WRI 83-4083, 20 pp.

Prych, E. A. *Flood-Carrying Capacities and Changes in Channels of the Lower Puyallup, White, and Carbon Rivers in Western Washington.* 1988, WRI 87-4129, 69 pp.

Stewart, J. E., and G. L. Bodhaine. *Floods in the Skagit River Basin, Washington.* 1961, W1527, 66 pp.

West Virginia

Carpenter, David M. *Floods in West Virginia, Pennsylvania, and Maryland.* 1985, WRI 88-4213, 86 pp.

Doyle, W. H., Jr., P. B. Curwick, and Kathleen Flynn. *A Flood Model for the Tug Fork Basin, Kentucky, Virginia, and West Virginia.* 1983, WRI 83-4014, 87 pp.

Erskine, H. M. *Floods of August 4–5, 1943, in Central West Virginia, with a Summary of Flood Stages and Discharges in West Virginia.* 1951, W1134-A, pp. 1–57.

Wiley, J. B. *Flood Discharges and Hydraulics Near the Mouths of Wolf Creek, Craig Branch, Manns Creek, Dunloup Creek, and Mill Creek in the New River Gorge National River, West Virginia.* 1994, WRI 93-4133, 27 pp.

Wisconsin

Conger, D. H. *Estimating Magnitude and Frequency of Floods for Wisconsin Urban Streams.* 1986, WRI 86-4005, 18 pp.

Krug, W. R., D. H. Conger, and W. A. Gebert. *Flood Frequency Characteristics of Wisconsin Streams.* 1993, WRI 91-428, 185 pp.

Wentz, D. A., and D. J. Graczyk. *Effects of a Floodwater-Retarding Structure on the Hydrology and Ecology of Trout Creek in Southwestern Wisconsin.* 1982, WRI 82-23, 75 pp.

Wyoming

Cooley, M. E. *Use of Paleoflood Investigations to Improve Flood Frequency Analyses of Plains Streams in Wyoming.* 1990, WRI 88-4209, 75 pp.

Linder-Lunsford, J. B. *Precipitation Records and Flood-Producing Storms in Cheyenne, Wyoming.* 1988, WRI 87-4225, 44 pp.

Rankl, J. G., and J. G. Wallace. *Flood Boundaries and Water-Surface Profile for the Computed 100-Year Flood, Swift Creek at Afton, Wyoming, 1986.* 1989, WRI 88-4064, two oversized maps.

Ritz, G. F. *Flood Boundaries and Water-Surface Profiles for the Computed 50-, 100-, and 500-Year Floods, Childs Draw and Tributary Near Cheyenne, Wyoming, August 1991.* 1993, WRI 83-4022, three oversized maps.

6 Audiovisual Aids

The audiovisual aids listed here provide a wide range of information on floods and their consequences. A graphic representation provides a portrayal of disasters more vividly than the written word. The films cover a wide variety of topics, such as disasters, dams, flash floods, and flood forecasting.

The following books list audiovisual aid sources in English:

AFVA Evaluations, 1992. Fort Atkinson, WI: Highsmith Press, 1992.

Educational Film and Video Locator of the Consortium of College and University Media Centers and R. R. Bowker, 4th ed. 2 vols. New York: R. R. Bowker, 1990–1991.

Film and Video Finder, 5th ed. 3 vols. Medford, NJ: Plexus Publishing, 1997.

Video Rating Guide for Libraries. Santa Barbara, CA: ABC-CLIO, various years.

Video Source Book, 20th ed. 2 vols. Detroit: Gale Research, 1998.

General

Flood
Coronet/MTI Film and Video International
4350 Equity Drive

Columbus, OH 43228
Phone: 800-321-3806 or 201-739-8000; fax: 614-771-7361
Color, 14 minutes, 16 mm/U-matic/VHS, n.d.

Tells story of a canoeist who seeks adventure on a swollen river.

The Flood and Double Trouble—Volume 2
Augsburg Fortress Publishers
PO Box 1209
Minneapolis, MN 55440-1209
Phone: 800-328-4648 or 612-330-3300; fax: 612-330-3455
Color, 45 minutes, VHS, n.d.

Animated format is used to tell the story of Chris and Joy and their travels through Biblical places and events. *The Flood* is the story of Noah and his ark, and *Double Trouble* tells the story of Jacob and Esau.

Flood of Fury
Critics Choice Video, Inc.
900 North Rohlwing Road
Itasca, IL 60143
Phone: 800-367-7765; fax: 708-775-3340
Black and white, 25 minutes, VHS, Beta, 1952.

From the television series *Sky King.* During the flooding of a town, prisoners escape from the jail and kidnap Penny and Clipper. The "Sky King" rescues the children and aids in capturing the prisoners. A story with good flood scenes.

Rivers, Floods, and People
University of Wisconsin–La Crosse
Film Library—Audiovisual Center
1705 State Street
La Crosse, WI 54601
Color, 11 minutes, 16 mm, 1974.

Shows how we build along major rivers on floodplains that are periodically flooded. The extensive and expensive efforts to keep the floodplain are shown to be futile attempts to control a river.

Flood Forecasting

Flood
U.S. Department of Commerce
National Oceanic and Atmospheric Administration

12231 Wilkins Avenue
Rockville, MD 20853
Color, 15 minutes, 16 mm, 1971.

Describes how flood predictions are made, including the fundamental precautions against the dangers and disasters imposed by floods. It stresses the importance of hurricanes, seasonal snow melting, and heavy rainfall in creating floods.

Flood Below
National Audiovisual Center/National
Technical Information Service
5285 Port Royal Road
Springfield, VA 22161
Phone: 800-788-6282 or 703-487-4650;
fax: 703-487-4009
Color, 14 minutes, 16 mm, 1975.

Shows how NASA weather satellites can give warnings to help save lives and property as it helped two cowboys whose ranch is threatened by a flash flood.

Flood Forecasting
Encyclopedia Britannica Educational Corporation
310 South Michigan Avenue, 6th Floor
Chicago, IL 60604
Phone: 312-347-7000; fax: 800-323-1229
Color, 20 minutes, VHS, Beta, 3/4U, 1987.

Presents the techniques of such items as weather balloons, satellites, and other tools meteorologists use to predict floods.

Flood Weather
United States Weather Bureau
Washington, DC 20242
Black and white, 32 minutes, 16 mm, 1937.

Describes weather forecasting for river navigation and flood protection. The floods of the Ohio and Potomac Rivers are shown.

Flash Flood

The American Experience: The Johnstown Flood
PBS Video
1320 Braddock Place
Alexandria, VA 22314

Phone: 800-344-3337; fax: 703-739-5269
Color, 60 minutes, video, 1991.

Tells the story of the Johnstown flood on May 31, 1889. A dam broke, sweeping Johnstown, Pennsylvania, away in a 30-foot wall of water, killing thousands of people.

Flash Flood
National Audiovisual Center/National
Technical Information Service
5285 Port Royal Road
Springfield, VA 22161
Phone: 800-788-6282 or 703-487-4650; fax: 703-487-4009
Color, 14 minutes, 16 mm, 1979.

Emphasizes the danger of camping in mountainous areas where flash floods occur. Stresses the need for a flash flood warning plan by National Weather Service advisories.

Flash Floods
Instructional Video
PO Box 21
Maumee, OH 43537
Phone: 419-865-7670; fax: 419-867-3813
Color, n.t., VHS, 1980.

Shows how to respond to a flash flood warning. Be prepared, for a tranquil stream can become a raging flood.

The Johnstown Flood
New Dimensions Media
85803 Lorane Highway
Eugene, OR 97405
Phone: 800-288-4456 or 541-484-7125; fax: 541-484-5267
Color, 26 minutes, VHS/U-matic, 1990.

Looks at the events leading up to and following the devastating flood of Johnstown in 1889. Mentions the reactions of such industrialists as Carnegie, Mellon, and Frick and the participation of Clara Booth after the flood.

Disasters

Disaster Aid: Public Health Aspects
National Audiovisual Center/National

Technical Information Service
5285 Port Royal Road
Springfield, VA 22161
Phone: 800-788-6282 or 703-487-4650; fax: 703-487-4009
Black and white, 11 minutes, 16 mm, 1955.

Uses a flood to show how local, state, and federal health agencies can help prevent public health dangers.

Disasters
New Dimension Media, Inc.
85803 Lorane Highway
Eugene, OR 97405
Phone: 503-484-7125; fax: 503-484-5267
Color, 25 minutes, VHS, Beta, 1987.

Considers the means of preparing for a natural disaster in order to save lives and facilitate recovery of the disaster area.

Disasters: Anatomy of Destruction
Karol Video
350 North Pennsylvania Avenue
Wilkes Barre, PA 18773
Phone: 717-822-8899; fax: 717-822-8226
Color, 70 minutes, VHS, Beta, 1985.

A compilation of several disasters providing information on types of assistance needed in the disaster area.

Flood Emergency Action
American Red Cross/Audio-Visual
Loan Library—American National Red Cross
5816 Seminary Road
Falls Church, VA 22041
Color, 5 minutes, 16 mm, 1968.

Gives instructions on how to protect family and property during a flood. Gives help with food and drinking water. Also warns about the use of electrical appliances.

Dams

Dams
Portland State University
PO Box 751

Portland, OR 97207
Color, 10 minutes, 16 mm, 1957.

Presents the history of dams from their first use for water storage to modern uses for flood control and hydroelectric power. Shows Hoover, Roosevelt, Bonneville, and Grand Coulee Dams. Shows the complete construction of a dam.

Flood
Warner Home Video, Inc.
4000 Warner Boulevard
Burbank, CA 91522
Phone: 818-954-6000
Color, 98 minutes, video, 1976.

Movie for television of the bursting of a dam and the resulting flood. Dramatic scenes of flood destruction and the rescue of people by helicopter.

Rivers

Colorado River: Water and Power for the Southwest
BFA Educational Media
Division of Columbia Broadcasting System, Inc.
BFA Films and Video, Inc.
470 Park Avenue South
New York, NY 10016
Color, 14 minutes, 16 mm, 1967.

Discusses the geologic history of the Colorado River and the development of the complex dams and canals that control the flow. Shows the dams and powerhouses built for flood control and the production of electricity. Describes the role of the American Canal to supply water to the Imperial Valley.

Columbia River
Simon and Schuster Communications
108 Wilmot Road
Deerfield, IL 60015
Color, 11 minutes, 16 mm, 1966.

Views the colossal, multipurpose dams in the Columbia River systems. Shows how man uses the Columbia River, including historical footage of floods, the construction of the Grand Coulee

Dam, and the United States Agreements to cooperate in the development of the river.

Columbia River Environment
National Audiovisual Center/National
Technical Information Service
5285 Port Royal Road
Springfield, VA 22161
Phone: 800-788-6282 or 703-487-4650; fax: 703-487-4009
Color, 29 minutes, 16 mm, 1970.

Discusses the development of navigation, irrigation, flood control, and wildlife and recreational areas in the Columbia River Basin.

Flood of 1953: Delta Plan
Modern Education Services
Modern Talking Picture Service
Customer Service Center
PO Box 17620
Clearwater, FL 34622
Phone: 813-243-6877 or 813-532-0706; fax: 800-237-7143
Color, 17 minutes, 16 mm, n.d.

Shows the different methods of flood protection used by the Netherlands since their flood of February 1, 1953.

The Flooding River
The Media Guild
11722 Sorrento Valley Road, Suite E
San Diego, CA 92121
Phone: 619-755-9191; fax: 619-755-4931
Color, 34 minutes, VHS, Beta, 3/4 U, 1973.

Presents the flood possibilities of the Connecticut River from its headwaters and floodplains to the ocean.

The Flooding River: A Study of Riverine Ecology
John Wiley & Sons, Inc.
605 Third Avenue
New York, NY 10016
Color, 34 minutes, 16 mm, 1971.

Uses the Connecticut River as a model to study the migrating shad, ducks, amphibians, and the land and plant life as they depend on the annual flood cycle. The complex ecological successions are explained through the river cycles.

Floods and People
Washington State University
Instructional Media Service
Pullman, WA 99163
Color, 20 minutes, 16 mm, 1923.

The study of floods and floodplain management in the Pacific Northwest. The advantages of floodplain management, zoning, flood-proofing existing structures, and the development of warning systems. Simulation studies were performed on flooding in the Albrook Hydraulic Lab at Washington State University.

Mississippi River
Lucerne Media
37 Ground Pine Road
Morris Plains, NJ 07950
Phone: 800-341-2293
Color, 17 minutes, U-matic/VHS/16 mm, 1979.

Shows how the Mississippi River has influenced the history of the United States as it travels from Minnesota to the Gulf of Mexico. Early settlements, farming, transportation, and problems of pollution and flooding are examined.

The Mississippi River: Background for Social Studies
Simon and Schuster Communications
108 Wilmot Road
Deerfield, IL 60015
Color/black and white, 14 minutes, 16 mm, 1960.

A tour of the river showing its economic and recreational uses. Depicts the role of the Mississippi River as a carrier of commerce, a water supply, and a carrier of sewage as well as a destroyer of property during floods. Maps show the area drained by the Mississippi.

Mississippi River: Lower River
Academy Films
PO Box 3414
Orange, CA 92665
Color, 15 minutes, 16 mm, 1948.

Reveals the physical and human geography of the Mississippi from Cairo, Illinois, to New Orleans, Louisiana. The trip shows the freight-carrying boats, bridges, dredging, and flood controls.

Mississippi River: Upper River
Academy Films
PO Box 3414
Orange, CA 92665
Black and white, 15 minutes, 16 mm, 1948.

Provides a view of the physical and human geography from its headwaters to St. Louis. Shows the many power dams, river traffic, how the locks work, and the regional economy. Uses animated diagrams and maps.

The Mississippi System: Waterways of Commerce
Britannica Films
310 South Michigan Avenue
Chicago, IL 60604
Phone: 800-554-9862 or 312-347-7900
fax: 312-347-7966
Black and white, 16 minutes, VHS, Beta, 3/4U, 1970.

Traces the development of the river and explores the Big Flood of 1927.

The River
National Audiovisual Center/National
Technical Information Service
5285 Port Royal Road
Springfield, VA 22161
Phone: 800-788-6282 or 703-487-4650
fax: 703-487-4009
Black and white, 32 minutes, 16 mm/U-matic/VHS, 1939.

Shows life in the Mississippi River Valley. Describes the results of floods and erosion and federal efforts to help in development of the valley.

River Valley
Encyclopedia Britannica Educational Corporation
310 South Michigan Avenue, 6th Floor
Chicago, IL 60604
Phone: 312-347-7000; fax: 800-323-1229
Color, black and white, 11 minutes, 16 mm, 1964.

Illustrates the main features of a river valley and explains how these features affect the activities of those who live along the river. Shows how the river provides food, water, minerals, power, and transportation.

River, Where Do You Come From?
Simon and Schuster Communications
108 Wilmot Road
Deerfield, IL 60015
Color, 10 minutes, 16 mm, 1970.

Scenic view of a river from its headwaters to the ocean. In its journey it serves man's need for water, transportation, recreation, power, and so on, but it also becomes polluted and wreaks havoc on the people during times of floods. The narration is a lyrical ballad.

Rivers at Work: An Introduction to Channel Processes
Lucerne Films, Inc.
37 Ground Pine Road
Morris Plains, NJ 07950
Phone: 800-341-2293
Color, 20 minutes, 16 mm, U-V, 1983.

Introduces the basic concepts of fluvial geomorphology—the science of how running water aids in the creation of landforms. Examines such concepts as flood erosion, deposition, velocity, and volume.

Tennessee River: Conservation and Power
Arthur G. Evans
460 Arroya Parkway
Pasadena, CA 91101
Color, 15 minutes, 16 mm, 1970.

The story of the accomplishments of the Tennessee Valley Authority. Describes the control of the rivers and the development of the regional economy to improve the quality of the life of the area.

Glossary

100-year flood standard A flood area that has a 1 percent chance of being flooded every year.

absorption The entrance of water into the soil or bedrock by all natural processes, including the infiltration of all types of precipitation.

aquifer A water-bearing rock layer.

atmospheric cell A small body of air with the uniform meteorological characteristics of temperature, pressure, and wind direction.

bank The edge of a channel of a stream. Banks are named right or left as viewed when facing the direction of flow.

bank protection To stabilize the bank of a river by such means as planting grass, shrubs, or trees to prevent erosion caused by flooding.

bund Another name for levee.

cold front A cyclonic storm where cold moving air comes in contact with warmer air. The cold air pushes the warm air upward, sometimes creating thunderstorms.

cubic feet per second A unit measuring the rate of discharge. One cubic foot per second is equal to the discharge of a stream with a rectangular cross section 1 foot wide and 1 foot deep, with water flowing at an average velocity of 1 foot per second.

current meter An instrument that measures the speed of flowing water.

cyclonic storms A large low-pressure area of more than 1 million square miles in which there are cold and warm fronts. The storm moves from west to east in the middle-latitude westerly wind system.

diversion channel A channel that diverts water from the main stream channel during flood stage.

drainage basin The area that is drained by a stream or river.

flood Water that overtops the natural or artificial banks of a stream, causing or threatening damage to the surrounding area.

flood control The techniques used in attempting to control the flooding of rivers.

flood discharge The amount of water carried by a river.

flood insurance Monetary protection against flooding.

flood stage The time at which a stream overflows its natural bank. Damage may begin at this point.

flood wall A wall of concrete or stone, normally in an urban area, to provide protection from floods.

floodplain A lowland along a stream that is flooded during high-water stages.

groundwater The amount of water held in the pores of rocks.

groundwater recharge The amount of water required for the ground to be completely saturated.

hydrologic cycle The endless natural cycle of stabilization of water on the Earth where water passes from the ocean into the atmosphere, onto the lands, through and under the lands, and back to the oceans.

isohyetal map The lines on a map that join points that receive the same amount of precipitation.

levee A structure of material built on the bank of a stream to increase the amount of water that a stream can hold under natural conditions. A major flood control device.

National Flood Insurance Act A federal program of flood insurance available in all communities subject to periodic flooding.

National Weather Service The federal agency that forecasts the weather.

overland flow The flow of water over land to streams or lakes.

oxbow lakes Large loops that are abandoned when a stream shortens its course. These abandoned channels fill with water.

porosity The amount of water that a rock can absorb.

reservoir A body of water, either natural or artificial, for the storage, regulation, or control of water.

reservoir capacity The amount of water a reservoir can hold.

river cutoff In a gentle-gradient stream, wide bends may develop. During flood stages, the river cuts across these large loops, isolating them from the stream.

river deepening Deepening the river channel so that it can carry more water during flood stage.

river realignment Changing the river channel to reduce flooding.

river widening Widening the river channel so that it can carry more water during flood stages.

runoff The precipitation that runs off the surface into streams or lakes.

satellite imagery An electromagnetic image from a satellite in space.

sedimentation The sediment deposited by a stream as its velocity decreases and it gradually loses its carrying capacity.

spillway A vertical pipe that conveys the water down a horizontal shaft or tunnel to a lower stream level.

stage Height of a water surface above an established datum plane (also gauge height).

stopbank Another name for a levee.

streamflow The discharge of water in a natural surface stream channel.

streamflow gauge The gauge to measure the discharge of water from a stream.

surface runoff The portion of precipitation that flows over the surface to the nearest stream.

surface water Water on the surface of the land.

thunderstorm A sudden updraft of air in an area of several square miles. The rapid upward air movement causes a release of energy, creating a storm with thunder and lightning. A major thunderstorm can release as much as 2 inches of precipitation in 1 hour, creating flash floods.

tidal flood Flood resulting from high tides caused by strong winds.

tsunami An undersea current that creates flooding when it reaches a land area.

U.S. Army Corps of Engineers The federal agency responsible for flood control developments on U.S. rivers.

U.S. Geological Survey The federal agency responsible for geologic work.

warm front In a cyclone, where warm moving air comes in contact with stagnant cold air. The warm air overrides the cold, causing precipitation, known as warm front precipitation.

water balance The stability of the total amount of water on the Earth through time.

water equivalent of snow The amount of water from snow as it melts. The water content varies according to the liquid water in snow at time of precipitation.

water level The level of water in a reservoir.

Index

American Meteorological Society (AMS), 68
American Red Cross, 6, 69, 104
Audiovisual aids, 265–274
  dams, 269–270
  disasters, 268–269
  flash flood, 267–268
  flood forecasting, 266–267
  general, 265–266
  rivers, 270–274
Automatic Local Evaluation in Real-Time (ALERT) System, 4

Bank protection, 7
Bedrock, 8
Bibliography, 117–264
Big Thompson Advisory Committee, 40
Big Thompson Flash Flood of 1976, 38–41
  Colorado Emergency Act, 40
  effects of the flood, 39
  floodwaters, 39
  governmental response, 40–41
  origin of the flood, 39
Big Thompson Flood, journal articles, 228
Big Thompson River, 38
Bipartisan Task Force on Funding Disaster Relief, 1955, 34
Books, 118–136
  bibliographies, 117–118
  dams, 128–129
  flash floods, 127–128
  flood damage, 129–130
  flood forecasting, 125–126
  flood frequency, 130
  flood hazard management, 124–125
  flood reservoirs, 131
  general, 118–124
  handbooks, 118
  tidal floods, 126–127
Books, specific floods, 131–136
  Acadiana, Louisiana, 136
  Big Thompson Flood, 134
  Mississippi Basin Flood of 1993, 132–134
  Mississippi River, 1982–1983, 136
  Pennsylvania, 134–135
  United States, general, 131–132
Boreholes, 8
Boulder Canyon Project Act, 109
Bunds (levees), 7
Bureau of Reclamation, 25
Bypass channels, 13–14

Calculated flood discharge, 9
California floods, journal articles, 229–230
Cambria Iron Company, 36
Carnegie, Andrew, 36
Channel, 9, 11, 13
Channel stabilization, 10–11
Channel widening and deepening, 9–10
Chicago Flood of 1992, journal articles, 217
Chronology, 51–62
Church World Service and Witness (CWSW), 69–70
Colorado Emergency Act, 40
Colorado River, 110, 112

Colorado River Flooding Protection Act of 1986, 110–112
  development of flooding, 111
  land control, 118
Colorado River floodways, 110, 112
Colorado River Storage Project Act of 1956, 108–110
  development, 109
  purpose, 109
  revenue, 109–110
Columbia River Flood of 1948, journal articles, 229
Community assistance and program evaluations, 22
Community Development and Regulatory Improvement Act of 1994, 35
Conemaugh River, 36–38
Contribution to American Red Cross for flood relief, 104
Coordination of flood insurance with land management programs in flood-prone areas, 94–95
  criteria for land management and use, 95
  identification of flood-prone areas, 94–95
  purchase of certain insured properties, 95
Costliest East Coast United States hurricanes, 1900–1995, 60
Cutoffs, 12–13
Cyclonic storms, 23–35

Dam Act of 1906, 106
Dam Acts, 61, 104–106
Dam breakage floods, 36–38
Damages of United States floods, 53–54
Dams, 6, 11, 12, 80, 105, 106
De Luz Reservoir, California Act of 1954, 108
Deaths from United States floods, 53–54
Defense Civil Preparedness Agency, 100
Department of Agriculture, 79
Department of Human and Urban Development, 92
Department of War, 79, 80
Development of the Coosa River, Alabama and Georgia Act of 1954, 107–108
Digitized Radar Experiment (D/RADEX), 4
Dikes, 10, 11
Directory of organizations, 63–75
Disaster Assistance Administration, 100–101
Disaster relief, 96–104
Disaster relief and emergency assistance acts, 61
Diversion channels, 7, 107
Doppler radar techniques, 4
Dredging, 9

Earthquakes, 45
East Coast floods, journal articles, 208–213
  East Coast Hurricane Flood of 1972, 210–211
  general, 208–209
  Johnstown Flood, 209–210
  Pennsylvania Flood of 1936, 212–213
  Pennsylvania Floods of 1942, 211–212
Economic aspects, journal articles, 184–186
Electromagnetic sensors, 4
Embankment, 42
Emergency action planning guidelines for dams, 65
Emergency Operation Center (EOC), 4
Emergency spillways, 11, 12
England, East Coast, 46–47
Environmental impact—human relations, journal articles, 195–200
Environmental Protection Agency (EPA), 63–64
Erosion potential, 8

Federal disaster assistance programs, 101
Federal Emergency Management Agency (FEMA), 31, 64, 96
Federal Flood Insurance Act of 1956, 88–89
  purpose, 88–89
  administration, 89

Federal government, journal articles, 194–195
Federal guidelines for dam safety, 64, 65
Federal gidelines for earthquake analysis and design of dams, 65
Federal guidelines for selecting and accommodating inflow design floods, 65
Federal Interagency Floodplain Management Task Force, 18
Federal laws, 77–115
Federal Power Commission, 105
Federal relief funds, 20
Federal Water Information Coordination Program, 67
Flash flood forecasting techniques, 4
Flash floods, 3, 4, 139–140
Flash floods, journal articles, 139–140
Flood banks, 7
Flood control, 5–14, 15, 18, 66, 77, 78, 80, 81, 82, 83, 84, 86, 106, 107, 108, 111, 141–160
Flood Control Act of 1917, 77–78
Flood Control Act of 1928, 78
Flood Control Act of 1936, 6, 77, 79–80, 81
  establishment of a national policy, 79
  flood control compacts, 80
  flood control projects, 80
  implementation, 79–80
Flood Control Act of 1937, 80–81
Flood Control Act of 1938, 6, 77, 81–82
Flood Control Act of 1941, 82
Flood Control Act of 1944, 77, 82–83, 108
Flood Control Act of 1946, 83
Flood Control Act of 1948, 83
Flood Control Act of 1950, 84
Flood Control Act of 1954, 84
Flood Control Act of 1958, 84
Flood Control Act of 1960, 7, 84
Flood Control Act of 1962, 84
Flood Control Act of 1965, 85
Flood Control Act of 1966, 85
Flood Control Act of 1968, 86
Flood Control Act of 1970, 86
Flood Control Acts, 61, 77–86
Flood control dam, 8
Flood control, journal articles, 141–160
  channels, 147–150
  dams, 151–154
  design, 144–146
  detention basins, 155–156
  dikes, 156
  flood walls, 157–158
  floodgates, 157
  general, 141–144
  lakes—water level, 158
  levees, 146–147
  protection, 159
  reservoirs, 155
  sea walls, 158–159
  spillways, 150–151
  transportation, 160
Flood control policy, 20
Flood damage, 6, 7, 16, 21, 90
Flood Disaster Protection Act of 1973, 96–98
  congressional findings, 97
  financial considerations, 98
Flood forecasting, 92
Flood hazards, 85, 91, 95, 98
Flood insurance, 7, 15, 20–23, 88–96
Flood Insurance, journal articles, 186–189
Flood Insurance Act, 20
Flood Insurance Advisory Committee, 93
Flood legislation dates, 61
  dam acts, 61
  disaster relief and emergency assistance acts, 61
  flood control acts, 61
  flood prevention, 61
  national flood insurance acts, 61
  proclamation on flood relief, 61
  river and harbor acts, 61
  water planning acts, 61
  water quality acts, 61
  water resources, 61
  wild and scenic river acts, 61
Flood losses, 90
Flood potential, 21
Flood prediction, 2–3
Flood prevention, 61, 86–88
Flood Prevention Act of 1944, 6

Flood-prone locations, 21
Flood proofing, 92
Flood protection, 5
Flood stage, 2, 11
Flood walls, 7, 9
Flood warning systems, 3–4
Floods in general, 136–139
Floods of 1849 and 1850, 5
Floodplain, 2, 6, 7, 9, 14, 15, 19, 21, 21, 25, 31, 98, 95
Floodplain, journal articles, 189–193
  alluvial fans, 192–193
  general, 189–192
Floodplain management, 14–20
Floodplain Management Review Committee, 35
Floodplain Management Task Force, 35
Floodplain resources (biological, societal, water), 16
Floodwater, 13
Floodways, 14, 107, 110, 111, 112
Forecast techniques, 4
Forecasters, 4
Forecasting, journal articles, 166–169
Frequency, journal articles, 169–173
Frick, Henry Clay, 36
Friends Disaster Service (FDS), 70

Gauges, 3, 4
Geofield-Oliver technique, 5
Government documents, 243–264
Government response to Big Thompson Flood, 40–41
  Big Thompson Advisory Committee, 40
  Colorado Emergency Act, 40
  Colorado Water Conservation Board, 40
  National Flood Insurance Program, 41
Gradient, 2, 12
Great Flood of 1927, 5, 6
Ground water table, 10
Groynes, 10
Gulf of Mexico, 47

Harrisburg, 43
Hawaii, 45
Herbicides, 10
Hurricane Agnes, 41
Hurricane floods, 41–45
Hurricane floods, journal articles, 206–208
Hurricanes, 3, 59
Hydrologic cycle, 2
Hydrological forecast program, 5

Integrated Floods Observing and Warning System (IFLOWS), 4
Interactive Flash Flood Analyzer (IFFA), 5
Interagency Committee on Dam Safety (ICODS), 64–65
Interagency Floodplain Management Review Committee, 1994, 29

Johnstown Flood of 1889, 36–38
  Cambria Iron Company, 36
  Carnegie, Andrew, 36
  Conemaugh River, 36–38
  dam breakage, 36
  effects, 37–38
  Frick, Henry Clay, 36
  Knox, Philander C., 36
  Mellon, Andrew, 36
  South Fork Dam, 36
  South Fork Hunting and Fishing Club, 36
Johnstown Flood of 1889, journal articles, 209–210
Journal articles, 136–230
Journal titles, selected, 230–243

Kansas Flood of 1951, journal articles, 216–217
Kingston, 42
Knox, Philander C., 36
Krakatoa Volcano, 46

Levee Act of 1917, 77–78
Levees, 5, 7–8, 24–25, 42, 107

Major world floods, 51–52
Management, journal articles, 177–184
Manually digitizing radar, 4
Mathematical models, journal articles, 160–166
computer simulation, 165–166

Mellon, Andrew, 36
Mennonite Central Committee (MCC), 70–71
Mennonite Disaster Service (MDS), 71
Midwest floods, journal articles, 213–217
  Chicago Flood of 1992, 217
  general, 213–214
  Kansas Flood of 1951, 216–217
  Ohio River floods, 215–216
Midwest Flood of 1993, 23–26
effects of the flood, 26–32
flood control, 24–26
Mississippi River, 5, 12, 28, 29, 30, 32, 78, 106, 107
Mississippi River Commission, 5
Mississippi River Flood Control Act of 1928, 106–107
  damage liability, 107
  flood control, 107
  purpose, 107
Mississippi River Floods, journal articles, 225–226
Missouri River, 29
Mitigation benefits, journal articles, 193–194
Mitigation Insurance Program, 35
Moisture-laden air, 3

National Association for Search and Rescue (NASAR), 71–72
National Association of Catastrophic Adjusters (NACA), 72
National Association of Flood and Stormwater Management Agencies (NAFSMA), 72
National Bureau of Standards, 106
National Dam Inspection Program Act of 1972, 104–105
National Flood Insurance Act of 1968, 15, 89–95
  National Flood Insurance Program, 91–93
  purpose, 90–91
National Flood Insurance Acts, 61
National Flood Insurance Fund, 93
  dissemination of flood insurance information, 93
  prohibition against certain duplication of benefits, 93
  properties in violation of state and local law, 93
National Flood Insurance Program (NFIP), 7, 21–23, 91–93, 96, 97
  establishment of chargeable premium rates, 92–93
  estimate of premium rates, 92
  nature and limitation of insurance coverage, 92
  scope of the program and priorities, 91–92
National Flood Insurance Program Act of 1989, 95–96
National Flood Insurance Reform Act of 1994, 35, 96
National Meteorological Center, 5
National Oceans and Atmospherlc Administration, 65
National policy, 79
National Weather Service (NWS), 5, 65
Native American archaeological sites, 32
Natural channel, 2
Natural disasters, 88
Natural Hazards Research and Applications Information Center, (NHRAIC), 72–73
Nature and limitation of insurance coverage, 92
Navigation, 83
Nevada, 256
New England, journal articles, 205–208
  general, 205
  New England Flood of 1936, 205–206
  New England Flood of 1938, 205–206
  1938 Hurricane Flood, 206–207
  Northeastern Flood of 1925, 207–208
New Guinea, 46
Noah, 1
North Sea, 47

Ohio River, 5
Ohio River floods, journal articles, 215–216

100-Year Flood, 22
Oregon Water Resources Congress (WRC), 74
Organic Act of March 3, 1879, 67
Organization and administration of the flood insurance programs, 94
  industry flood insurance pool, 94
Origin of floods, 39
Overflow land, 14

Pacific Ocean, 45
Pacific Rim, 45
Papua New Guinea Tsunami, 45–46
Passaic River Coalition (PRC), 74–75
Pennsylvania Flood of 1936, journal articles, 213–214
Pennsylvania Flood of 1942, journal articles, 211–212
Penstock (flood gate), 83
Physical properties, journal articles, 200–204
  hurricanes, 204
  wave and tide actions, 203–204
  weather and climate, 200–203
Plans and projects, journal articles, 175–177
Potential flood discharge, 8
Power generation, 8
Precipitation, 2, 3, 8
Private associations, 68–74
  American Meteorological Society (AMS), 68
  American Red Cross National Headquarters (ARC), 69
  Church World Services and Witness (CWSW), 69–70
  Friends Disaster Service (FDS), 70
  Mennonite Central Committee, (MCC), 70–71
  Mennonite Disaster Service (MDS), 71
  National Association for Search and Rescue (NASR), 71–72
  National Association of Catastrophic Adjusters (NACA), 72
  National Association of Flood and Storm Water Management Agencies (NAFSMA), 72
  Natural Hazards Research and Application Information Center (NHRAIC), 72–73
  U.S. Committee on Large Dams (USCOLD), 73–74
Private insurance, 89, 90, 94
Proclamation on flood relief, 61
Profile of equilibrium, 12
Program for reducing the national flood damage potential, 7

Radar systems, 4
Rainfall rates, 5
Rainfall runoff, 8
Regional floods, journal articles, 205
  East Coast, 208–213
  Midwest, 213–217
  Mississippi River, 225
  New England, 205–208
  Southeast, 226–227
  Upper Mississippi River Flood of 1993, 217–225
  Western, 227–230
Reservoir capacity, 11
Reservoirs, 8–9, 25–26
Revetments, 10
Risk zones, 95
River and harbor acts, 61, 112–115
River channel, 7
River floods, 55–58
River Forecast Center, Harrisburg, 42
River stage, 3
Riverbank stabilization, 111
Robert T. Stafford Disaster Relief and Emergency Assistance Act of 1974, 98–103
  Disaster Assistance Administration, 100–101
  disaster preparedness assistance, 100
  economic recovery for disaster areas, 102–103
  federal disaster assistance programs, 101–102
  functions of the act, 99

Robert T. Stafford Disaster Relief and Emergency Assistance Amendment of 1988, 33–34
Rocky Mountains, 38

Sacramento River, 78, 107
St. Patrick's Day Flood 1937, 42
Satellite imagery, 4–5
Sensors, 4
Siphon Spillway, 11
Sloughing, 25
Soil Conservation Service, 6, 7, 25
South Fork Dam, 36
South Fork Hunting and Fishing Club, 36
Southeast floods, journal articles, 226–227
Specific floods, 23–47
  Big Thompson Flash Flood of 1976, 38–41
  Midwest Flood of 1993, 24–36
  Johnstown Flood of 1889, 36–38
  Susquehanna River Flood of 1972, 41–45
  tsunami floods, 45–46
  wind and tidal floods, 46–47
Specific river acts, 106–112
Spillways, 8, 11–12, 107
State agencies, 74–75
Stop banks, 7
Storage capacity, 8
Storm surge, 47
Sunbury, 43
Surface water, 2
Susquehanna River Flood of 1972, 41–45
  Chemung, 44
  Chemung River, 44
  Colorama Creek, 44
  Corning, 44
  flood damage, 41–45
  Forty Fort, 42
  Harrisburg, 43
  Hurricane Agnes, 41
  Kingston, 42
  National Guard, 42
  origin of the flood, 41
  River Forecast Center, Harrisburg, 42
  St. Patrick's Day Flood, 1937, 42
  Sunbury, 43
  Susquehanna River, 41–45
  Wilkes-Barre, 41–42
  York, 43–44
Synoptic analysis branch, 5

Tennessee Valley Authority (TVA), 7, 64, 94, 105
Thunderstorm flash floods, 3, 38–41
Thunderstorms, 39
Tidal floods, 47
Topography, 11
Training courses related to dam safety, 65
Tsunami floods, 45–46, 61, 65
Types of flood control, 7–14

Underground reservoirs, 14
United States river floods, 55–58
Upper Colorado River Basin Compact, 109
Upper Mississippi River Flood, 1993, journal articles, 217–225
  flood control, 220
  frequency, 220
  general, 217–219
  government, 224–225
  impact of floods, 221–224
  recovery, 220–221
  weather and climate, 219–220
U.S. Army Corps of Engineers, 5, 7, 12, 22, 25, 28, 29, 34, 42, 43, 44, 65–66, 79, 85
U.S. Committee on Irrigation and Drainage (USCID), 66
U.S. Committee on Large Dams (USCOLD), 73–74
U.S. Geological Survey (USGS), 66–67
USGS professional papers, by state, 243–247

Velocity, 1

Wall, 42
Warning, journal articles, 173–175
Water level, 2, 10
Water planning act, 61
Water quality acts, 61, 64
Water resource investigation, journal articles, 247–264
Watershed management, 19, 82

Watershed Protection and Flood Prevention Act of 1954, 86–88
  congressional funding, 86
  development of projects, 87
  requirements for implementation, 87
Western floods, journal articles, 227–230
  Big Thompson Flash Flood of 1976, 228
  California floods, 229–230
  Columbia River Flood of 1948, 229
  general, 227–228
White, Gilbert, 6
Wild and scenic river acts, 61
Wilkes-Barre, 41–42
Wind and tidal floods, 46–47
Wind velocity, 5

Yellow River, 1
York, 43–44

E. Willard Miller is a professor of geography and associate dean of resident instruction (emeritus) at the Pennsylvania State University. He received his A.M. degree at the University of Nebraska and his Ph.D. from the Ohio State University. He is a fellow of the American Association for the Advancement of Science, the American Geographical Society, the National Council for Geographic Education, and the Explorers Club. In 1990, Dr. Miller received the Honors Award from the Association of American Geographers. He has published more than 100 professional journal articles and 30 books. He is listed in *Who's Who in America* and *Who's Who in the World.*

Ruby M. Miller is a map librarian (retired) at the Pattee Library at the Pennsylvania State University. She received her B.A. degree at Chatham College and did graduate work at the University of Pittsburgh. She established and developed the map collection at Penn State, and at her retirement the collection had over 250,000 maps and over 3,000 atlases. She is the coauthor of 6 books and over 100 bibliographies. The Pennsylvania Geographical Society has honored her with its Distinguished Scholar Award. She is a member of the Association of American Geographers and the American Association of University Women.